外黒人

GAIKOKUJIN - THE STORY

Contributors

Edited by Joshua S. Yeley

Proofreading by Tracy M. Riva

<u>Cover Art</u>

Drawing: Griffin Reid

Calligrapher: Minori Ito

Note: If you wish to make a contribution, please leave a review of the book here:

https://www.amazon.com/review/create-review/?ie=UTF8&channel=glance-detail&asin=4908556016

https://www.goodreads.com/book/show/28349177-gaikokujin---the-story

Thank you in advance!

Copyright

Publisher's Cataloging-In-Publication Data
(Prepared by The Donohue Group, Inc.)
Names: Amaru, Takuan.
Title: 外黒人 = Gaikokujin - the story. Book I, Hip hop, race, and
   pursuing the American Dream / Takuan Amaru.
Other Titles: Gaikokujin - the story. Book I, Hip hop, race, and
   pursuing the American Dream | Hip hop, race, and pursuing the
   American Dream
Description: Nagoya, Japan : AfroAsiatic Books, [2016] | Book I of
   a trilogy. | Interest age level: 014-030. | Includes
   bibliographical references.
Identifiers: ISBN 978-4-908556-07-4 (set) | ISBN 978-4-908556-
   01-2 (print) | ISBN 978-4-908556-00-5 (ebook)

Subjects: LCSH: Racially mixed children--United States--Fiction. |
    Child abuse--Fiction. | Urban fiction. | Race--Fiction. |
    American Dream--Fiction. | American literature--Japanese
    American authors. | LCGFT: Biographical fiction.
Classification: LCC PS3601.M37 G351 2016 (print) | LCC
    PS3601.M37 (ebook) | DDC 813/.6 [Fic]--dc23

Published by AfroAsiatic Books
www.afroasiatic.jp
www.takuanamaru.com

外黒人

GAIKOKUJIN - The Story

Book I: Hip Hop, Race, and Pursuing the American Dream

Takuan Amaru

AfroAsiatic Books

Nagoya, Japan

Author's Note:

In Japanese, the word *Gai-koku-jin*, literally meaning outside-country-person; i.e. foreigner, is traditionally written as 「外国人」. I, however, am coining terminology by replacing the middle character 「黒」, which is pronounced identically but means 'black' instead of country. Not only does this symbolize my own cultural perspective, but it also represents a set of circumstances which is not limited to any race or country. This book is a spiritual rags-to-riches adventure. I have been blessed to live a 'storybook life' but not in any glamourous way. Writing this has allowed me to examine my role as a person of color—which I refer to as melanin-rich—in a society which has proven itself to be hostile toward non-Caucasian people.

Who is Takuan Amaru?

The son of an African/Native American man and Japanese woman, Takuan is a writer, teacher, counselor, and youth-advocate specialist. The author of hundreds of articles on topics ranging from popular music and culture to ancient philosophy and spirituality, in order to connect with readers, Tak taps into experiences from his past as a U.S. soldier, social worker, athlete, and music artist. Throughout his life, he has traveled extensively and now makes his home in Japan.

Website: www.takuanamaru.com

Email: takuanamaru@gmail.com

Table of Contents

A Probe into Generation X

In the 1980s, the economic policies of the Reagan Administration, policies widely known as "Reaganomics," created such astronomical unemployment for young blacks that John E. Jacob, president of the National Urban League, labeled the decade a "Depression Generation." Since that time, black and brown people have been murdered and incarcerated at such a disproportionate rate compared to Caucasians, that nowadays brothers beyond the age of thirty who are *not* on probation *and* have a job (not to mention all their teeth) are such rare figures in our community children see us as old men.

The only adult guidance many of our youth receive comes from gang members, drug addicts, or neighborhood bums. Since these are the adults the youth emulate, trying to put something over on people—we called it 'getting over'—rather than succeed through meritorious achievement, replaces true ambition. The result: crime and other forms of deceit become a normal way of life. Despite being a dangerous game to play, many have been led to believe this is the road to the American Dream.

This book is about one such misguided youth.

I am the youngest of three children born to two people of color: an American man and a Japanese woman. Since both of my parents were ostracized by their families for marrying foreigners, my siblings and I were robbed of an opportunity to meet our relatives. Lacking a sense of identity, we allowed friends and classmates to label us as *'Haafu,'* 'Jap,'—or even worse. Back in those days, I wish I'd known about the term "Asiatic." Not in its contemporary usage but in an earlier, perhaps an even ancient one.

Many conscious brothers and sisters understand this word to encompass something much deeper than meaning a person was born on the Asian continent.

In fact, the term was popularized in the early twentieth century by three, prominent spiritual leaders. Timothy Drew, better known by his title, the Noble Prophet Drew Ali, founded the Moorish Science Temple in 1913. Elijah Poole, known as the Honorable Elijah Muhammad, along with his predecessor, Master Fard Muhammad, is credited with forming the Nation of Islam in 1934. From them, we learned that 'Asia' was one of the names for Mother Earth millions of years ago when the continents were still connected.

The discovery of this hidden jewel of knowledge was eye-opening because racially divisive terms like African-American, Black, Indian, or even 'mixed' never sat well with me. In elementary school, I hated being forced to choose one ethnic group from the very limited options on the Metropolitan Achievement Tests. Since my teachers did not allow me to darken all the ovals except 'White,' I took turns filling-in the other choices; so every year I was a different ethnicity. Even at a young age, I understood the terms listed were neither satisfactory nor sufficient to describe my lineage. I was also confused about why people would identify themselves with colors. Due to the popularity of the Black Power movement during the 1960s and 1970s, black was the only color that made any sense. And now I believe this is because, even in our "dumbed-down" state of mind, we are still interacting with the magical substance called Melanin[*].

The word "autochthonous" traces its roots to the Greek word *autokhthon*, which literally means "sprung from the land itself." In recent years, archaeological evidence has established that autochthonous people existed much earlier than historians of the western world are willing to admit. These "original human beings"

---

[*] For more information, check the Glossary of Terms, Historical Figures, and Events

are not to be confused with prehistoric man. Like our ancestors, we have billions of melanocytes in our epidermis layer. This clearly illustrates our blood-ties to them. And while this cannot be overstated, what has proven to be more significant than the color of our skin is the volume of usable *melatonin*—known as 'Neuromelanin'—in our nervous system. This is because it is believed that neuromelanin connects us to the divine source of the universe.

Melatonin is produced by the pineal gland. This small, pine-cone shaped, endocrine gland is located in the center of the brain. Throughout the ages, spiritual systems have laid claim to the paramount importance of interacting with melatonin in order to evolve to higher states of consciousness. In his book, *From the Browder File,* Anthony Browder writes: "The relationship between melatonin and spirituality is certainly nothing new. The revelations of the Bible, Torah, Koran, and of the Buddha were all inspired by melanin-induced visions of people of color." Another expert on the subject, Dr. Aseer Ali Cordoba, states that prior to the emergence of western civilization, most Asiatic people had a healthy, functioning 'third eye' (i.e. pineal gland). Dr. Cordoba claims this was the "normal condition."

For these reasons, I use the term 'Melanin-Rich' interchangeably with Asiatic to mean black and brown people.

However, before I would stumble upon any of this profound knowledge and come to fully understand it, I had to search far and wide to unravel the riddle of life. Along the way, I experimented with everything this world had to offer. From drugs and petty crime to illicit sex—why I even tried becoming a 'saved' Christian during my three-year stint in the Army.

Gaikokujin - The Story is based on true accounts in my life.

The names and certain details of this fictional memoir have been altered to protect the innocent—as well as the guilty. While steering clear of embarrassing anyone other than myself, this survivor's guide has been written for sincere people trying to make sense of the world we live in. The brutally honest perspectives I express are due to the wonderful (and not so wonderful) people and situations I found myself involved in. Transcending the boundaries of the box called society—which has been dubbed "The Matrix" by the conscious community—my quest for self-worth and redemption defies the logic and reasoning that today's world has come to accept as normal.

Throughout my journey, especially in my times of need, I learned to depend on a dynamic energy-force which, bizarre as it may sound, appeared out of nowhere. Because this entity always showed up in my most desperate moments, and only to protect me, I assumed it was my guardian angel. Barely averting disaster time and again, I eventually became disgusted with my rock-bottom existence and began searching for the missing link in my life: God. After sifting through the seemingly endless religious options at Ft. Bragg, I realized each house of worship was just a different version of Christianity. This did not surprise me because it is no secret that military installations are saturated with chapels and cathedrals of the various sects. Having no alternative, I immersed myself in a non-denominational church to give thanks to Jesus...hallelujah!

It took almost two years but in the course of time my angelic protector gradually led me away from the "Synagogue of Satan." Taking small steps, little by little, it never stopped performing its divine alchemy; and just like the biblical parable of turning water into wine, it spun my orthodox circumstances into an opportunity to illustrate the infinite power of the universe. At that time, I didn't know the Sanskrit word, *Kundalini*, meant a "coiled power" which resided at the base of the spine. Or, if this vital force traveled upward it resulted in achieving Christ Consciousness. Thus, I never suspected the benign apparition lending me a helping hand was none other than my Higher Self.

Book I

Chapter 1: White Flight of the '70s

Growing up on military bases was cool. All of them were virtually the same: no pollution, lots of parks, and loads of children to play with. Following the Vietnam War, McGuire Air Force Base became one of the military installations designated for racially-mixed-couple marriages; so once we moved there all of my friends were multiracial. Though most of my playmate's fathers were black, their mothers usually hailed from Korea, the Philippines, or somewhere in Europe.

One of my earliest childhood memories is being in the commissary, the BX, and the Asian food-market. There, I always wondered why Oriental women warmly greeted each other in their native tongues but always addressed my mother in English. Being one the few Japanese, she would basically get dissed by these ladies. Knowing nothing about the history or politics involved, I thought rudeness was part of their culture.

My sister and I soon realized the number of Japanese people on the base was sparse in comparison to Filipinos or Koreans. My mother claimed this was because the Japanese had more pride than other Asians. When she saw the confused look on our faces she used this opportunity to explain why we could never visit any of her relatives.

"As you already know, I am from a traditional Samurai family," she said, looking back and forth at us with a

1

solemn expression on her face. "I am the only daughter with seven brothers…"

Since we understood whenever our mother began by citing this introductory phrase she was about to drop a historical gem, we remained quiet.

"When I was a little girl during the war, everyone was poor because every person was required to sacrifice for the good of the nation. Poverty was new to my family. Despite the meager conditions, every day, one of my classmates always had the cutest rice ball in her *bento*[†]. It was neatly rolled in *nori* and when she bit into it the prettiest apricot would be revealed. Every day, as I watched her enjoy this delight, I came to covet it. I decided to steal it. The next day at lunch, when she opened her bento and loudly complained she had been robbed, all eyes were suddenly on me. This was the first, of only two times, that my father ever raised his voice to scold me. The other time was when I announced my intention to marry your father." Following a long, cold stare, she summed-up her account. "Then he kicked me out of the family."

The strongest man I have ever met in my life is my sire. Interestingly, this may have been both his best and worst characteristic. Growing up in rural Alabama during the Jim Crow Era of the 1930s and '40s, his native features suggest an ancestry deriving from the Napochi, Muskogee, or Choctaw Nations. These clans were known to have resided along the Black Warrior River, which flowed through his hometown.

Similar to Eve of the Old Testament, my father was

[†] For English translations, check the Glossary of Terms, Historical Figures, and Events

seduced by the *Serpent*. Moreover, like the mythic Genesis story, this viper poisoned his mind, body, and soul. A warrior by nature, I have oft-times reflected how in another more epic era, my father may have conquered or cultivated an entire society. However in these so called modern times, legendary personas have become as outdated as platform shoes and bell-bottom jeans.

A career military man who devoted twenty-one years to Uncle Sam, his tours featured perilous pit stops in both Korea and Vietnam. Following another twenty-plus years as a corrections officer in NJ, he became a dual pension recipient when he retired. Always impeccable in appearance, he was the type of man who arrived fifteen minutes early for any appointment. As a result he could never understand why I was always late to school.

My parents met while my father was stationed at Tachikawa Airbase during the early postwar years of Japan. This military installation, which was located in Tokyo, was not far from where my mother worked part-time in a cafe owned by her brother. However, because Tokyo was reserved for white military personnel only, plus the fact my mother was hiding her boyfriend from her family, the two lovers had to meet in nearby Yokohama to go on dates.

Whenever I tell this story, most people naturally assume my mother wanted to keep my father a secret because he was a 'Negro.' However, according to her, black or white was the same because her family equally looked down on both as *gaijin*. Describing her family as outdated, conceited people who relied heavily on traditional values, she was searching for a way out of the strict, Japanese caste-system. Nevertheless jumping into the shoes of a black woman might have been more than she bargained for.

"So you see, as the only girl, even had I married a low-class Japanese, I would still be in the same boat," she nonchalantly joked one evening about her castaway status.

Despite her carefree sentiments, we knew she was deeply scarred and she wanted to reunite with her family. In the mid-90s, some forty years later, she finally realized her dream. But only after my grandfather died. *He was that stubborn!*

Because my brother, Kensuke, grew up in the decimated *Nippon* of the '50s and '60s, he was a victim of Japanese bigotry on a daily basis. Enduring racist names like gaijin and *kurombo* for over a decade, this type of *ijime* left an indelible mark on his psyche. To this day, he hates Japan and cannot understand why his brother chose to settle down there. Nonetheless when he arrived in the U.S. at fifteen years of age with a lopsided afro, funny accent, and strange customs, it is debatable as to whether or not his situation improved. Facing a different kind of discrimination, one which included the threat of physical violence, his new adversaries prompted him to become active with the Black Panther Party.

Since Ken is twelve-years older than me, this is the time I remember him best: as a militant who loved funky music! Every morning, I woke up to the soulful sounds of Earth Wind & Fire, Kool & the Gang, or Mandrill during the years we shared a bedroom together. In fact, these are some of my fondest childhood memories. After yawning and sitting up, I would stare at a poster of BPP Chairman, Huey P. Newton as he looked down defiantly from his wicker-chair throne. He seemed to be offering me a choice between a rifle and a spear. *I wanted to use both of them!*

In 2004, I sat in an airplane bound for Brazil with a

4

good friend. Out of the blue, he asked me about my conception of God. He claimed no matter how much he studied the work of Dr. Ben and Dr. John Henrik Clark, he was unable to erase the 'white Jesus' imagery which had been implanted in his mind. Knowing my Japanese background and the fact I had not attended church growing up, he wondered if I had been spared this mental torture. When I closed my eyes to visualize 'God,' a picture of my brother Ken jumped into my mind. After blowing it off, I tried again only to have the same apparition disturb my thoughts. Following a moment of deliberation, I recalled the statue of Buddha we had in our living room. As a child I thought this traditional figurine with its *chinky* eyes and *nappy* hair was Ken dressed-up in a funny robe. Consequently, my elder brother sitting on a lotus flower had become my image of the Creator.

I was a curious third-grader when I stumbled upon a letter from Kensuke addressed to my parents. This was a couple months after Ken joined the Air Force. In it, he thanked them for being gracious enough to adopt him as a baby. Reading this, I was shocked like any child would be who was finding out for the first time his brother was adopted. When I asked my mother about this, she scolded me for snooping into her affairs–*without ever answering any of my questions.* It was not until many years later, while I was studying at Rutgers that Ken finally told me his story.

Back in the mid-50s, Ken's biological family lived next to my parents on Tachikawa Air Base. A week after the airplane his father was on crashed in Korea, his mother fell into a deep depression. Prior to ingesting a lethal dosage of prescription drugs one afternoon, she abandoned Ken in the common, playground area within the housing complex. In her suicide note, she apologized for her inability to raise the boy but laid the blame on society for cursing the 'half-breed' baby. She also requested that one of her neighbors take care of Kensuke. Having no children of their own, my parents welcomed the discarded orphan into their home. The irony of this tragedy with a beautiful ending is: had I not been such a nosy boy, my sister and I would have never found out about this. Despite the fact my and Keiko's facial features did not resemble Ken's, since he was 'mixed,' it never occurred to us we were not related. My question is: why was it kept a secret? *Why is everything about my family a shameful secret?*

Since my siblings hated their Japanese names, they shortened their titles to 'Ken' and 'Kay' in an attempt to sound more American. When I tried to follow suit by nicknaming myself 'Tak,' people inadvertently called me 'Todd,' which I regarded as a whiteboy's name. I decided the better of two evils was to endure the ethnic jokes and for that reason always made sure to introduce myself as 'Takuan.' In spite of that, to this day, most of my friends call me 'Tak.'

A couple weeks after my birth, my father left for his *second* tour in Vietnam. At that time, I was still a bouncing, bald-headed, baby boy. My sire, believing his son should have already started growing hair, worried his seed had been born defective. Therefore, my mother vowed to keep my mane uncut until he returned from the war. This was why many of our neighbors thought my mother had two daughters.

Keiko is a year-and-a-half older than I am, and as children we were very close. When she started kindergarten I was lonely. Every afternoon, I raced my mother to the door to greet my sister upon her arrival from school. With her short afro, she smelled like *Jergens* lotion when I hugged her. Like all siblings, sometimes we got into fights. Although I could beat Kay up by the time I was seven, she would still defend me from the bigger boys on our street. Completely unafraid, she was ready to fight them if they picked on me. Witnessing her bravery always pumped my heart up and once these bullies realized they were about to get jumped by both of us, they left me alone. Keiko was my big sister and I was proud of her.

At the age of nine, Kay was diagnosed with severe astigmatism. Once she was required to wear glasses, her self-esteem plummeted. Other kids wore glasses too but Keiko's were different because she had really thick 'coke bottle' lenses. The final blow came when Ken dubbed her the 'Four-eyed Monkey' in front of her friends.

Later the same year, we moved from the base to a civilian neighborhood in the suburbs. For a couple weeks, the three of us were terrified. Thank god the town was only an hour from McGuire because this enabled us to visit our friends while we gradually adjusted to our frightening surroundings. The scary thing about our new block was every family was Caucasian. We already had white friends so this was not a case of us not liking them. Like most children, we chose our playmates based on their personalities—and perhaps their toys. None of us cared one way or the other about ethnicity. However my European friends on the base were a different breed. Their mothers were warm and friendly, and they spoke English with a foreign accent just like my mother did. Besides the color of their skin, these people had little in common with my new neighbors who were very standoffish and bigoted.

Luckily, one of our next-door-neighbors was Jewish and their youngest son, Samuel, was my age. Since Sam was also considered strange, as outcasts normally do, we became friends. Even with Sam by my side, it took a couple months for me to become comfortable enough to stray away from my house. If Kay or Sam did not want to play outside, I always stayed home. Ken, Kay, and I looked forward to our trips to McGuire every weekend. While my parents went shopping at the commissary and BX, Ken visited his friends and Kay and I played at the park near our old house.

The allure of these weekend trips ended a couple months later after a Filipino kid moved in across the street. In fact, everything changed for us misfits once *Ant's* family arrived on the scene because this commenced the 'White Flight' era. As we witnessed our neighbors leaving in droves almost overnight, their sentiment was clear: "There goes the neighborhood!"

Anthony Asuncion had three gorgeous sisters. The oldest, Antonia, used to babysit me and Keiko sometimes. The next two girls, Karen and Roslyn, were about Kay's age and they became friends. It only took a couple days for Ant to gain immense popularity as an all-around jock. Seeing this encouraged me to play a variety of sports too. This introduction to athletics at a young age played a crucial role in my youth. Most of my earliest memories of the suburbs are of Ant teaching me to play baseball. Being three years younger than Ant, I was too young to compete with him but I was athletic enough to practice.

Ant maintained his 'All-Everything' status for many years. It was not until high school when his short physique limited him to the baseball diamond. By this time I wondered how he was able to hold onto his suave reputation while playing only a 'white sport.'

The white kids in Jersey and Philly were avid stick-ball enthusiasts. Realizing this, I started taking my practice sessions with Ant very seriously and soon I was smacking home runs in our pick-up games instead of grounding out. Once this occurred, suddenly everyone knew my name. "We got Tak!" This is what the kids yelled if I approached a contest already in progress. Then a debate would erupt between the opposing team members about why it was fair for me to be on their team.

Because Ant joined Little League he rarely played stick-ball with us. But on those few occasions when he did the dynamics of the game were drastically altered. Not only did he thoroughly dominate the contest, he accomplished the feat while seeming to be joking around. The fact that he managed to appear humble in his starring role is what impressed me the most. Even though I was the youngest player, and initially one of the worst, Ant always picked me on his team. *And we always won!*

All the kids on my block respected Ant. I did my best to emulate his example and just being around him boosted my confidence 150%. Thanks to Ant's tutelage, by the time I was old enough to play on a Little League team myself, I was able to strike out older batters quite easily. This was because at eight-and-a-half, my pitching repertoire not only included a wicked fastball, it also featured a curve. You should've seen the angry look on my coach's face when the umpire prohibited me from throwing my specialty pitch.

In our first game of live pitching, following three innings of watching me strike out every batter I faced, the ump gestured for a timeout and called my manager to the mound. After Coach Sherry jogged over in his ill-fitting Giants t-shirt, the umpire said it was dangerous for such a young boy like me to throw a breaking-ball. He claimed I could badly injure my elbow. While this may be debatable, one thing is not: the fact that my curve ball was very effective!

In retrospect, it was probably disheartening for youngsters being weaned off a batting tee to try hitting a curve. In spite of hurling a number of shut-outs that season, once most of my stick ball buddies left town, I discarded my baseball glove for a basketball.

Although Caucasians still outnumbered everyone else, the complexion renovation in our town became obvious by the time I entered the fourth grade. Not surprisingly, this was the same year Samuel and I stopped hanging out with each other because after *Roots* hit the TV screen, it became dangerous for white kids to walk home from school. Many years later, one of my teachers joked this was the safest period for black people in U.S. history. This was just before the asinine slogan 'black on black' crime surfaced in the media—along with crack, AIDS, and MTV. But the trend that left the biggest impression in my mind was seeing guys chasing whiteboys down the street almost every day.

Dashing by my sister and me, neither group would pay us any attention during their high-speed pursuits. By the time I was in middle school, I used to worry about some of my white friends. That said, I *never* volunteered to walk with them. Once, I expressed these feelings to a white classmate in secret. His response surprised me.

"Tak," he said nodding his head, "you're different from the other black kids."

This confused me so I approached my father and asked him if I was indeed black like him. After staring at me for a long second my sire punched me in the chest. "You're *my* son!" he boomed. "That means you're black! Don't ever forget that!"

This was one of the last pleasant phrases my father said to me. But it was not the last time he punched me.

Chapter 2: "Jap!"

"Ahh...Freak Out!"

The 1978 hit by *Chic,* called *Le Freak,* was a new dance craze that hit our classroom every winter afternoon. Whenever there was inclement weather, normal outdoor recess was moved indoors. Once inside, hands down, the girls controlled the activities. Like most of the newest residents, these strong sisters had just migrated from Philadelphia. Under their rule, *Scrabble*, checkers, or playing with paper airplanes became a distant memory. Instead, the record player was pulled out and we danced. Well not everybody. I surely didn't.

In spite of learning how to do the *Hustle* at home watching *Soul Train* with my sister and brother, I was way too shy to get up and *Shake my Groove Thing* in front of my classmates. While getting loose with my siblings in the living room was just for play, the thought of dancing with a girl— especially slow-jams—was completely out of the question. This was underscored when Ken left for the Air Force. Unable to learn the latest dance moves from a teenager like my friends Earl and Eugene, who had older siblings in high school, I tried to quietly fade into the background. But the girls in my class were not satisfied by dancing with them only. They wanted to dance with me too because I had "good hair."

The first time I heard such a phrase I did not know

what to make of it. Although I came to realize it was a compliment, it made me feel uncomfortable. In fact, anything that alienated me from other black kids, good or bad, was unwelcome. The only exception to this rule was my status as a sort of a teacher's pet.

Despite being quick-witted and bright, many of the newly arrived students could barely read or write. Therefore my elementary school teachers purposely sat some of the boys having difficulty next to me for private tutorials. In most cases not only did we become friends, their grades improved because I allowed them to copy my test answers. In spite of this, I may have been the one who benefited the most from these pairings due to the lessons I received on 'being black.' In addition to this, another perk enjoyed by the teacher's apprentice was the privilege of collecting my classmate's lunch money every morning. Learning to tally figures and count money was not the only thing I aspired to practice.

This was my first crack at trumping the System.

At first, it was a nickel here or a dime there; just enough to buy one of the ice cream sandwiches which were sold at Friday lunches. These delectable treats were my favorite snack. So naturally, when the delicious desserts began being offered two-days-a-week, I started dipping in the pot twice as much. Sometimes I hooked my friends up too, but usually, I would *loan* them money to be paid back with interest. Having learned to charge interest from Samuel, to this day, it still baffles me that kids actually paid it.

Everything was rolling along smoothly until the cafeteria manager brought me into the school's kitchen to question my calculations. As you can guess I was terrified. While Mrs. Wainwright was speaking, I was about to confess but she never allowed me to speak. When she continued babbling about some incoherent figures, I nodded my head realizing she did not suspect any dishonesty on my part. I can still see the looks of astonishment on Earl, Brian, and Terrance's faces when I returned to my seat and handed them their complimentary ice cream sandwiches. Smiling back at them, this was the moment I began thinking I was smarter than everyone else.

"Takuan, you ain't black! You're a Jap…hahahaha!"

This is how Pam responded after I turned down her request to dance when 'her song' came on. It never dawned on me girls so confident would get their feelings hurt just because I didn't want to dance with them. What I did realize was, soon everyone was jumping on the 'chink joke' bandwagon.

"Yo, I saw Tak's mom in a Godzilla movie!"

After verbally painting me as Bruce Lee, Jackie Chan, and every other Kung-Fu personality they could bring to mind, the crowd was in an uproar. However the joke which showed the most imagination by far was by my friend, Kris. He used to call me the great, great, great grandnephew of the famous detective, Charlie Chan. Lacking any knowledge of my Japanese heritage, I had no way to defend myself. And honestly, until that joke about my mother surfaced, it had never occurred to me to get angry.

On the East Coast of the late '70s, gangs were a dying breed. This was the disco-drug generation inserted between the demise of the Black Panthers and the rise of the *Bloods* and *Crips*. Throughout this era, most brothers belonged to some kind of posse because to be alone was to stand-out as a

15

target. Like many kids, I learned this the hard way by getting my butt kicked a couple times. One day, a representative from a group of roughnecks who were known for beating up weaker kids approached me with an offer to join their clique. Being six of them, they called themselves the 'Super Six.'

"If you join us, I guess we'll change our name to the 'Super Seven,'" the boy admitted. His name was Louis but everyone called him 'Wink.'

Wink had a crush on Kay a couple years back. At that time, he used to visit our house on his skateboard every day. Wink's brother, Buck, was the leader of the Super Six. By the time we were teens, these delinquents had moved up to peddling drugs and committing other petty offenses, just like me.

For my initiation, Buck ordered me to *sneak* a random whiteboy on our elementary school's playground. I cannot recall how I rejected their membership request but there was no way I could punch a kid in the face I didn't even know. Once again, my socialization woes were mended with the camaraderie provided in sports.

"Tak, baseball's for whiteboys. You should play basketball!" exclaimed my friend, Earl.

Earl Tomlinson was one of the first kids I met from Philly. He used to tell me how everyone in his old neighborhood was tough, hip, and cool. Earl was also the first person to encourage me to participate in 'black activities.' The first time he emphasized baseball was a sport for whiteboys, I pointed out that the 1979 Pittsburgh Pirates–who happened to be the reigning World Series Champs–were comprised almost entirely of melanin-rich players.

"Shut up!" I scolded him before singing the hook-line in *Sister Sledge's* hit, *'We are Family.'* This was the tune the major-league team adopted as their theme song on their run to the pennant. "The Pirates destroyed teams last year!" I claimed. "And for your information, their captain happens to be a black man named Willie Stargell, and their all-star, right-fielder, Dave 'the Cobra' Parker, is black too!" Crossing my arms as if I had deliberated an air-tight case in front of judge and jury, I then smugly waited for his response.

Earl stared with a blank expression before shrugging his shoulders. "Baseball's still boring," he replied looking unimpressed. "You just stand out in the field and wait for the ball to get hit to you. Or you sit on the bench waiting for your turn to bat. It's nothing like basketball. Basketball's fun all the time!"

I never thought of it that way.

I found the best time to work on my skills was in the morning. By myself. Although I wanted to play with my friends, in order to improve as quickly as possible, practicing alone was critical. My intense enthusiasm for the sport had nothing to do with any 'hoop dreams' in the NBA, or even playing for a big-time university. No, I realized being recognized as a 'baller' in my *hood* meant instant prestige. So I decided to devote my time and energy toward enhancing my reputation. Hence any talk about baseball or any other 'white activities' ended in elementary school. The black-versus-white paradigm that America offered influenced me to devote myself to black activities only. And so far that meant playing basketball and having fun.

As winter melted into spring, my weekend routine included early-morning practices. Minutes after the sun skirted the horizon, I would already be drenched with sweat, dribbling back-and-forth in deep concentration. Shooting at both hoops I would be so absorbed in the moment sometimes men on a morning stroll would startle me with applause, claiming they had witnessed me hit fifteen or twenty jumpers in a row. Whenever I conducted these magical sunrise sessions, the touch on my shot was perfect for that evening's matches. *"And one, chump!"* This is what I said when an opponent fouled me but I still managed to score. The accuracy of my jump shot eventually earned me the nickname 'Money' at the courts where I played.

Although having 'game' was socially beneficial, it was not the only way to reach celebrity status. Emcees, deejays, poppers, and break-dancers were also popular figures in our community. However neither jocks nor musical talents could compare with the legendary fame enjoyed by my friend, Jo-Jo.

"I'm shooting fair ones! What's up cuz?" This was one of the bellicose phrases Jo-Jo used to challenge another tough guy to a fight. Following this, he would launch into his pre-bout routine consisting of various, jerky movements of his head, legs, and arms to loosen-up his body.

During these moments it seemed everyone, excluding his opponent, knew Jo-Jo was about to record another knock out. Allow me to emphasize that Jo's KOs are not to be confused with a clumsy demonstration of brute strength. I'm talking about super-crisp, boxing technique. A technically-efficient fighting machine, it appeared his foes would put their guard down, stick their chins out, and blindly take a step forward. In the '80s, as far as I'm concerned, only Iron Mike Tyson knocked more guys out with such precision.

Many years later, I ran into Jo-Jo and a few of the fellas at a local bar. After a couple drinks, we began reminiscing on some of Jo's 'greatest hits.' What made our conversation more amusing was the fact that three of the guys who happened to be in the bar were on the list. At that time, I told Jo he missed his calling as a professional boxer. In a joking tone, I said he should be the light-heavyweight champion of the world by now. Although everyone laughed, we knew it was no joke!

More than just a fighter, this talented, young man realized the prized status he enjoyed in our neighborhood. And like most people, given the chance, he abused it at times.

"My ball!"

This is how Jo-Jo indicated he had been fouled in a pick-up, basketball game. In fact whenever he missed a shot, even if no defenders were nearby, he was more than likely to yell this out. To make matters worse, he was infamous for getting *very* physical on the defensive end, all-the-while daring his opponent to charge him with a violation. If no older guys were around to curtail his antics, Jo-Jo was notorious for messing up games. Although many ballers hated when he showed up at the courts, few vented their complaints. I can remember being quite nervous whenever this guy was around. That is, until Jo himself taught me to conquer my fear.

"My ball!" Jo uttered between his labored breathing even though I hadn't touched him.

It was sudden-death, game-point in our one-on-one competition. In our hood, we played 'make it – take it' which meant there was no change of possession after a scored basket. Scoring and then getting the ball back put a lot of pressure on the defender. After I hit five straight shots to tie the contest—despite being hacked viciously each time—Jo-Jo realized my confidence was soaring. With the momentum on my side, there was no way he would allow me to get the rebound after his missed shot.

"Jap!"

"Ball in," I announced as I handed him the *rock*. Following a faked shot, Jo dipped his shoulder and bulldozed into me but I was ready for him, having already gotten run over by his fullback-type drive to the basket several times in the previous game. I also knew he was going to try what he called his 'Akeem the Dream' drop-step because he always used it whenever he was in trouble. Despite my stellar defense, which resulted in an air-ball from a partially blocked shot, he again penalized me for another phantom foul. Nonetheless after his third miss in a row, even he felt embarrassed and decided to 'man up' and play some defense of his own.

Knowing I would not question his fouls, nor make any calls against him, Jo-Jo had slapped, scratched, and elbowed me for the last game-and-a-half. With caked-blood mixed with dirt and determination smearing my wrists and forearms, I had gradually acclimated to being brutalized. After losing the first game, my plan was to use that experience to learn how to score when I got fouled—as if I had another option!

The good news was, by this time, I had formulated a theory on attacking his peculiar style of defense. Realizing he was going to whack me no matter what, I stopped being afraid of getting hit. Once I was able to concentrate, I determined if he smacked me on the way up I normally missed. However if I could delay his assault until I was in the act of shooting, I found it was possible to score. First, I had to create enough space between us to get out of his reach. To do this, I exploded hard to his left or right before lifting off the ground. From that point it was simply a matter of learning to absorb the blow to my shooting arm while simultaneously compensating with an equal amount of extra force on the follow-thru. Although it had taken the better part of two games to tweak my technique to perfection, after my series of swishes, even Jo seemed impressed. That said he still had his sights set on claiming a victory.

Putting my winning formula in motion one more time, I released a fade-away jumper. Before the ball had time to bank off the backboard and slice through the chain, however, Jo barked out a make-believe dribbling violation. In spite of this small delay, it was not Jo-Jo's day and I persevered to the end. When I eventually hit the winning basket, he just stared at me and grinned.

Sucking in oxygen with both hands on his knees, Jo then paid me a compliment I will never forget. "Damn Tak! Your skills got nice as shit since I been away! You've really been practicing, huh?"

Jo-Jo had been locked up for the past six-months in the juvenile detention-center we called 'DC.' Although he was only half-way through his one-year sentence, recently the judge allowed Jo to come home Friday afternoons for weekend-furloughs. The first morning he had showed up to play with me, I was scared to death. However once it was apparent he lacked much of his normal swagger, I was able to relax. Since our contests were staged so early, with no audience to impress, this probably factored into his unusually laid-back demeanor.

"Tak, why don't you play like this all the time?" Jo-Jo asked while he checked the ball in to commence our tie-breaking match. He then added another unforgettable quote. "By the way, don't let any of those muthafuckas call you Jap anymore! You hear me?"

"Gotcha," I replied. "And I do play like this all the time, you just ain't been around." Following a series of fakes, I dashed out of his reach and launched a three-pointer from the left baseline. This time, instead of slapping my wrist Jo drew his hand back at the last moment. Perhaps he wanted to see the effect if he didn't foul me.

Swish!

For the next two years, even after Jo came home from DC, we continued our private matches on the weekends. Playing against Jo-Jo really brought out my competitive nature because week-after-week he showed up bristling with confidence, bragging about how he had been practicing too. During this time, both his skills and mine vastly improved. Nevertheless fouls or not, Jo-Jo never beat me again. Despite tallying victory after victory, there was nothing but admiration in my heart for Jo-Jo. Proof of this was I never mentioned these games to any of our friends. To this day, besides his younger brother, I don't believe anyone else knew about them. Through these physical contests, not only did I earn Jo's respect, I was no longer afraid of other kids.

By the time we entered middle school, playing ball and street-dancing had become serious business. However street-fighting—we called it boxing—was in a class by itself. To hone our hand-speed and harden our bodies, we *slap-boxed* and *body-boxed* to no end. At this level of rough-housing, as to be expected, occasionally someone would get punched in the face by accident. Then an authentic 'fair one' would take place.

Following a year of being on the receiving end of these play-fights, I began lifting weights in the summer between seventh and eighth grade. I was intent on paying back the hard-hitting body-boxers who had taken advantage of a lightweight Tak. When I coincidentally hit puberty, which added four inches and a couple pounds to my stature, I couldn't wait for September to arrive.

"I gotta surprise for them muthafuckas this year!" I exclaimed one evening in August, following a set on the bench press.

On the first day of school when my boy Joel challenged me to a 'toe-to-toe,' which was another name for body-box, I was ready. And exactly as I had imagined, within seconds, I connected with a left-hook that sent him flying back into his hall locker. After his head smashed into the metal door with a loud crash, he collapsed onto the floor. Once we ascertained he was okay, I looked around and smiled at all the surprised expressions.

"Books! Books!"

As my friend Marcus teased me on the way home from school, I looked down at the hard-covered texts in my hand.

Once elementary school ended, not only was carrying books considered corny, studying was viewed as something only white people did while the black folks chilled out and had fun. With this theory in effect, I wondered what kind of grades Marcus got before concluding he either had a bunch of easy classes, some lenient parents, or both. Unfortunately my situation was altogether different as *any* negative reports sent home from my teachers resulted in an instant ass-whipping. My father did not listen to excuses, nor did he play around when it came to our education. Although I do not recommend scaring children in order to motivate their study habits, considering I made the honor-roll every semester until halfway through my senior year, it could be argued that this brutal system was effective.

Contemplating my dilemma, I felt damned if I did and damned if I didn't. In order to be accepted as cool, it was necessary to face the wrath of my father–*which was completely out of the question!* On the other hand, if I carried books home, I might get beat-up for being a whiteboy. With options A and B both registering as absurd, I was forced to come up with a plan C.

For the next two weeks, I concentrated on stealing all the textbooks for my classes. Sometimes this was as easy as snatching a spare copy left on a shelf. However at other times I stole my classmates' books when no one was looking. Once I had a full set at home, I simply folded my worksheets and carried them in my pocket. Aside from a few complaints from teachers about creased assignments, my new plan was a success. In some cases, this was the difference between my receiving an A or a B. I can recall my Latin-studies teacher, Ms. Abernathy, chastising me. "Takuan, with a little more effort, you could be a Dean's List caliber student."

No thank you, please!

These white ladies, from far-off neighborhoods, could never understand that academic trophies only alienated me from 'being black.' As far as I was concerned this issue was resolved. I had given myself an A for effort and I executed plan C every year until I graduated high school. An added benefit was each fall I made a little chump-change by selling books to younger students who wished to emulate this nonsense. To this day, I'm sure there are still a few dusty textbooks in my parent's attic.

Following any heavy snowfall, the 'books dilemma' became most apparent in our after-school snowball fights. Since making snowballs requires two-hands, students carrying books became the easiest targets. Far from simply not taking part in a fun activity, the inability to retaliate was dangerous because our version of this wintertime activity was nothing like the Christmas specials on television. This drama was absent of any smiling snowmen, or giggling children tossing balls of white powder. *No, ours was a full-contact sport!*

Fights erupted when kids got blind-sided with chunks of ice to the cranium. Many students got injured just from slipping on the frozen pavement in their desperate attempt to escape being assaulted. Every afternoon the infirmary was filled to capacity due to our winter festivals. We disregarded the daily pleas over the loudspeaker warning of the repercussions and numerous dangers. Drivers on the roadways, along with dogs, cats, birds, and other pedestrians, were pummeled without mercy. *Talk about fun!* We even wrapped our arms around the rear fenders of moving vehicles to hitch rides along the icy roads. To miss out on this excitement in order to do homework was just not going to happen!

Middle school was a crazy time of transition. No longer a child but far from being an adult, I evolved in many ways. My fondest memory, by far, was learning how to 'french-kiss' from my girlfriend, Patrice. *What a great kisser!* In addition, my street-entrepreneurship blossomed as my friend, Terrance and I set-up shop between classes by selling the candy and gum we shoplifted at the nearby *7-Eleven.* Perhaps the most significant change was the 'Jap name-calling' had become a thing of the past. Having worked diligently to prove myself, I felt accepted among the 'cool society' and life was fun!

On June 18, 1982, we graduated from Kennedy Middle School. At that time I was looking forward to expanding further upon my 'blackness' in high school. I actually thought we were being promoted into nothing more than the senior level of snowball fights and slap-boxing. *Man was I in for a rude awakening!*

Chapter 3: Only a Freshman

"If you don't leave now, you'll be late!" my mother scolded loudly from the kitchen in Japanese.

I had been in the bathroom for over twenty minutes. Excited as I was to enter legendary Garfield High, I was having second thoughts as I stood there looking in the mirror. Thanks to a cluster of acne that seemed to have spawned overnight, my face looked like a pepperoni pizza. The truth was, with so many girls wanting to touch my 'good hair,' beyond believing the hype that I was handsome, I had become somewhat of a narcissist.

"How can I face the beautiful honeys with all these pimples?" I complained to my ghastly reflection.

"Is that what you're worried about?" my mother inquired with a chuckle. "Girls?" She was now standing outside the bathroom door so she had overheard me talking to myself. "Boy, no one's thinking about you, you're only a freshman. Come on, hurry up!"

I opened the door and angrily brushed by her. *"Itte-kimasu."* As I was leaving I mumbled under my breath while I considered playing hooky on the first day of school. Luckily, I ran into Quinton and Earl on the way. As usual, they were smoking *cheeba*.

Now everything was all right.

"Damn cuz! What happened to your face? You look like 'Bumple-stiltskin'!" Quinton said in between tokes of the aromatic herb.

"Fuck you! And pass that before it becomes a roach," I said trying to defer attention away from my complexion challenges.

Over the summer, the three of us had decided to experiment with marijuana. Although we did not consider weed to be a 'real drug' like cocaine or heroin, we also never thought we would become regular users so quickly.

By the time we staggered onto the school grounds, we were high and also quite drunk. Before puffing on our last two joints, we had stopped to pick up another friend named Keith. Everyone knew Keith's father promoted events in Philadelphia nightclubs; so there was always an abundance of liquor at his house we could drink without his parents noticing.

"Welcome to mighty Garfield High! What up G-men?" I saluted my inebriated mates in a mocking tone as we sauntered between the Roman Coliseum-like pillars at the main entrance.

"Yo Tak, you got that Visine?"

"Yeah," I responded, reaching into my pocket.

After making sure no one was watching us, we took turns squirting the eye drops into our eyes next to the main entrance. We entered the building just as the bell signaling the end of second period sounded. *My head is spinning!* In spite of feeling dizzy, I had no trouble focusing on the voluptuous upper-class chicks in the stairwell before a purplish-white blur caught my attention. Snapping my head upward, I caught a glimpse of a white kid tumbling down the stairs.

From our vantage point, it was hard to tell if the boy had tripped on his own, or been pushed. However the situation became curiously amusing once he crashed onto the ground floor. Instead of standing up, the boy crawled on all fours in a vain attempt to gather his scattered books and worksheets from underneath a stampede of students changing classes. After a girl accused him of being a pervert, people began kicking him in the butt. The comedy-relief really escalated when another group of guys picked his books up and began tossing them to one another. As the hapless boy ran back-and-forth in a ridiculous game of monkey in the middle, Earl grabbed my arm.

"Yo, ain't that Jeff?" he asked.

Reaching into my pocket, I pulled out my glasses and put them on. "Oh shit! You're right, that is Jeff!" I exclaimed shocked to discover it was indeed the goofy kid who lived behind me.

In elementary school, Jeffrey Chason had been famous for his uncanny ability to talk himself into a beat-down. With the exception of Quinton, who had moved from Canada just a year ago, all of us had kicked Jeff's ass at least once. Now as a high school sophomore, he still seemed like a strange guy. At that moment, if someone had predicted I would be friends with this nerd before graduating from Garfield, I would've looked at him like he was drunk. Wait a minute, we were drunk...*I almost forgot!*

As to be expected in an 'ethnic town' surrounded by predominantly Caucasian districts, every year the G-men ranked high in the 'black sports'; i.e. basketball, football, and track. Only celebrated Camden High, who boasted NBA players like Milt Wagner and Billy Thompson amongst its alumni, had a better reputation. Woodrow Wilson High, which was also in Camden, and our cross-town rival, Eastern High, were the only other schools that could compete with the G-men in all three sports.

29

Over the summer, I had formulated my blueprint for success at Garfield. Having nothing to do with academics—or reality for that matter—it consisted of playing basketball, being popular, and most of all, chilling the fuck out! Although I imagined my skills would eventually lead to collegiate opportunities, I decided to worry about scouts and scholarships later. Despite my optimism, there was one major flaw in my scheme: I wasn't as good at basketball as I thought I was.

Sure, I was a talented shooter. Nevertheless having a laser-tight jumper outside on the playground does not always translate to success inside the gym. In a regulation game, a player is required to operate within the parameters of a rigid system. On the other hand, street-ball is the complete opposite. Absent of clocks and referees, it was more like organized chaos; and this is the game I loved! However, since the list of 'black-approved' activities was limited, the obvious choice within this narrow spectrum was basketball.

To make matters worse, I was a prima donna before I even mastered the fundamentals of the game. This was due largely to the broadcasted imagery of the 'million dollar athlete' which had become commonplace in the eighties. Because these media caricatures were projected as both cocaine fiends and sexually promiscuous, I saw no conflict of interests between my ritual at the playground, which included smoking and drinking, and the life of a varsity player wearing a blue-and-white Gryphons uniform.

The Courts

For the disenfranchised inhabitants of America, the barber shop and the playground basketball courts are two of the remaining bastions of culture which we can still call our own. Our neighborhood was no different. Thus everyone paid the courts a visit at some time or another. *Flygirls* stopped-by to check out the ballers; street dancers blasted funky-fresh mixes from huge *boxes* while they busted head-spins on large pieces of cardboard. As homeboys shot fair-ones to settle their beefs, graffiti artists spray-painted murals or just tagged their names on the backboards, poles, or the concrete below our feet. Even hustlers dropped by to shoot dice and handle their business; which of course, led to *Johnnie-Law* showing up to keep those dealings in check. In spite of these regularly scheduled police-harassments, the courts were 'the place to be' for black and brown folks. This was where we congregated to relax and release stress.

Oftentimes chased out of the house by my enraged father, terrified and in tears, what does a disheartened boy like that do? He searches for a friendly face. Actually, friendly or not, any face will do. This is the type of situation which sets youngsters up for various forms of child exploitation.

More than a decade later, as a social worker, I had the opportunity to assist kids who had been betrayed—sometimes violated—by adults. Considering all the unspeakable things that happen to vulnerable children every day, I consider myself very fortunate.

Following my near-escapes, the courts served as my personal mental-health facility. Possessing nothing but a faded t-shirt and my 'skills,' after wiping the tears from my face, I would be mystically transported to an enchanted place where I always felt welcome and everyone knew my name.

"We got Tak! We got Tak!"

The moment my silhouette was sighted walking behind the elementary school, the debate would commence. Although these honored receptions made me feel special, they were not reserved for only me. Quinton, Wayne, Earl, Terrance, and even Jo-Jo—for slightly different reasons—received equal fanfare. Furthermore there were old-heads like June-bug, Mann, and Ernie whose red carpet treatments dwarfed ours by comparison. This was because these veterans had played with the old-school legends like 'Money Mike,' the guy I was named after, and 'Jack Frost,' the phenom who could rock-the-cradle like 'the human-highlight-film,' Dominique Wilkins.

As the sun began its descent out west, most of the serious ballers would be preparing for the evening tournament. In addition to stretching and shooting jumpers, puffing on a Newport cigarette or a joint were mainstays to getting warmed-up. While beer and wine were also common refreshments, they were normally reserved for the nightcap.

After two captains were selected, one of them would shoot a 'do-or-die' from the top of the key. If he drained it, he had the right to choose the first player.

"I got June," says Keith.

"I'll take Mann," Scottie quickly counters.

"Gimme Ernie."

"Okay, I got Wayne."

"Yo *ET*? You running?" Keith yells over Scottie's

shoulder.

When everyone turns their head in the direction Keith is yelling, we see Earl emerge from behind the nearby public pool.

"Damn!" Scottie curses for failing to notice the lanky teen first.

"Yeah," Earl responds jogging onto the court. After one of the younger guys passes him the ball, Earl nets his first jumper of the evening. Due to his crazy leaping ability and electrifying dunks, ET was usually the first amongst us younger guys to be selected.

"Aiight, I got E." Keith states with a smile. By the confident look on his face, it is apparent that Keith believes he has the cornerstones to a winning squad.

Following a careful scan for any other newcomers, Scottie chooses his next player. "Gimme Tak."

Once the teams were decided, the unpicked talent which we referred to as B-players were sent over to the far, more dilapidated courts. When the game was finished, a new captain then selected another squad to challenge the champs.

"I got next!" This is what I would say whenever my team failed to produce the sixteen or twenty-one baskets needed to win.

Despite the blow to our pride, losing had its benefits too. This was especially true if *flygirls* happened to be present that evening. Also since most ballers moonlighted as break dancers, they had a couple minutes to *uprock,* or hit some back-spins, before taking another shot at the title.

"Ill! What happened to your face?"

This is how my ex-girlfriend, Patrice, greeted me at her locker after I spotted her talking to an upper-class jock. Since our lockers were in the same hallway, diagonally across from each other, I had deliberately waited until the older boy departed before making my approach.

"Oh, I know you ain't trying to get wrong!" I snapped back. "With your generic *jheri curl* and matching plastic jacket, you over here lookin' like an extra at a *Beat It,* video audition!"

This was the type of humor that had produced gut-wrenching laughter from Patrice back in middle school. Nonetheless after two weeks at Garfield, the fact I was the low-man on the totem pole still had not sunk in. To quote my mother verbatim: "No one's thinking about you, you're only a freshman!"

"Well if you don't like my hair, stop trying to talk to me all the time. Last year is over! And by the way, you really need to see a dermatologist about your...condition." After Pat replied in an irritated tone I had never heard before, without a second thought, she closed her locker and made a hasty exit in the same direction as the older boy.

Following some investigation, I found out my new rival was named 'Justin.' In addition to being a starter on the JV basketball team, homeboy had a full mustache and beard. *How could I compete?* I brooded realizing that rekindling my flame with Patrice was going to be more difficult than I had anticipated. Furthermore it was torture pretending I did not see them cuddling across the hallway every morning. When I saw Justin give her a *Starburst* candy, which was exactly how I had wooed Pat last year, I was jealous as hell!

I concluded the only 'black way' to confront the issue was to pick a fight with Justin. Considering he was two years older—not to mention two inches taller and ten pounds heavier—I decided to get a second opinion first. Since Kay was in Justin's class, I asked her one day when her friend Lizzie was at our house. After they both busted-out laughing, Kay made her point loud and clear.

"Justin will fuck you up!"

And in case I had wanted a third opinion, which I certainly did not, Liz added her two cents for good measure. *"Boy please!"* she exclaimed with a frown. "Go and sit your freshman ass down somewhere before our class of '84 brother smacks you in the mouth!" Almost a second sister to me, in recent years Liz and I had developed our own sibling-like rivalry.

Before I had time to respond, my mother yelled down the hallway that I had a phone call from Quinton. With no rebuttal in mind, I hurriedly walked away from the two snickering girls.

"Wassup man," I said after grabbing the phone.

"Check-it-out," Quinton started in. "I was talking to the freshman football coach today."

Quinton was originally from Barbados but his family moved to Jersey from Toronto last year. Therefore he was one of the few guys I knew who, like me, did not have any extended family in Philly.

"Word? What'd he say?"

"He said he wants you and me to start at linebacker on this year's squad," Quinton got right to the point.

"For real!"

Although I was not interested in playing football, I was elated to hear any man bearing the title 'coach' was acknowledging my athletic prowess. Even though my football experience up-to-that-point had been limited to playing two-hand-touch in the street, I had no trouble believing the head-coach had randomly spotted me in the hallway and decided, from one look, that I was his starting linebacker. *Feeling left out in the cold, I was desperately seeking any form of acceptance.*

The next afternoon, Quinton and I showed up at practice. Following a week of boring drills and predominantly watching from the sideline, after our team lost its opening game, the coach inserted both of us into the starting lineup. By mid-season, Quinton had established himself as the star linebacker he had predicted while I played a significant role by starting on both offense and defense as well as on all the special-teams.

As champs of our division, we finished the year with only that one blemish on opening day. From our second game on, we spanked our opponents by an average margin of thirty-six points. Although playing football had not been part of my plan, considering it qualified as a 'black activity,' it turned out to be a great idea.

When basketball season rolled around, I was worried my patented jump shot would not be ready. In spite of this, I made the team easily but became disappointed when I was not named a member of the starting unit. Nevertheless, having already played a non-starring role on the football squad, this helped me deal with my sixth-man designation. Although I never would have admitted it, playing off the bench actually suited me. With the crowd, the lights, and the referees blowing their whistles, I was too nervous to play well at the beginning of the game. However once it began, I was able to relax.

The star of our team was our point-guard, Fraheim. *Frah* was both a scorer and a great passer. The guy starting over me at the two-guard position was a cool dude named Raheim. *Rah* understood his priority was not to score, but instead, to compliment Frah. 'Frah and Rah' was a tandem unit that played well together. Anytime I went in the game as a small-forward, with both of them playing, it was easy for me to blend-in and play team ball. However, whenever I replaced Raheim, I would start *gunning*.

'Gunning' simply means shooting the ball a lot. For some players it was okay to gun because they were the stars of their team. I was not. This conflict of interests reached its apex during our most important game of the season.

"For Chrissake Amaru! Run the play the way we did it in practice!" Coach DeUriarte, who we all called Coach D, screamed from the bench when I ran past him.

"But Coach, I scored!" I responded.

In my book, it was all about scoring.

"Shut-up and get back on defense!" Throwing both hands up in disgust, Coach D was furious.

There was no playoff system in-place for freshman teams, so the champion of the division was decided by the best record. A couple weeks earlier, we dropped a double-overtime thriller to undefeated, Holy Saints High for our only loss. Ironically, this game had been my best performance of the season. Scoring twenty-four points and even dishing-out a few assists, I was a big part of the comeback which barely fell short. With only one game remaining, both teams understood this contest would decide who took home the Liberty Division crown.

Holy Saints, a private, Catholic school in a neighboring town, boasted an all-Caucasian squad. Many people thought it was unfair they could recruit players from both North and South Jersey. As a parochial institution devoted to winning basketball games, the Saints were often compared to Duke University. And just like the Blue Devils, these 'white devils' were known for winning championships.

At half time, we trailed by twelve.

Similar to our first match, the Saints' star, Bobby Lehman, was scorching Raheim. He scored fifteen points in the first half alone. When Rah committed his fourth foul in the final seconds, everyone knew he would not be starting the third quarter. With a look of disappointment on his face, Raheim had jogged off the floor believing he was letting us down. Seeing this, I checked the scoreboard before entering the locker room. It was obvious someone besides Frah needed to step-up in the second half.

For most of the first half, I had sat on the bench analyzing Bobby's game to a tee. Not only was I convinced I could shut him down defensively, I was also confident I could score on him too—*just like I did in our first game.* This challenge had my name written all over it. Furthermore, I was ready. Unfortunately Coach D did not see it that way.

"We're gonna go with a smaller line-up to apply some pressure on the ball. Tak, you go in the game for Kam. Kenny, you sub for Rah," our coach barked out following his half-time speech.

Being sent in the game as a forward meant I would not be able to match wits against Bobby. Although I realized the risk, considering this was equivalent to our championship, I decided to inform Coach D of my first-half observations.

"Coach, I've been really watching Lehman's

footwork. I'm sure I can shut him down if you let me—"

"Amaru," he interrupted, "when I want your coaching advice I'll let you know. Do you understand?" Stunned by his cold reaction, I was slow to reply. Coach D, registering my silence as disrespect, snapped at me. "Big mouth, you're on the bench in the second half!" he yelled before pointing behind me. "Tony, get in there at forward."

Fighting back tears of frustration, I bit my tongue and ran over to join the reserve players who had already started shooting layups. A couple minutes later, I took a seat on the bench, no longer upset. I cheered for the entire quarter along with my teammates. During this time, nothing really changed. We basically kept pace with the Saints in spite of Lehman's continual heroics. With no time on the clock, I stood up with everyone else when Kenny came down awkwardly with a rebound and collapsed in a heap.

During the short intermission, the coach examined Kenny's condition. When he tried to stand, it was apparent he could barely walk. Crossing my fingers, I got my wish.

"Tak," Coach D pointed at me. "You're in for Davidson."

Hearing this, I ripped off my sweats and ran over to place them on a chair. I did this quickly to illustrate there was no lingering attitude problem. When I rejoined my teammates, Coach D was all business.

"Let's switch to man-to-man defense," he said. "On offense, keep working the ball into the post like we did in the third quarter." Then Coach D looked at me. "Amaru, this Lehman kid knows how to score. Stay on his right hand. Force him to his left and make him take tough shots," he instructed.

"Yessir." Nervous I might mess this up by talking too

much, this was all I said.

Down by fifteen, I started the fourth quarter by in-bounding the ball to Fraheim. As we crossed the half-court line, a double-team was waiting for him so he passed it back. Kam, also having re-entered the game, posted-up near the basket like we had drilled in practice. However, since I had played small-forward all week, I was not comfortable making this pass into the low-post.

Seeming to sense my uncertainty, Lehman started talking trash. "Ah, a new nigger for me to torch! Now I see why you're all so dark!"

After repeatedly being showered with racial epithets by their players and fans, we disliked the Saints almost as much as they hated us. Once Lehman started popping junk, which was the only language spoken at the courts, our team's game-plan vanished from my memory in a flash.

I'm gonna bust this whiteboy's ass! I thought with a grin a split-second prior to exploding to my right and quickly dribbling the ball between my legs to change direction. Bobby, seeming unfamiliar with a ghetto cross-over, stumbled and was left in the dust. After swishing a midrange jumper, I heard the crowd gasp on my way back on defense.

I was set-up well before my opponent arrived. Since he wanted to talk junk, I stared hard into his eyes. My challenge was clear. "Lehman?" I taunted him. "Ain't that a Jewish name? You should be ashamed of yourself…what a sell-out!" By saying this, I was attempting to reverse the head-game. Once he did not respond, I clamped down on defense.

A few seconds later, a lazy pass intended for him floated in our direction. Jumping up, I managed to get a hand on it; however instead of chasing down the loose ball, I sprinted to the opposite goal hoping it rolled to one of my teammates. There was one problem with this tactic: should the other team get to the ball first, it would be a four-on-five because I was running toward the opposite end of the court by myself. Luckily, on this occasion, my 'cherry picking' gamble paid off.

Receiving a long pass, I laid the ball off the glass and smacked the backboard with both hands on my uncontested lay-up. *Four points for me, and zero for the superstar,* I reflected. Despite the presence of eight other players on the floor, I imagined I was playing one-on-one.

"Bobby, you getting tired?" the Saints' coach asked while his team inbounded the ball.

"No, I'm okay Coach," Bobby assured the balding middle-aged man dressed in a blue, pin-striped suit.

"Well I need a little more effort outta you. That's twice-in-row your man scored."

"I got him Coach," Bobby reaffirmed his previous statement.

Having overheard their exchange, I waited until Lehman crossed beyond half-court before pressing my psychological advantage. "Bobby-boy, where you at? Thought you were supposed to be good?" I teased with a grin on my face.

"Tak, shut-up and play ball!" Coach D yelled from the sideline.

"You better listen to your coach before he puts you back on the bench!" the Lehman kid growled back. Nevertheless, he seemed less sure of himself.

After a Saints' big man scored a hook-shot, once again, I beat their star down the floor and caught another football-like pass for my second stylish layup. This time, however, Bobby was close enough to shove me out of bounds. The ref blew his whistle just as the ball rolled around the rim and plopped through the net.

"Shooting one plus a technical foul on number ten for unsportsmanlike conduct!" yelled the referee pointing at Bobby.

I was picked-up off the floor by my teammates. Following high-fives all around, I sank both free throws. As the second shot swished through the net, I winked at Bobby.

For the next couple minutes, both teams traded baskets but we clearly held the advantage. Since defenders swarmed Frah whenever he touched the ball, he continually fed me where I could best operate. This brought out all my offensive talents. Bobby scored once during this time but I was getting the best of the matchup. With time running out, Coach D instructed us to go into a full-court press on defense. This resulted in me stealing the ball twice, scoring once, and even tallying two assists. At this point, the Saints were in disarray.

"Timeout!" yelled their coach.

With two minutes remaining, it was 58 – 56.

Walking toward our bench, my eyes were glued to the scoreboard. I did not dare look at Coach D, fearful he might take me out of the game. To my surprise, he called a play designed for *me* to be the primary shooter. *I was ecstatic!*

"Men, it's crunch-time and we got 'em right where we want 'em!" he roared looking in my direction. "Amaru, that Lehman boy looks tired. For the rest of the game, I want you to take him off the dribble and look for the open man or get to the foul line."

His words were music to my ears! At this moment, my ego took center-stage telling me my super-stardom had finally arrived. For a fleeting instant, I felt disappointed because Pat and Justin were not present to witness me single-handedly slay the Saints. If only this were a home-game, I lamented in silence. Then, I blew it off figuring it was just as well if they heard the highlights from one of our managers.

As the horn sounded and a referee blew his whistle, Coach D repeated his last directive in my ear. "Go strong to the hoop! No jumpers, you hear me?"

"Blue ball…here we go!" the ref barked before handing me the leather-bound, Wilson basketball.

In-bounding the *rock* to Frah, I immediately noticed their team had switched to an aggressive man-to-man defense just like Coach D had predicted. When Bobby got real close in an attempt to deny me from receiving the ball, I smiled knowing he could never keep up.

Bursting to my right, I ran under the basket and through a screen set by our power-forward. I caught the ball near the top-of-the-key with enough time to face the basket and scan their defense. By the time Bobby showed up, I was confident I had found their weakness and I was determined to exploit it in convincing fashion. Faking both ways, I crossed Lehman up again and easily blew by him. Being in one-on-one mode, I sprung off the floor before realizing their center was stepping toward me. By the time I noticed the double-team, it was too late.

Trapped in mid-air, I stared at the gigantic, white jersey bearing down on me as Coach D's last words in the timeout replayed in my mind: *"No jumpers!"* Caught in no man's land, I blindly flung the ball into the throng of players under the basket. Luckily a Saints player was a half-step late on his shift. Although he managed to smack the ball, it magically deflected into the hands of our center who

Only a Freshman

promptly jumped up and dunked it with two hands. The score was tied. This caused the Saints to call their last time-out.

To the average fan, since we had scored, it may have appeared we executed our offense. Well, Coach D was no novice spectator.

"Tak, sit down! Rah, get back in there and this time stay on Lehman's right hand!" After smacking Raheim on the backside, the coach turned away from me in disgust.

How could that be? I complained in my head. *I was the star of the game!* Staring at the scoreboard, I remembered the fifteen-point margin when I entered. After taking a seat on the bench, I sat up feigning a positive attitude, hoping this would convince the coach to put me back in the game.

With under a minute remaining, Lehman hit a baseline jumper and resumed talking trash. Seeing this, I could not bear to watch any longer. I decided to take my chances. Standing up, I walked over to Coach D. "Coach—" I began before he cut me off.

"Amaru, I swear to God if you ask me to put you back in the game, you're off this team!" Coach D was so livid he was trembling. "How many times do I have to tell you? You are *not* the coach! Our whole season's on the line and all you care about is how much playing time you get. Get outta my face!"

When some of the home-court cronies spotted the opposing coach yelling at the cocky kid who had been mocking their star player, they recognized this as an excellent heckling opportunity.

"Yeah Coach, you tell him," one guy yelled. "There's no letter 'I' in T-E-A-M!" Hearing their timely sarcasm, a couple other spectators giggled along.

Brooding on the bench, I quietly reflected: *But there is*

44

an 'M' and an 'E'! Fuck this bullshit...I'm outta here!

When Coach D called a time-out and walked onto the floor to yell at the referees, I excused myself to the locker room. There were still thirty-eight seconds remaining. By the time the final buzzer sounded, I was already walking home. It never dawned on me this stunt would cancel any chances I had to play for Garfield in the future.

"Yo Tak, why'd you quit the G-men?"

Hearing the question asked by one of the younger boys named Rudy, everyone at the courts became dead silent. Rudy was one of the kids in middle school who looked up to us. After I rehashed my version of the story, Rudy cheered me on.

"Yeah cuz, them *cracka-ass* coaches always trying to dim a brother's shine! You gotta let them know you ain't no sucka!" As he said this, we bumped our fists together. This was our favorite way of showing solidarity. We called it giving each other 'a pound.'

"Shut-the-fuck-up youngboy!"

As Mann approached the sea of players parted to allow the old-head to pass through. Mann, in his early 20s, was a quiet baller who usually kept to himself.

"So lemme get this straight," he said once he reached me. "You walked out before the game ended? That's *wack!*"

Astonished at his rare show of emotion, I listened in silence.

"Tak," Mann continued, "your game has improved more in one year than any baller I've ever seen! Before last

45

summer, you were strictly a B-player. Word is bond, I didn't even know your name. Nowadays, your ass is *money!* You hit all kinda crazy jump-shots even when you're just playin' around. And though I heard you try to keep it on the hush, Quinton and Earl told me you're a brainiac in school too." Pausing to look at me up-and-down, he then pointed in disgust. "So what's up with you? You out here smoking weed and drinking forties like you got no other options." Stepping forward, he punched me in the chest.

Not very hard, it jolted me back to the time my father had jabbed me in the same area after I asked him if I was black.

"I actually believed we were gonna see you playing in March Madness in a couple years. Damn cuz!" With one last look of disappointment, Mann turned and walked away.

"You will Mann! 'Cause I'm gonna play next year!" I clamored at his receding silhouette. "Wait 'til you see how nice my skills are by next year!"

From that moment, Mann was always cold toward me. In fact, he never spoke to me again.

Chapter 4: Injured – Almost Incarcerated

"Shit!" I cried out in agony.

Feeling close to fainting from the intense pain, this was the only word I could utter as Quinton and Terrance carried me to a grassy area near the pool. My head was swimming in dizziness. Once they set me down, I removed my sneaker and, together, we stared at my swollen ankle.

"Damn, it looks like a purple tennis ball!" exclaimed Terrance to my dismay.

Since quitting the G-men four months ago, it seemed like I hurt myself every week. I feared this injury was more serious than my normal sprains, and my intuition was proven correct the next morning when the doctor diagnosed it a mild fracture. This resulted in my ankle being wrapped in a soft-cast. At home, instead of receiving sympathy, my father accused me of being accident prone and grumbled about having to use his days off to drive me to the hospital.

"Boy, you been wearing that ankle brace I bought you? Ain't nobody got time to be driving your ass to McGuire every weekend."

To make matters worse, two days later, my father had to take me to juvenile court. Six months prior, three of my football teammates got picked up by *five-o* for committing numerous acts of vandalism. When they implicated me as one of their partners-in-crime, I was arrested a week later. Even though I was terrified of getting sent to the juvenile detention center, after the judge sentenced me to a year of probation and house-arrest, I almost requested to go to DC rather than to be trapped inside a car with the Serpent.

Surprisingly, after leaving the courthouse, my father paid little attention to me. Like most Asiatic men, he was inherently terrified of courtrooms. In fact, the only time I ever saw my sire look frightened was during those court proceedings. Perhaps he was exhausted from the entire ordeal. At any rate there were no incidents before we got home.

In a nutshell, house-arrest meant I was only able to leave home for school or if I was accompanied by my parents. During the first two weeks, my probation officer surprised me with several unannounced visits. Had I been healthy, I certainly would have been outside by myself on a few of those occasions. So it was only thanks to my injury, I never got sent to DC.

For the next couple months, I enjoyed tranquil moments at home with my mother and sister. A throwback to my childhood days, on most nights, we played board games or watched television until it was time to go to bed. Since Kay and I were in the same Spanish class, we also found time to practice dialogues from my plan C textbook. However, the vibe took a serious dip whenever my father was off from work. With him stretched out on the living room couch, it was impossible to relax under his omniscient wrath.

Like many descendants of the conquered, original inhabitants, my father suffered from emotional trauma that was exacerbated by his addiction to over-the-counter pharmaceuticals—plus a few of the street variety as well. Forced to suppress his manhood at work due to the peculiar parameters of society, he unleashed his pent-up fury on everything and everybody when he got home. This was not limited to the confines of our house either. I can recall three instances when bigoted neighbors made the mistake of expressing their biased views my way. Whenever this occurred, I couldn't get home fast enough to tell my father. Upon hearing the slightest hint of racism, my sire was at their doorsteps ready to shoot a fair-one! In each of these cases, after numerous apologies, these cowards generalized the incident into a 'big misunderstanding.'

Unfortunately, there weren't enough open-racists around for my father to channel his anger on a regular basis. With no other outlet available, the enraged Serpent usually vented his aggression toward our black-shepherd named 'Shogun.' Since the pecking order was *Sho,* then me, I probably owe my life to this loyal dog.

Sho received even more beat-downs than my eccentric neighbor, Jeff. It was rare to go an entire day without seeing my father kick Sho at least once. And God forbid we neglected to let the dog outside to relieve himself and, having no other option, he handled his business on the carpet. For those special ass-whippings, broom handles and tree branches became the preferred instruments of punishment.

Back in first grade, I came down with a bad case of the flu which kept me out of school for two weeks. On the third morning, my parents got into a heated argument. When I heard my father walk outside and slam the door, I was relieved the altercation had not turned into a violent episode. Before I could thank God, however, I spotted an apparition slithering across the snow in our backyard.

Shogun, still a pup at the time, was already well-acquainted with his role as crash dummy. For this reason, he

49

had tried to hide when my father first raised his voice in anger. In spite of his efforts, there was no escaping our fenced-off backyard.

Burning up with fever, I watched the chase scene under the dreamy influence of Nyquil. The two bodies splashing through the wet snow appeared to be running in slow-motion as they moved in-and-out of my field of vision. Lying on a couch near a sliding glass door, I clenched my eyes shut when Sho started yelping in pain. Fearing for my puppy's life, I vividly imagined every wicked blow being administered.

Suddenly, the canine's body slammed hard against the back door. This caused me to open my eyes. Once I did, I saw Sho staring at me with both ears pressed-down against his head and his tail between his legs. He looked terrified. I understood he was begging me to open the door and I will never forgive myself for not helping him. With my head throbbing and body aching, I laid there paralyzed with fear as a dark shadow descended on Sho.

The Serpent struck but the dog was quicker. I watched Sho duck under a kick vicious enough to crack his skull had it landed. By the time a piercing crash shattered my eardrums, Sho was scurrying passed his stalker to safety. I don't know how I summoned the will to flip my lethargic body over the back of the sofa, but I vacated the couch an instant before shards of glass showered the area where I had been watching cartoons.

From underneath the couch, I watched my father retrieve his foot from the shattered door. Despite wearing only sweat pants and a pair of low-top sneakers with no socks, the Serpent did not sustain even the slightest hint of an injury. Seeing this, I imagined the scales which shielded him were grafted from high-grade steel. I was convinced he was invincible.

Since this occurred in February, old-man winter was lurking outside. In an attempt to keep him from entering our house, we used duck-tape and cardboard cut from a neighbor's discarded refrigerator-box to seal the hole for a couple days until a repairman came to our rescue. In the evening, we bundled up in our coats and blankets just to watch television and we were still cold. Even with this inconvenience, unlike the rest of my family, I felt sorry for my father. It was obvious he felt ashamed whenever he looked in the direction of the insanity he had perpetuated. More than anything, I wanted to believe his out-of-control behavior would stop.

Like Shogun, I was prepared to evacuate the area at any hint that my father's Emotional Pain Body had been pierced. However, unlike Sho, there was no trapping me. For as long as I can remember, the Serpent was not quick enough to catch me. Some of my friends claimed these daily escapes from my living room had enhanced my ability to play two-hand-touch-football, saying it was almost impossible to place both of their hands on me at the same time.

Nonetheless with my leg now in a soft cast, I was a dead-duck in the event of any such outburst. In total silence, I laid in the darkness of my bedroom reviewing the hopelessness of my situation. Even fearing to use the toilet, my goal on my father's days off was to make him forget I was home. Beyond despair, I felt my will cracking under the stress. It was then I heard a knock at our front door.

"Who is it?" the Serpent snapped.

My father detested visitors in general, so this is how he normally responded. It was so bad, many of our friends were afraid to come over whenever his silver Cadillac was in the driveway. Although I could not understand the guest's reply, I was surprised to hear my father's voice soften up and become friendly.

"Yeah Ant, come on in. Tak's in the back. How's your father doing?"

"He's fine, thank you," Ant responded politely. "Mr. Amaru, forgive me for not coming in but I'm on my way to my part-time job. Could you give Tak a message for me, please?"

"Sure, what is it?" inquired my father, demonstrating the decent side of his personality.

"Please tell him from now on, I can give him a ride to school. One of my friends saw Tak crutching down the highway this morning. He doesn't have to do that. I'll be happy to give him a lift."

If Ant had not already been revered as a god in my eyes, he certainly would have become a saint that afternoon. Until that moment, I had been singing the blues. Besides my football season and the 76ers trading for center, Moses Malone, this school year had been a terrible experience; I detested my life at Garfield. But suddenly the clouds were giving way to a bright sunshiny day because I was about to start hanging-out with certified, G-men All-Stars!

A far cry from a simple ride to school, this was the deluxe package. Not only did Ant and his friends hustle weed, they were also amongst the top personalities in the graduating class of '83. For a disgruntled freshman experiencing growing pains under the new caste-system, being seen in Ant's car was the difference between night and day. At the end of April, on the spur of a moment, I could not have drawn up a more favorable set of circumstances.

Ant liked to get to school well before the eight o'clock bell so he could open-up shop by selling joints for a dollar a stick. Before arriving, we usually picked up his girlfriend, Rita, and one or two of his friends. On my first morning riding with the senior crew, Rita was not with us. Due to an early, six o'clock workout with the track team, she was already at school. Rita was G-High's top, female 400-meter-hurdler. Many people joked that she and Ant were a match made in athlete-heaven. After hearing Ant mention to his friend, Chauncey, that she would meet us later we entered the student parking lot.

Almost immediately, I spotted three chicken-heads gawking hard. Squinting my eyes allowed me to recognize the uppity trio that had 'gotten new' this year. Back in eighth grade, Candis, Ronda, and Laticia were cool as hell with everyone; they were always in the middle of whatever was going on. However once we got to Garfield they refused to speak to any freshman, especially the guys. If they acknowledged us at all, it was done with contempt.

The threesome was waving their arms to get Ant's attention. Since Ant was staring at the girls as we approached, I thought he was going to stop and talk to them. For this reason, I busted-out laughing when he continued to taxi right by.

In response to being *dissed,* the three biddies looked at one another and exclaimed, "Ant's so crazy!" This was followed by a round of cackling laughter.

When the gray Ford Granada reached an area where students had not yet convened, Ant circled around and stopped. By the time I looked up, *Larry, Moe,* and *Curly* were already there.

"Hi Ant!" the three of them chorused together.

Pushing with their elbows, each girl was visibly jockeying for the best position in front of the driver's window. "Let's see, who else is riding with you today?" one of them asked way too loudly. Although she used the word 'you' and it was obvious she was speaking to Ant, by her body language it appeared she was asking one of her girlfriends. This was because Ant had yet to acknowledge their presence.

"Oh is that Chauncey?" Another one asked, pretending she didn't quite recognize the All-State linebacker riding shotgun. Following the feigned question, the three-chicken-headed ensemble once again chimed-in together. *"Hi Chauncey!"*

Like me, Chauncey was busy rolling a joint so he never bothered to look at them. It took a couple seconds for Ant to finally say something. But he never spoke to them. Looking in the rearview mirror through his stylish Ray-Ban sunglasses, he asked me a question.

"Ay youngboy, you know these chicks? They down with you?"

He set me up beautifully! Since the rear windows were tinted, the girls had not yet noticed me. Before they had a chance to, I lowered my window just enough to show my face. "Nah," I casually responded, staring right at them, "I've never seen 'em before. They must be freshman."

Before the trio's caked-on makeup had time to crack, I spied Ant's girlfriend making her way through the crowd. "There's Rita!" I said while Ant and Chauncey exploded into laughter. Then Ant put the car in drive and the three girls with smashed pie streaming down their faces vanished from my peripheral vision.

"Yo Tak," Chauncey said, still chuckling as he handed me a flaming spliff.

54

Smiling a look of satisfaction, I grabbed it from Chauncey and took three long drags before I tapped Ant on the shoulder to pass it to him.

Until this moment, I had been so caught up feeling sorry for myself I never recognized everyone in my class was experiencing the same freshman pressure I was. Although I had talked badly about those sisters, now that I was equipped with a senior platform to stand on, I proved to be just as eager to 'get new' as I accused them of being.

Thanks to Ant, I became cool with the coolest dudes and the flyest females in G-High. All in all, I had some good times that spring and summer. In fact, this was my most stable four months of high school. During this period, I spent a lot of time at home with my mother and sister. However, once August starting heating up, now armed with healthy ankles so did my desire to get back to my magical ritual at the courts.

Although I had been sneaking away most mornings once school ended, I needed more action. Incidentally, whenever Jo-Jo showed up with his 'cage-match' style of play, he teased me about how the tables had been turned. He claimed that now he was free and I was the convict. But as far as changes were concerned, all else was business as usual. He kept on slapping the hell out of my wrists and I continued draining 3's right in his face. *Swish!*

In my irresponsible way of thinking, these early basketball workouts were within the limits of house arrest. Since my probation officer had never shown up in the morning, to me, this registered as being 'safe to leave.' Nevertheless my mother did not share my cocky attitude. She always appeared stressed-out when I returned home sweaty and famished. I thought she was silly to fear any random police officer might somehow know I was outside illegally. Thank goodness this was a few years before people on house arrest were mandated to wear electronic bracelets around their ankles. One morning, after my shower, I tried to console her while sipping down a bowl of miso soup.

"Mom don't worry," I said. "I leave here at five and get back before nine."

"That's not the point! You promised the judge you would stay home," she lashed out, absolutely despising whenever I patronized her. "And what do you mean, 'Don't worry?' Takuan, you talk like a big man but you don't know anything. You're as stubborn as your father!"

She knew I hated any comparisons with my sire.

"Mom, I know the streets. You don't!" I snapped back. "It's hard times for black people in America! What do you know about that? You don't know anything about being black!"

Even though my mother was getting on my nerves, this was as far as I dared to back-talk her. Not only was my mother a foreigner, she was married to a man who was a member of the disenfranchised class of her new country. Having raised three 'mixed-race' children alone much of the time while her husband was stationed away from us, she had received a crash-course on being a target of discrimination. When I saw her eyes flash at my mention of 'hard times,' I knew she was about to break me down. Nonetheless what she told me that afternoon about her childhood astonished me.

"*You* are questioning *me* about hard times? Well before I answer, let me ask you the same question. What do you know about them? Look around Takuan, you don't live in the ghetto. Even though you and your friends pretend that you do. No, you live in an air-conditioned house in the middle of the suburbs!"

"Yeah but—" I tried to interrupt.

"Urusai! Shut up and listen! This is your problem. You always want to talk and you never listen! This is not your fault because you were never taught properly."

Although I disagreed at the time, she was absolutely right. Whenever she was speaking, instead of listening to her, I was busy thinking about what I wanted to say next.

For close to a minute, my mother waited until she was convinced she commanded my attention. Only then, did she begin speaking in a relaxed tone. "I was still a little girl when the huge B-29s began flying over our village. Because we lived in Kyoto, we were spared much of the firebombing which consumed other towns. But we had nothing, everyone was poor! I mean real poverty: no food, money, running water, and definitely no air-conditioning! Do you know what that does to people?" Pausing here, she pierced my soul with her eyes. "No you don't, so I'll tell you. It turns them into savages, that's what! People fight and steal just to stay alive!"

For the next twenty minutes, my mother spun ghastly tales about WW II and postwar Japan that were completely unknown to me. Sobbing in frustration at her inability to convince me of anything, she understood I considered her to be old-fashioned. Beyond the shadow of a doubt, she also knew her son had a lot of potential but lacked any guidance or direction. By my teenage years, my mother gradually withdrew from the dysfunctional activities occurring within her home. Instead she spent more time with her friends / sorority group.

This club was a cultural organization. It consisted of middle-aged, Japanese women who were married to Americans. Together, they sponsored events in the Tri-state area and volunteered to do the *Bon-odori* at summer festivals. In addition, I remember those women played a lot of *Hanafuda* and drank their share of sake too!

The more I spiraled out of control, the less I spoke to anyone in my family; so besides occasionally yelling back and forth, there was little communication occurring within our home. Recalling this period, I am ashamed of how I disrespected both my mother and father. That said, think about it: How many well-intending parents mindlessly guide their children toward a lifestyle which is similar to their own, despite knowing damn-well they've never known happiness themselves? This struck me as being illogical then, just as it does now.

Free at Last!

"Wait a minute, I can't believe my eyes!" When Pookie approached me, I thought he was happy to see me. Then he revealed this was not the case. "Damn! What the fuck did you use to get rid of all those zits? Oxy-10…million?"

There was nothing phony about Pookie. That's what I liked about him; he was always loud and straight to the point. Even though I was cool with Jo-Jo's uncle, at that moment, he was embarrassing the hell out of me. This was because on my first evening back from exile, there were flygirls at the courts who were new faces to me.

"Ah shit!" June yelled from midcourt after he stopped dribbling to point at me. "Check-it-out y'all, tonight we gettin' a blast from the past! Wassup stranger?"

With the game delayed, the other ballers looked at

who June was pointing at.

"Money's back!" Brian hollered before jogging over to show me some 'love.' While in *B's* embrace, I heard other familiar voices.

"What up, boyee!"

"Tak, you runnin' with us next, a-ight?"

After B released me, Jo-Jo stepped forward and gave me a pound before I could respond to Terrance or Lacy. "You out for good now?" Jo asked with a grin.

"Damn right!" I exclaimed. Looking around, I was humbled that both the A and B games had come to a standstill. Raising my fist, I addressed my adopted family all at once, "Ssup everybody!" Then I made my rounds to give pounds, hugs, and even a few kisses on the cheek to the girls I knew. I was elated to finally make it back 'home.'

Every morning since the summer began, I had snuck-out to this exact location. This is why I was astonished to find it felt like I had not been here in years. This was because the energy at the courts in the evening was altogether different. Under the setting sun, the courts were a divine oasis consecrated to the transformation of common hood-rats, ragga-muffins, and b-boys into their finest glory. With no parents or teachers around to hassle us, this was our time to be ourselves. In early-80s lingo, we were *cold chillin'!*

Once the games resumed, I walked back over to Pookie.

"Really Tak, talk to me…" Pookie continued his previous interrogation, seeming unfazed by my hero's welcome. "So what'd you do? Use some of that fabled Chinese, herbal medicine on your face?" Stepping closer, he carefully inspected my complexion. "Homie, I can't see no marks or nothing! And believe me when I say, your grill was fucked up!"

Hearing some snickering in the background, I realized Pookie wasn't finished clowning with me yet. During my months of seclusion, I had not only dreamt of busting my friends on the court, but also verbally matching wits with them like this. More than ready, I was dying to get busy!

"Oh hold up, I know *you* ain't trying to crack jokes! Not with a name like 'Spookie!' Bring it on, cuz. This is gonna be *too* easy!" Saying this, I scanned my adversary from head to toe for every shred of joke material.

Before either of us could set it off, the loud drone of 808 speakers pumping the dance-club rhythms of the *Latin Rascals* got everyone's attention. Once I recognized the mix being played, I turned around and started walking. When a brown Honda Accord rolled into the parking lot, Quinton yelled over to me.

"Who's that Tak?".

"It's Ant," I responded. "He got a new ride."

For a graduation present, Mr. Asuncion had bought his son the trendy hatchback.

"Word? That joint's fresh!" screamed Earl. "Yo, ask him if he got any cheeba-cheeba?"

"A-ight, lemme find out the deal. I'll be right back," I replied breaking into a slow jog.

Ant rarely came to these courts, preferring to ball across town with a different group of playground legends. Since everyone knew I was his official youngboy, no one else walked toward the parking lot.

With his music still blaring, Ant stepped out of the car to give me a half hug-half handshake. "What up youngboy?" After releasing me, he looked at me in astonishment. "Oh shit, your pimples are gone!" he exclaimed, shaking his head before resuming in his normal tone. "I've been trying to tell your dirty ass for years. You finally took my advice and used some soap, right?"

"Fuck you!" I responded with a grin as he broke into a hearty laugh.

A week ago, Ant had accepted a scholarship from a small college in Florida to play second base. That night, Rita and Chauncey threw him a farewell party. *Man, did we get fucked up!* During the festive gala, Ant announced he was leaving in a few days. For this reason, I was surprised to find him still in town.

"Get in man," Ant said. "Since this is like your first week out the crib, I know you wanna showcase your skills to June and the rest of them. Don't worry, we'll do the quick five-minute, get-high tour."

"Yo Tak! Tak! You running or what?"

Barely able to hear Quinton and Ernie over the high-tech speakers, I understood their gestures more than actually comprehending their words. Reaching through the open car-window, I turned the volume down before responding. "Nah, y'all go ahead. Lemme run with whoever got next. I'll be right back." Then I jumped in the passenger seat, knowing that all eyes—especially those of the luscious ladies I had not yet met—were checking me out in Ant's fresh ride.

Returning the music to its previous decibel level, Ant treated the courts to a masterful mix of *Shannon's 'Let the Music Play'* blended with the unique scratching-pattern of *GrandMixer D.ST.* The crowd of teens were on their feet expressing their musical appreciation; especially once Herbie Hancock's electro-classic, *'Rockit'* got faded-in completely. Watching my peers sway to the groove, I knew if we stayed any longer, a block-party would soon erupt.

"Yeah cuz, so I'm about to hit I-95 right after I drop you off. I'm ready to go down-south and steal some bases on them hillbillies, nah I mean?"

Despite hearing what seemed like a question, I said nothing, knowing Ant was not finished talking.

"So I just came here to tell you to 'be cool' and…" Ant intentionally paused here. "To give you the Lady's phone number."

"What?" I barely got my question out before I started coughing from inhaling too much smoke. Thirty seconds later, when I stopped, the look of surprise was still plastered across my clear complexion.

'The Lady' was a moniker given to a woman who sold dime-bags in neatly-folded, manila envelopes. Since the quality of the Arizona-brown was only mid-level, not to mention her sacks contained lots of seeds, she needed a gimmick. Hers was consistency. From ten-in-the-morning until ten at night, seven-days-a-week, rain or shine, she had the goods. That is if, and only if, you were blessed to be on her short list of customers. For those bold potheads who were not in the member's only loop but decided to ring her bell anyway, the Lady never answered the door.

Since I remained in the parking lot whenever Ant completed our transactions, I had yet to meet this mysterious Lady. Nevertheless, I imagined she never had any drama dealing with uninvited solicitors, like the Jehovah's Witnesses. Although I was happy to receive the consistent weed hook-up, it seemed odd Ant had tracked me down before embarking on a twenty-one-hour road trip just to fork over the number of a second-rate herb dealer. Seeming to read my thoughts, Ant cut to the climax of the conversation.

"She likes you," he simply stated as we began to

circle back toward the courts.

"What? Who likes what? What're you talking about?"

Listening to me trip over my own words, Ant wore an amused grin. "The Lady, that's who. She asked me to give you her phone number."

Stopping alongside the same curb we departed minutes ago, I caught a glimpse of Earl rejecting a lay-up attempt by Terrance. Then I felt something hit my lap. Looking down, I saw a complimentary nickel-bag.

"Don't lose this betting on games with these muthafuckas!" Ant stated. "This here's the *blazingest* cheeba you've ever smoked in your life! It's called 'Northern Lights'."

As I examined the light-green bud in the small plastic bag, Ant jotted a number down on a napkin. Once finished scribbling, he extended it toward me between his fingertips. "Here," he said. Before I could grab it, Ant pulled it away in a teasing manner. "Oh yeah, almost forgot, she also said don't take it if the only thing you got on your mind is cheeba." Then he gave me the napkin.

"Thanks," I said while placing both items in my pocket and reaching for the door handle. Then it dawned on me I had never seen the Lady before. "Wait a minute. I don't know anything about this girl...or woman. First of all, how old is she? And how does she know me?" In addition to wanting more information, I realized this was the last time I would see Ant for some time. So naturally, I wanted to spend a few minutes with my old-head.

"Chill out! Now you really sound like a youngboy!" Ant replied laughing at me. "The Lady's a good friend of mine. Don't worry, we're just friends...meaning I never knocked it down. Last summer, we used to chill in this parking lot and get puffed. That's when she saw you. Lucky for you that was before you came down with that 'bubonic-chronic plague' on your face, nah I mean?" Saying this, Ant broke into another chuckle. "Youngboy don't *lunch* on this chance! Now get out, I gotta hit the road."

Chapter 5: The Lady in my Life

Like tree climbing and skateboarding, riding my bicycle was a hobby I enjoyed as a child but found little time for as a teenager. However on this sunny, autumn afternoon, I took advantage of a rare opportunity to cruise my blue St. Tropez BMX. After arriving at a tiny playground located right behind the Lady's apartment, I skidded to a stop in the sand before putting down the kickstand and taking a seat on a jungle gym. Reaching into my pocket, I pulled out the napkin Ant gave me three weeks ago. Next to the logo of the Golden Lady restaurant, he had scribbled a telephone number but neglected to write a name. Looking at it, I considered whether he wrote the number next to the logo on purpose and snickered at the thought of ringing the doorbell and asking for 'the Lady.'

Before contemplating my next move, I put the hood over my white Puma cap. Then I reached down to wipe my white-on-white, shell-top Adidas and examine the white *New Yorkers* accentuating my light-blue, Lee jeans with its crease ironed so tightly it could slice your fingers! Once I unzipped my jacket to ensure my chrome name-belt-buckle spelling 'MONEY' was showing, I was certain my gear was *funky fresh!*

In spite of my confidence, I still lacked a plan. Standing up, I spun around to check-out my surroundings. Doing so, led me to notice some interesting things. First, the

Lady's apartment complex was comprised of modest, family dwellings built around a central playground area. This was where I currently rested. With a slide, swing set, and seesaw situated within each square section, it resembled the family-housing units on military installations. When a lady pushing a baby carriage sat down on a nearby balance beam, I wondered where Ken's biological mom had abandoned him— under the swing set or next to the sliding-board?

Since 'family occasion' contained little meaning in my personal experience, I had forgotten Labor Day was a holiday when kinfolk traditionally came together. Sitting back down, I gazed at people of all ages and skin tones celebrating under the Indian-summer sun. This brought to mind my second revelation. I tried to imagine being surrounded by people who not only loved me, but also had a vested interest in me. As a crisp, autumn breeze penetrated my blue Izod Lacoste windbreaker, I began to feel sorry for myself. Just as I decided to quit that sad train of thought, I heard a familiar voice call my name.

"Takuan? Takuan is that you? What're you doing way out here?"

Glancing in the direction of the approaching female forced me to shield my eyes from the sun's dazzling rays. Before I moved my hand, I knew the voice belonged to a blazin' sista who was in my gym-class last year. "What's up, Rina?" I said, standing up to greet her. Having overlooked the possibility I might need an alibi to explain my presence so far from home, to stall for time, I asked her a question. "You live here?"

"No, my aunt does. She's having a cook-out today." Turning around, Rina pointed at the residence across from the one I was staking out. "That's my family over there."

Looking where she was pointing, I saw about twelve adults and a whole tribe of children enjoying a barbecue. "Wow!" I expressed my surprise. "You got a big family!"

"Yeah I know," she admitted. "But actually, a few of those folks are our neighbors. "What about you?" she asked. "Do you have relatives out here too?"

Even though I bought myself a couple seconds to come up with something, I stammered badly when I tried to explain. "My friend...I um, am here to see a friend."

Rina's facial expression revealed she knew I was lying. Seeing this, I decided to tell her a glossed-over version of the truth. Once Rina had a general idea of the situation, she began cross-examining me.

"So your *friend* told you some girl you never saw before likes you—"

"No, I said a lady," I replied, trying to act more relaxed than I felt.

"Oh, she's a lady?" Rina asked this like she had picked up a clue. "We'll come back to that," she stated with a grin. "You said he gave you her phone number, right? Why didn't you just call her?"

"Because I-I, umm, forgot her name," I stuttered.

"You don't know even this *lady's* name, but you're sure she lives in these apartments?"

"I said I forgot her name," I corrected her.

Seeming to disregard my response, she then unraveled the mystery out of thin air. "By any chance, is the friend that put you up to this named 'Ant'?"

At that moment, I swore Rina was psychic!

"Lemme get this straight," she continued between chuckles once she saw my astonishment. "You never met this girl, and you don't know her name, but you're here for a date anyway?"

"A date? I didn't say nothing about no 'date'!" I blurted out defensively.

Being classmates, Rina was familiar with my wardrobe selections. When she began staring at my clothes in exaggerated fashion, I realized how obvious my extra effort to look sharp this afternoon must have been. "What you looking at like that?" I snapped in a playful tone while pointing at my apparel. "Sista, my gear's *always* cold-crush like this! If you don't know, you better ask somebody!" Saying this, I folded my arms into a mock b-boy stance and we both busted-out laughing.

Before we could resume our conversation, a female voice called Rina's name. Turning our heads, we spotted one of the ladies from her party approaching.

"Hey girl, everybody's waiting for you so we can start eating. I'm on my way to get some barbecue sauce." Then she looked at me. "Ri-ri, who's your friend? He's cute."

Once I got an eyeful of the voluptuously curved, hazel-brown woman, I felt *Jimmy* quivering in my pants. In her bright-yellow, spandex leggings under a tight pink, one-piece mini-skirt, she resembled one of the sexy models in the *Cameo* video for their song, *'Strange.'*

"Tak, this is my Aunt Belkis," Rina gestured toward the stacked woman in her mid-30s.

In spite of Belkis' 36-24-36 'brick house body' and attractive face, I soon came to regard her like an elder sister. Even before she spoke, I sensed she was a friendly person.

"Nice to meet you," Belkis said politely. "Did Ri say your name was 'Todd'?"

"The pleasure's mine," I replied. "And no, my name's Tak—"

"Tock!" Rina cut me off before I could finish. "Like tick-tock, you know the sound a clock makes."

Rina's interruption startled me. When I looked at Belkis, she likewise looked puzzled but instead of pushing that envelope she asked the question foremost on her mind.

"Tak, are you here to see Rina?" Belkis asked with an inquisitive grin. "Because if you are, you came on a great day because our entire family's here to interrogate—umm excuse me, I mean *meet* you. Please, won't you come and join us?"

"Aunt Belkis, leave Tak alone!" Rina chastized her aunt. "You said you were going to get some barbecue sauce. Go ahead, I'll be right there."

"Alright, alright I'll leave you two in peace," she replied with a chuckle. "I just had to make sure he wasn't no stalker, or a thief. You can't be too sure these days," she added sarcastically before concluding in a sincere tone. "No really Tak, please come and join us for a plate of food."

"Thank you very much," I responded with a polite smile.

After Belkis was barely out of earshot, Rina shocked me with her next question.

"You came here to buy weed, didn't you?" she inquired in a tone of suspicion.

"No!" I exclaimed.

Since the primary reason I came was to uncover the mystery about the Lady, I considered my answer to be mostly true. However once the fellas at the courts heard me bragging about the Lady liking me, of course no one believed it, so they collected a cheeba fund and gave it to me. Ernie called it a 'win-win' situation, saying they'd either get to clown me for lying or get puffed.

"Tak, everyone knows you get high. You do know

that, right?"

Feeling like Rina was attacking me, I had no idea where her conversation was going.

"The reason I asked about the weed was," Rina continued, "if you wanted some, I was going to tell my aunt to bring it back with her when she returned with the barbecue sauce, that's all."

I was still adding two-and-two together and coming up with three when Rina lost her patience and spelled it out.

"Tak, my Aunt Belkis is the 'Lady' you came here searching for."

Even though I heard her clearly, the meaning didn't sink in until I spotted Belkis' sexy figure entering the apartment I had under surveillance. Needless to say, I accepted her invitation to join their family that afternoon. What a great decision that turned out to be!

Not only did we eat, drink, and be merry until late into the evening, after dinner, Rina and I spanked all challengers at the card game, Spades. When the party finally broke up at eleven o'clock, I could not believe how fast the time had flown by. It was easily one of my best Labor Days ever. In addition to meeting the legendary Lady and becoming her newest approved customer, I enjoyed two delicious meals and met some good people.

At some point during the Spades tournament, I realized without a shadow of a doubt that Ant had lied to me. Not only did Belkis not have a crush on me, she was a grown-woman who had never seen me before. *The question was why?* Having spent the majority of the evening answering questions about myself, I only had one opportunity to grill Rina for information. Yet, when I tried, she beat me to the punch by asking the same question which had rattled me earlier.

"Tak, you sure you don't want to buy a dime? You don't have to be shy. I saw you smoking with Ant in the student parking-lot last year," Rina stated nonchalantly.

Even though I had several ten-dollar-bills in my pocket, I could not bring myself to admit the truth. Even after seeing Belkis leave several times to take care of business, I still felt it would somehow desecrate their family get-together. With this in mind, I had decided to delay commencing business operations with the Lady. This determination to stand my pious ground quickly disintegrated when Rina reminded me the first day of school was in a few days. This is because Quinton, Earl, and I had another opening-day bash scheduled at Keith's house. And this year, I was in charge of supplying the ganja. Luckily, I caught Belkis alone before leaving that night.

While everyone knew Belkis' weed did not qualify as the highest grade of cannabis, since it was always available whenever my friends wanted some, I started paying the Lady a visit almost every day. For a couple weeks, I managed to stay high by simply bumming buds from my buddies for my messenger services. As far as I was concerned everything was cool. Once again, Ant had hooked me up lovely! Nevertheless it was not long before Belkis, realizing the earning potential I represented for her, made me a business offer I could not refuse.

Lunch with Rina

My first day as a sophomore had much in common with the start of my rookie campaign.   Meaning that after

71

getting fucked up at Keith's house, when I walked into 3rd period, it was my first class of the day. This year I had biology. After wobbling passed the various test tubes and flasks which normally decorate a classroom devoted to the study of a natural science, I spotted Rina sitting at a round table with a skinny guy I had never seen before.

To avoid being a 'third wheel,' I decided to sit in the back of the classroom with Quinton. Nonetheless when I greeted Rina on my way by, she grabbed my arm and playfully gestured with her eyes she wanted me to sit at her table.

Let's get something straight: *Rina was fine as hell!* A little shorter than the average female, Rina's mahogany-complexion perfectly complimented her burgundy lipstick and pearly white teeth. Her smile, which commanded every guy's attention in the room with the simplest smirk, was evenly distributed across her face by prominent cheekbones and matched her mysteriously dark eyes. Having been involved in gymnastics since childhood, Rina's athletic figure was the exact representation of an hour-glass. With seductively shaped, muscular thighs leading to a slim waist and lusciously-full breasts, Rina's physique was far from masculine. In other words, just like her auntie's, it had all the curves a man likes!

Garfield High had a reputation for having the most gorgeous, female students throughout Philadelphia's Tri-state area. I didn't know it back then but I was privileged to attend a school with so many girls who had both a good-looking face and a stunning body. Yet, it was Rina's hair that elevated her above the next pretty face in the crowd.

Extremely thick and curly, she wore it in exquisite locks which fell down her back, almost to her waist. Darker than the blackest moonless night, her hair was too wavy to be dreadlocks and too natural to be a weave. Appearing to have at least a hint of Taino-Arawak blood running through her veins, she once told me her family originally came from California, but one of her grandmothers was born in a village called San Jose de Las Matas, in the Dominican Republic. For this reason, she called herself an 'American Moorish Princess.' Rina was the first person I ever met who called herself a *Moor.* Up to that point, I thought Moors looked like the whiteboy on the oatmeal box. Then I recalled they were 'Quakers.'

In biology class, instead of listening to Mr. Riley's boring lessons on photosynthesis or cell theory, we engaged in philosophical discussions about the world and our futures lives in it. After a couple weeks, Rina started hinting we should study together on weekends or catch an afternoon matinee. It was apparent she wanted to be more than just friends. Even though I thought she was one of the finest females in our school, hearing this made me nervous. Somehow I could not imagine Rina as my girlfriend but I feared revealing this would hurt her feelings, if not ruin our friendship altogether. So, for a while, I played dumb.

Rina was a different person in class than at Belkis' apartment. In her aunt's presence she was shy and quiet but at school she really opened up and relaxed. This was a good thing because the more she expressed her feelings about me, the less I had to say in our conversations. By listening to Rina speak freely I was able to collect enough information to connect the dots between her, Belkis, and Ant.

When she said Ant had encouraged Belkis to sign-up for an accounting class with him, I was surprised. Although Ant ended up quitting the course when he left for Florida,

Rina reported that Belkis had recently received her CPA license. I contemplated that meant she had customers coming for both dime bags as well as tax returns. *Impressive!* I thought, reflecting on her street-entrepreneur tactics.

Hearing Rina talk about Ant like he was her uncle, I understood how tight he was with their entire family. That said, I never figured out if he had dated Belkis or not. Something which did become obvious was that it was Rina all along, never Belkis, who was fond of me. Even when Belkis called me cute, she said it like I was a child. So Ant did play a joke on me after all.

At the end of class one day, Rina confessed she told Belkis I was the nicest-looking guy in any of her classes last year. Hearing this, I figured she must've really liked me because that was when the 'bubonic-chronic plague' was on my face.

"That's why I was careful to introduce you as *Tak,* instead of Takuan," Rina admitted. "I didn't want my aunt to know you were the guy I had been talking about. But I think she knew it anyway," she said blushing.

Rina divulged this just as the bell rang. This was the only thing which saved me from having to respond. At this point, only one loose end remained: If Ant was hooking me up with Rina, why did he write Belkis' phone number on the napkin? It's difficult to fathom he wasn't aware that Rina lived with her parents and two brothers in a different town. It took a couple weeks for this mystery to unveil itself.

On that October morning, the sun's rays had beamed the temperature several degrees higher than usual. The other guy at our table, a cool dude named Mike, was absent. While Mr. Riley's lecture digressed from pitifully dull to mind-numbingly boring, I noticed Rina looked depressed. As my

74

classmates' heads gradually lowered onto their desks, I watched her face stretch from a snivel to a sniffle, before eventually breaking down into a grief-stricken sob. Somehow Rina was able to position her hair and coat in such a way as to conceal her weeping appearance. By the time I handed her the tissue I received from a girl sitting nearby, she was already calming down.

After wiping her tears, she explained that her father suffered from symptoms of Post-Traumatic Stress Disorder. A veteran of the psychological horrors known as the Vietnam War, like my sire, he had been prescribed psychotropic drugs to cope with his bi-polar condition. Rina said, at first, the meds were effective. However, over time, his body had gradually developed a tolerance to them, and now his temper tantrums were out of control. She went on to explain that last April, one of his outbursts had resulted in her oldest brother's arm being fractured, and the other one suffering bruised ribs.

"I haven't been home ever since," she said wiping her re-emerging tears.

Fortunately, her father's sister had moved to a neighboring town. So every afternoon, Rina elected to bypass the scene of the hostilities in favor of a three-mile hike to Belkis' apartment. Once she moved in with her aunt, although physically safe from her version of the Serpent, she felt guilty for what she called 'abandoning her family.'

"He's much worse toward my brothers than me," Rina whispered between sniffles. "So why am I the one who's s-so weak I-I have to run away?"

Fear, running away, and an abusive household; these were themes I was all-too-familiar with.

"Believe me," I stated with confidence. "Your folks are happy you're safely tucked away at Belkis' place. I've played ball with both of your brothers and neither one of 'em is a punk. And like you said, your mother deals with his eruptions better than you can. Think about it: if you were at home, they'd have to worry about you as well as their own hides, 'cause you know you can't fight!"

Hoping some light-humor might turn her tears of misery into those of happiness, once my efforts failed to bring any smiles to her pitiful condition, I decided to share some of my own harrowing home experiences. Minutes later, the bell rang. During our emotional conversation, I lost track of the time. Embarrassed I had become so misty-eyed, I put my head down to hide my tears. While a few classmates yelled my name on their way out the door, I feigned like I was sleeping. Then I heard Quinton's familiar voice approaching.

"What up Ri?"

"Hi Quinton," Rina replied in a sullen tone.

Since my head was still on the table, Quinton plucked my ear. "Yo homie, wake up! It's time to get out there and *'make make the money!'*" he jokingly harmonized the anthem made popular by the *Furious Five*. Seeing I was slow to pick my head up, my friend grabbed both of my shoulders and shook me. "Time's a wasting Speedie! Wake up, wake up! Up you wake, wake you up!" Revved-up and overly excited, Quinton appeared ready to sprint into the hallway to find some mischief.

Realizing there was no way to avoid detection, I lifted my head and snatched what tissue remained from the pile I had handed to Rina earlier. After I had wiped away most of the evidence, I blew my nose and stood up.

"What the hell's going on with you two?" Glancing back-and-forth at both of our melancholy mugs, Quinton gave us a quizzical look. "Y'all might be getting a tad too sentimental about dissecting them frogs next week. Don't worry, they're already dead."

Without saying a word, I reached into my jacket pocket and pulled out a plastic sandwich bag containing thirty-five joints. Before Quinton could ask what I was doing, I handed it to him in order to bypass this embarrassing moment. "Take one for yourself," I said, practically giving them away for free while he stared in disbelief. "Whatever you sell after that, I'll split half the profits with you. Deal?"

"Are you serious? A free joint!" Quinton exclaimed in a hushed voice while checking for the whereabouts of our teacher. "And," he continued to whisper, "we go fifty-fifty on whatever I can unload? Lemme outta here, I got work to do!" With that emphatic reply, Quinton vanished so fast it seemed he had been a figment of our imaginations all along.

As Rina and I collected our books and prepared to exit the room, my heart skipped a beat when Mr. Riley approached us because I feared he had witnessed the exchange with Quinton. Fortunately this was not the case.

"Rina, Tak, is everything okay? You two seemed a bit out of it this morning," said the soft-spoken teacher. Seeing the mournful glaze tinting our eyes, it's likely he dropped his intended purpose for paying us a visit, which was probably to admonish us for talking too much. "If either of you have any questions, or just need an ear to listen, I'll be here after-school until five."

"Thanks Mr. Riley," we chimed in unison. Pushing in our chairs, Rina and I shuffled out the door and nearly collided with some students arriving for the next period.

"Yo Sev, what up home-slice?" said a solidly-built brother wearing a Dr. J t-shirt.

"Ssup," I responded, checking out his shirt. I had the

same poster on my wall. It showed the *Doctor* soaring through the air before dunking on Bill Walton. After we exchanged a pound, the brother then whispered something.

"You got that?"

Although I was familiar with this guy's face, I don't think he ever told me his name. "Check out Quinton," I replied. "He's holding shit down right now."

At the moment, I wanted to defer my 'ganja-dealer' status so I could chill-out with Rina. However since business was booming this was not possible; it seemed like every other person I saw wanted to make a purchase. *"Yo Tak!"* This is all we heard as we aimlessly sauntered down the hall.

After directing five others in Quinton's direction, Rina shook her head. "Takuan, you sure are popular this year. Is all this commotion over buying cheeba?" she naively asked.

"Yeah! Lots of potheads in Garfield, huh?" Laughing, I considered how much my circumstances had changed. With my consistent supply of weed from the Lady and other sources, my sophomore year at Garfield was much different than my first one had been. In short, I was no longer a freshman.

When the bell sounded for 4th period, I watched some last-minute laggards sprint toward their closing classroom doors. For me, I was unconcerned because I had a blank pass in my locker for exactly this type of situation. After forging Mr. Riley's signature on it, I knew it would be easy to fool my History teacher, thereby keeping me out of detention. However I was surprised at Rina's unusually laid-back attitude in regards to being late. Since I normally walked her to the gym after biology, I wondered why we were not heading toward the girl's locker room. When I looked at her to ask where she was going, I was astonished to find her staring at me. It seemed she had been waiting for me to stop daydreaming.

"I'm not going to gym today," Rina opened up by stating the obvious. Her next question more than hinted at her plans. "Tak, where do you go when you cut school?" she asked.

Gazing into her still-moist eyes, I imagined Rina had invested some time contemplating this enigma. "I dunno...different places, why?" I felt she was invading my privacy, so I tried to avoid her question.

Rina, knowing my penchant for beating around the bush, quickly made her point. "Because I wanna know where *we* are going until two-thirty?"

In Garfield, playing hooky with the opposite sex was synonymous to engaging in sexual relations. Although I was known for cutting school, what most people did not know was that I was still a virgin. And, that I was quite comfortable with the masturbation stage of my adolescent development. Rina sensed my apprehension.

"Tak, I'm not asking you to sleep with me, but we have to get outta here before a hall monitor comes. After we get outside, if you want to be alone that's okay, I understand." Saying this, Rina lowered her head like her feelings were hurt.

"No, it's not that…" Since the last thing I wanted to do was to add to her misery, I had to lie. "It's, how should I put it? I can't take you to a house where a bunch of old-heads are getting high, watching re-runs of *Good Times*, that's all."

As our discussion slowly transformed into a debate, the clickety-clack of high-heels striking the polished floor caught our attention. The sound, coming from around the corner, was undoubtedly a monitor making her rounds. Being experienced with dodging these teacher's aides, I adopted the use of hand signals to indicate we should escape into the stairwell. After jettisoning down to the ground floor, we were far from home free. When Rina walked toward one of the emergency doors, I grabbed her forearm.

"While classes are in-session," I whispered, "if we open any door besides the main entrance, an alarm will automatically sound!" Then, with my eyes, I gestured toward the doors beyond the main office. "That's the only way in or out."

Normally, during my solo escapes, I simply waited until the secretaries in the office were not looking in the direction of the door. Then I walked right by them. By the time they noticed me, if at all, they saw the shrinking image of my back. I fully understood that in my standard Hip Hop gear, I could never be mistaken for an adult who had business at the school. But, as with most of my shenanigans, I relied on people not expecting a teen to be so bold; or just not giving a damn! But, with two of us, I felt this plan was too risky.

Creeping close enough to peek at the four people inside the office, I winced when I spotted Mr. Thomas, my assistant principal. Although I did not recognize the three women, I knew we could not afford to be seen by any of them. *Damn!* I reflected, knowing our chances of getting caught had been quadrupled. Despite this, or the fact I had no idea what to do next, it never entered my mind we would not be successful. Since I had never been caught, this sense of invulnerability was the best drug to boost my confidence.

"What're we gonna to do?" Rina asked excitedly.

With a delighted expression on her face, she phrased the question like she expected me to have a *007* trick up my sleeve to distract the adults while the two of us shimmied out the door disguised in UPS uniforms. And of course, not to mention, making our clean get-away in a brown delivery van.

Staring into Rina's dark eyes, I imagined if I told her the truth she would panic. Following an indecisive pause, I asked her about the time instead. "What time you got?"

After she checked her wristwatch, she opened her mouth to reply. At that instant, our escape plan became loud and clear. *Ding-ding-ding-ding!* It was a fire drill.

Without a second glance at the occupants in the office, we grinned at each other and strolled out the door. Once we were outside, we took swift strides to put the tennis courts between us and the school. Before we disappeared around the corner, we saw some students and teachers exiting the building.

As soon as we had traveled a little distance up the street, Rina, who had been laughing the entire time, grabbed my arm. "How did you know we had a fire drill today?"

"What're you talking about?" I was genuinely surprised by her question.

"Why do you think I'm so naïve? Ant always thinks I'm slow to what's going on too," she complained. After Rina accused me of "insulting her intelligence," she explained her take on what had just occurred. "You asked me what time it was right before the alarm went off, right?"

"Right," I responded trying not to laugh. More than curious to hear her theory, I was amused by her grand assumption.

"So you expect me to believe that was a coincidence?" Rina asked, glaring at me with an 'I'm not stupid' expression on her face. "You knew the bell was going to ring at the beginning of 4th period, didn't you? Don't even lie!" Rina appeared genuinely flustered. "Okay," she composed herself and resumed in a bartering tone. "I'll tell you a secret, if you tell me how you knew about the fire drill. Deal?"

Considering she was convinced I had a butler named Alfred assisting me from an undisclosed cave in the vicinity, even though it was impossible to fulfill my end of the bargain, I had no choice but to play along. I knew if I refused she would get upset. "Okay, it's a deal," I agreed. "But you go first, because revealing my secret could get me expelled." I said this not only to stall but also to add more drama to the plot. This was the first time I realized dealing with females was tricky business.

Rina, grinning like a little girl in a candy shop, was ecstatic. After clearing her throat, she looked around for any lurking FBI informants before murmuring in a low tone. "Last week, I started helping Aunt Belkis sell dimes." Pausing, Rina scoped-out her surroundings once more and, despite being the only two people walking down the tree-lined street, she continued whispering. "My shift's from seven to ten in the evening, so I work after dinner while I'm studying."

I was not pleased to hear Rina was dabbling in a street hustle. Before I could express my distaste, my sixth-sense alerted me to potential danger. Without warning, I grabbed Rina by the hand and pulled her behind a parked car. After ducking down, we peered through the car's side-window at a gas station across the street.

"Who's that?" Rina asked.

Momentarily ignoring her question, I was more concerned with the two customers my homeboy Dan was talking to. "He's a friend of mine," I responded seconds later.

Watching Dan hold what appeared to be a pleasant conversation with two police officers, when one of the cops pointed at the squad car's rear tire, the other one laughed at something Dan said. Suddenly I became aware Rina and I were still holding hands. Before this became an uncomfortable situation, the conversation across the street ended. Seeing the cops get in their car, I realized if they turned left after exiting the station, they would pass within a few feet of our hiding place. Therefore we had to move. *Fast!*

Releasing her hand, I gestured for her to follow me. After indicating she understood, we crawled to the front of the vehicle. We were careful to remain below the windows. Once we neared the headlights, Rina squatted down while I rested on one knee. "Chill here for a second," I said before rising to peek through the windshield again. I saw the patrol car turn left onto the street. "They're coming this way," I warned. As the squad car approached from the rear of the brown Nissan Altima we were concealed behind, I continued whispering. "When they get closer, stay low and start moving back toward the rear of this car." Before I finished explaining our objective was to keep the Altima between us and the cops' line of vision, Rina pantomimed she understood what to do.

As five-o rolled past, we executed the plan to perfection. Staying low, we inched our way backward until we were crouching behind the car, next to the tail-lights. Once certain we had given them the slip, Rina and I high-fived to celebrate another near miss. This is when Dan noticed us.

"Hey! Ya damn hooligan! If you weren't over there with that fine honey, I'd call five-o back here myself!" he playfully stammered while breaking into a slow jog to greet us.

"Shhh!" I scolded him playfully, gesturing toward the

receding image of the squad car.

Already half way across the street, Dan was preparing to hug me when he waved his hand condescendingly at the still visible black-and-white. "Don't worry, you good cuz! Them fools ain't looking back here no mo'!" Saying this, he waved his hand again. "Word up, I heard they got a blue-light special at Dunkin' Donuts this afternoon. What's up playa?" Bellowing this, the huge titan then crushed me in a brotherly embrace.

"Ssup ock!" I replied, happy to see my friend.

Releasing me, he then looked over my shoulder. "But more important than yo' ugly ass, who's your gorgeous accomplice?"

"Dan, Rina. Rina, Dan," I said gesturing back-and-forth between my two friends.

Following my introduction, Dan walked over to Rina and executed a ceremonious bow in her honor. "The pleasure's all mine, Queen." After greeting her in his most chivalrous voice, he then took her right hand in his.

Rina, not knowing what to make of this gentle giant, looked intimidated until Dan deliberately went down on one knee like a squire waiting to be knighted.

Thinking Dan's dramatization was corny, I broke-out in laughter; however Rina seemed moved.

"Queen, what're you doing hanging out with this thug?" Wearing a disgusted frown, Dan hooked his thumb at me as he slowly rose to his feet. Once he was standing next to Rina, he continued holding onto her hand—the same hand I had let go of minutes ago.

Daniel Bailey, a muscular brother whose physical dimensions brought to mind the physique of an NFL defensive end, was both buffed and handsome. Nonetheless due to his 'old man' personality he was not a hit with the ladies. The kind of guy who would rather spend hours in his garage repairing a transmission than waste his time hanging out with us 'hooligans,' Dan had dropped out of school after ninth grade to start working. For this reason, even though we were the same age, Dan was more mature than me and most of my friends.

Watching his awkward attempt to *kick game* to Rina, had there been any doubts about my feelings for her, they were now laid to rest. Even though I was certain Dan was about to get shot-down, had I been courting Rina, his behavior would have irked me. Nonetheless as it stood, since Dan's theatrics had distracted attention away from Rina and I being viewed as a couple, I was glad this happened. By the time Rina shook her hand free from the behemoth's grip, I was comfortably back to being my distant-self.

Since Dan got paid on Thursdays, I always stopped by on Friday afternoon so he could pay on his running tab. Being a big weed-head, I hoped to use ganja as a bargaining tool to borrow his mother's car. Having given my loose joints to Quinton, after walking around to the back of the station, I handed him buds straight out of a Ziploc bag.

"Where's your boss?" I inquired after looking around to ensure no one else was there.

"He's on his lunch break but Javier's in the office," he said referring to one of his co-workers. "Damn Tak, you got a lot of cheeba!" exclaimed Dan. Staring bug-eyed at the plastic baggie, Dan acted like he never saw an ounce of marijuana before. "And it's a good thing," he resumed, "'cause I need a big favor. My cousin and his friend are coming over this weekend, so can you hook-me-up with an extra quarter-ounce 'til next week?"

That was my cue. To make a long-story short, I traded a quarter-ounce of herb for the privilege of borrowing his mother's old, white Chevy Impala. Even though Dan was too young to get a driver's license, he drove it to work sometimes. After reluctantly agreeing to let me use it until six o'clock when his shift ended, in addition to forking over a free sack, I had to promise not to be late.

"Not by one minute muthafucka!" he reiterated.

"Yeah I gottit, shut-up already!"

Grumbling about the loss of profits to Quinton, and now Dan, in addition to the trickiness, I also noted that being in the company of a girl was expensive! Thinking this, I recalled Chauncey telling me one time that, 'A woman ain't nothing but another bill.'

"Here." This is all Rina said after she removed a twenty-dollar-bill from her purse and stuck it in my jacket pocket. *This was the second time she seemed to have read my mind.*

"No, it's okay. I don't need it," I lied.

After we got into the car, I placed the legal tender on her leg.

"Like I told you earlier, I have a part-time job now," Rina replied, "so let me help." Cheerfully replying thus, she placed the money on my lap while I was adjusting the rear-view mirror. "And I'm still waiting to hear how you knew about the fire drill," she playfully reminded me.

I was moved by Rina's selfless gesture. And Dan was right, why would any young lady who desires a dignified existence choose a deviant drug-dealer over a hard working stick-in-the-mud? Had she been dealing with a mature gentleman like Dan, perhaps this would've been the beginning of a grand love affair; one that developed into something truly special.

"What the hell?" I protested after Dan reached through the window and snatched the cash off my leg.

Without replying, he pulled a ten-dollar-bill from his wad of greenbacks and gave it to me. "Gas!" the muscular gas-attendant stated with a grin. "It's not part of the deal. And I heard Rina mention something about going to the Gallery. If y'all go to Philly, you're gonna need a full tank."

I was unable to argue. After Dan performed his job, we hit the road. Once the huge Impala was zooming down Rt. 130, I felt free as a bird let out of its cage. In spite of the car's rustic appearance, it was a real American car. Therefore it was made to cruise in style and comfort.

"You really feel like hitting the Gallery?" I asked, believing what Dan had said earlier.

"Not really, unless you do. But I do know one thing, I'm gonna be hungry soon—*hey!*" After interrupting herself, Rina stared in amazement. "You don't have a driver's license…you're only fifteen, like me!" Saying this, she broke into a hearty laugh; she seemed to be having the time of her life.

Since Dan had started using his parents' spare car a year ago, all of his friends had driven it many times. Hence I had almost forgotten this was against the law. This is the type of reckless behavior my future drill sergeants would define as "a total disregard for authority."

While scanning the approaching signs for the Betsy Ross Bridge, it occurred to me the only reason I ever went to a mall was to meet girls. With this in mind, I decided against bringing 'sand to the beach' and started to consider alternate destinations. Glancing over to the northbound side of the interstate, I spotted a restaurant with a sign in the window. It read: "Philly Cheese Steaks." Activating the turn signal, I pulled into the exit lane and looped around to the other side. After passing under a 'Bound for Trenton' sign, I realized Rina did not know my plan.

"Let's get some cheese steaks and go chill-out at Indian Creek Park. If we stay in the car, we shouldn't have any problems with the cops. Whaddya think?"

Seconds after Rina agreed with my hastily construed lunch-plan, we banked a right into the parking lot of 'Gaetano's Famous Subs.' To take advantage of having a car at our access, we decided to use the drive-thru. During our wait, I watched Rina enjoying her opportunity to say 'the hell with everything!' and just relax. When I eventually pulled-up to the window, I greeted a friendly, middle-aged Sicilian woman. Following her cheerful reply, I ordered a half-hoagie with french fries, a small salad, and a 7-up.

"Gimme the same order please," Rina stated from the passenger seat. "Except I'd like a small-order of fries and, can you switch the 7-up for a ginger ale?"

After the smiling lady consented with a simple nod, I gave her the money and she disappeared from our view. A couple minutes later, she reappeared and handed me the drinks along with a bag containing an appetizing aroma. Once back on the highway, in order to take our minds off the delicious smelling grub, Rina inserted one of Dan's WKDU mixtapes into the stereo. It did not take long before I was passionately rapping along to a song entitled, *'Sucker MCs.'*

"Two years ago, a friend of mine, asked me to say some emcee rhymes..." Only my friend Wayne knew *Run-DMC's* lyrics better than me. Before long, I was really getting into the groove: *"Dave cut the record down to the bone, and now they got me rockin' on the microphone..."*

"Takuan, you have such a nice voice," Rina commented. "Why don't you emcee for real? I bet you could rap better than Hi-C and Stevie-Gee!"

Rina was trying to gas my head up by comparing me with two well-known emcees in our school.

"Me? What about you sista?" I countered. "I believe I heard you spit a freestyle in gym last year. What's up with that?"

Just as I completed issuing my challenge, the deejay, *Master J*, mixed-in *'Sucker DJs,'* which was the ladies' rendition of the same song. Rocking the same beat, it featured none-other-than the female-sensation, *Dimples D*, on the vocals. Hearing this, I gassed Rina up to grab the imaginary microphone.

"Ahh shit, get some Rina! Lemme hear that raw, feminine flow!"

As I playfully encouraged her to express herself, she swayed to the music sporting a big grin. Then she jumped in with fervor.

"I was at a jam the other night, I was feelin' real good so the feelin' was right, I went to the party for a different kinda action, the next thing you know I was doing the Michael Jackson..."

Rina flipped the lyrics until Master J faded the song back to the original version. When she got quiet, which indicated it was my turn again, I turned the volume down so only the beat remained audible. Instead of simply rhyming along with DMC, this time I blessed the mic with a slightly modified remix.

"Tak-money's in the place to be, chillin' with my homegirl named Ri-Ri. A super-sophomore that's filled with knowledge, and after 12th grade I'm headed straight for

*college. Just a crush, black brother who's Nihon-jin, so you
know I love sushi and collard greens..."*

I flowed until only the scratching of the record could
be heard. Once it was evident Dimples D was being mixed
back in, I reached out to readjust the volume. However, not to
be outshined, Rina grabbed my wrist without disturbing her
flow. Then she likewise spit her own freestyle.

*"So listen Tak-money while I got your attention,
there's a few more things I'd like to mention, my name's Rina
but please call me Ri, and ain't a female in G-High can flow
like me. With my dark-brown eyes and sexy physique, I keep
the party rockin' in-time with the beat..."*

When she ended her verse right on time to allow
Marley Marl's ill echo scratch to be heard, I complimented
her effort. "Damn girl, you tore it up!" I exclaimed.

Going back-and-forth in this manner, both of us
demonstrated our lyrical prowess again-and-again at the
whim of Master J. Whoever wasn't rapping understood it was
their responsibility to contribute background vocals and other
sound effects to keep the party moving. By the time we
arrived at Indian Creek, we were laughing so hard I nearly
slammed into a stray dog that was walking near the entrance.
After screeching to a halt, I stuck my head out the window to
lyrically chastise the mutt to move.

*"Get out the way or be hit by this car, send ya black-
ass back to the Dog Star!"*

Once the jet-black hound scurried into the woods, we
tested the Impala's shocks by following it down a crude dirt-
road that was created for the park's ground-maintenance
vehicles. Separated from the paved thoroughfares jutting
throughout the park, there were signs posted which prohibited
visitors from using these utility pathways. Nevertheless many

people used them anyway.

"Go over there!"

By the time Rina pointed her finger and said this, I was already taxiing in that direction. It seemed we had spotted the perfect setting simultaneously. Soon I was parked next to a majestic oak tree situated under a canopy of crooked branches which illustrated every shade of autumn. For over a minute, we remained silent marveling at the picturesque view of red, orange, and yellow leaves fluttering into a sparkling pond.

"That's funny," Rina sounded surprised as we watched a family of mallard ducks swim by ten yards in front of us. "I've never noticed this pond before, have you?"

"Hmm, good question," I asserted. "They must've cleaned it up recently or something."

When Rina bowed her head to bless her meal, I became silent and followed suit. Ancestral rites completed, we broke out the food and tore into the hoagies, salads, and sodas in record time. With the music thumping in the background, we nodded our heads eating every last, finger-licking fry. In those fifteen minutes, no words were exchanged as we focused on savoring our meals.

I finished a couple minutes before Rina did. Grabbing some napkins, I wiped my mouth and turned off the music to conserve the battery. Feeling content, I reclined my seat back and noticed Rina was almost finished with her lunch too. "Here," I said handing her an empty bag so she could put her trash inside it. Once she stuffed the bag and put it down, she likewise reclined back in her seat. With a bursting-at-the-seams look of satisfaction scrawled on both of our faces, we soon realized how exhausted we were. Considering the extreme range of emotions we had experienced that morning, not to mention the daredevil escapes, we needed some rest.

"Do you think it's safe to stretch-out on the grass?" Rina asked as I was considering the same question in my head.

Following Rina's suggestion, we got out and searched the trunk. Spying some picnic blankets, we looked at each other and grinned. While I shook them out, Rina took a look around the mostly deserted park. "If we lie down right here," Rina said pointing behind the car, "joggers or other pedestrians can't see us. Whaddya you think?"

Instead of responding with words, I spread the blankets where she was pointing and collapsed onto the ground.

"I guess that means you agree," Rina replied plopping down beside me.

Forty seconds later, we were fast asleep in the shade provided by the mighty oak. In my dreams, I was getting chased through the woods by the canine we spotted at the park's entrance. Looking back, I recognized the dog. It was Shogun and he was trying to tell me something.

Two weeks ago, Kay and I knew Sho's fate when he did not greet us at the door after school. After more than a decade of ducking kicks and dodging sticks, my loyal dog's hind legs had worn out. Reflecting how I had been robbed of the opportunity to say good-bye before he was put to sleep, I felt sad until I realized the black shadow was now galloping next to me.

Kicking into high-gear, we agilely maneuvered amongst the trees and shrubs decorating the forest. We expressed our joy of being reunited by sprinting to our heart's content like we had done numerous times together. Just before emerging from the tree-line into the sunlight, Sho abruptly stopped in his tracks. When I likewise tried to put on the brakes, I found I was unable to do so. Despite having stopped my feet, my body continued floating forward.

Turning back, I caught one last glimpse of the Anubis-like creature before its outline darkened into a black dot and disappeared altogether.

Summoned from the depths of REM 4 with a jolt, I was suddenly wide-awake. Unsure of how long I had slept or why I woke up when I did, nevertheless I sensed danger. Rolling over onto my stomach, I checked my surroundings and made some important observations. By the position of the sun, I surmised it was around one-thirty. Understanding school was still in-session prompted me to peer underneath the car to search the roadway. In addition to two middle-aged joggers, I saw a slowly approaching automobile. Considering how our day had been going, even before squinting my eyes to confirm its identity, I already knew it was five-o.

"Shit!" Blurting this under my breath, I rolled back over to wake Rina up.

Seconds later, the aging couple had jogged out of view and there were no other people in sight. It was obvious the occupants of the slowly moving patrol car were eyeing us. Rina, now awake, took one look at my face and tensed up.

"Don't move," I began, "there's a cop car approaching, so whatever you do, don't look in their direction. Pretend you don't see them." Taking another peek, I resumed my report. "They're definitely checking us out. A-ight, let's stand up to show them we're not doing anything suspicious. *Slowly!"*

"Okay," Rina nervously replied.

As we stood up, I stretched my arms and faked a yawn. "Now remember," I advised. "We're two nice people…two college students enjoying a picnic on a beautiful day. We gotta sell that story, okay?"

"Okay," Rina again answered.

"They can't be sure of our age. Since we drove here in a car, from that distance, we can easily pass for adults." Using basic logic, I was attempting to keep both of us from panicking. Glancing over at Rina, since she had said nothing to this point except 'okay,' I continued making my case that everything was fine. "Let's move into plain view and start cleaning up," I suggested.

In order to subtly promote the idea of a lovely picnic in the park, we placed the bags bearing the Gaetano's logo on top of the blankets, in plain view. Once the municipal tank pulled onto the grass barely twenty yards away, we understood this was the moment of truth. If they got out to question us, we knew we would soon be calling our parents from the police station. *I had to do something!*

"Let's pretend we're lovers," I blurted out. "Gimme a kiss!"

"Huh?" This was all Rina could utter before I pulled her close.

Perhaps I really felt the cops were not convinced. Or maybe I saw an opportunity to do something I secretly wanted to do. Probably a little bit of both. To be honest, everything happened so fast I can't remember. What I do know is: it worked like a charm!

Far from resisting, Rina actually beat me to the kiss. Sneaking a peek over her shoulder, I was relieved to see the officers had not exited their car. Up to this point, I had played my hand pretty cool. All this ended once our lips and tongues connected. In spite of our precarious situation, Jimmy was rock-hard in a flash. With her arms wrapped around my neck,

Rina unerringly began to grind her precious yoni against my erection. Once my thoughts started swimming toward satisfying my physical appetite, I forgot about our dire set of circumstances. It was then a loud voice rang out.

"Hey kid!" yelled a man's voice through the megaphone attached to the patrol car. "This is a *public* park! Take that action back to your dorm room!"

"Or stop being a cheapskate and spring for a room!" his partner added in a heckling tone.

Now it was time to look at them. Turning my head, I raised my hand in a triumphant thumbs-up pose and grinned like I didn't have a care in the world.

When the cops drove off, we heard them laughing inside their car. Following a deep sigh of relief, Rina finally regained the use of her vocal cords. "Let's get outta here!" she said, expressing the exact vibe I was feeling.

Without wasting another second, we threw the blankets and trash into the trunk before jumping into the Impala. It was still before two o'clock but we decided to gamble on being caught by Belkis rather than chancing a third encounter with the cops. Fortunately, when we pulled in front of her building, Belkis' Toyota Camry was not in the parking lot.

We were greeted at the door by Belkis' younger sister. Once we saw piles of textbooks lining the coffee table, we knew Tracy was studying for her exams.

Tracy was a student in her final trimester at Temple University. Rina told me she was in an accelerated program designed for students to graduate in three years so they can start medical school. After Tracy scolded us in an irritating tone to be quiet, she explained that Belkis had taken the children to a dentist appointment. By her attitude, I gathered she was not thrilled with being delegated the dime-selling duties until Rina's shift began at seven.

"Tak, have you started studying for next week's Biology test?" Rina inquired out of nowhere.

In spite of sensing something out of the ordinary, I simply responded 'no' before sitting on the floor, grabbing a joystick, and flipping on the television to play *Pac-man*. As I guided the yellow icon to munch on a power-pill, I overheard Rina exaggerating about the importance of our upcoming test. Although I thought the girl had flipped her wig, with my mind riveted on avoiding *Blinky*, *Pinky*, *Inky*, and *Clyde*, I shut-out most of their conversation. Nonetheless when Rina offered to swap shifts with Tracy so we could study in the apartment, this caught my attention. Especially because her aunt jumped at the opportunity.

"Rina, you always were my favorite niece!" Tracy exclaimed as she hugged Rina. "If I leave right now, I can still make it to campus for a study session!" It took Tracy five minutes to throw her books in a bag, grab her car keys, and jet out the door. Following her departure, it took Rina even less time to start harassing me with the same question over-and-over again.

"What do you wanna do?"

"I wanna bust your cousin's high score!" I replied as the Pac-man barely made a narrow escape. "Whoa, that was close!" With my eyes glued to the screen, I was oblivious of the orgone energy gathering behind me.

"No, I mean *now!* What do you wanna do right now?" Rina repeated in a whiny tone.

Noting the emphasis on the word 'now,' I paused the game and put the joystick down. Rina looked more beautiful than ever when she sat down next to me on the beige-and-white rug.

"What do you wanna do?" she asked again.

Even before we touched, my skin was tingling like it was on fire. The magnetic attraction was irresistible but once we started kissing, I was petrified. Two of my friends, Earl and Brian, liked to tease me by claiming I was "scared of pussy" whenever they recounted the details of their sexual encounters. They were the only ones who knew for sure I was still a virgin. Though a side of me wanted to pull away, the lustful spirit in the atmosphere aroused my libido. Soon my inhibitions, along with our clothing, began peeling away.

Seeing Rina in just her bra and panties for the first time, I realized her body was even sexier than I had imagined. *I almost came on the spot!* Then we cuddled and caressed for several minutes, using our hands to explore each other. "Come on, let's go in the back," Rina almost moaned as she spoke. After I agreed to move to a bedroom, Rina led me by the hand. With each step, my heart was thumping wildly in my chest.

Lying down on the bed together, we commenced the next level of foreplay. While kissing beyond her lips, I continued fondling every luscious curve of her body. After leaving her cheek, I spent time applying hickeys to her neck. She really liked that! By the time I finished sucking on her dark nipples, I was intoxicated to receive her deepest treasures. As Rina's sheer pleasure became my carnal delight, I was gradually seduced to her most sacred gateway. No longer in control of my actions, my only desire was to satisfy her deepest passions.

Moments later, Rina's body started to quiver. "Unhh, don't stop!" she shrieked pulling my head into her. We continued for another minute until Rina had enough. "I want to feel you inside me," she said staring at me. Then she grabbed my hand and guided me to lie on top of her, between her thighs.

The first penetrating sensation was inviting, warm, and seductively satisfying. Once inside, I pumped my hips slowly at first. Moving in circular patterns, I imagined I was stirring a cup of hot cocoa. Rina's flexibility as a gymnast raised the sexual experience up a notch. After Rina coached me to push her legs back behind her head, I entered her yoni so deeply she howled in ecstasy.

"You like that, Ri?"

"Unnhh…yes!" she passionately replied.

The faster I thrust my hips, the louder and stronger Rina's moans grew. *We really tested those bed springs that afternoon!* It took several minutes but eventually we wormed our way up the mattress until Rina's head was knocking against the headboard.

"Takuan, stop for a second," she whispered between breaths.

Hearing her, I stood up. Once on my feet, I grasped her hand beckoning her to stand as well. Smiling, she stood up and we embraced in a slow kiss before I spun her into an exotic, salsa step. Releasing her hand, I grabbed both hips from behind and grinded my phallus snugly against her ass. Kissing her neck, I reached under both arms to squeeze her mango-sized breasts. The sound of Rina's rhythmic breathing growing louder and deeper aroused the dog in me. "Bend over," I said coaxing her to bend at the waist. Then I expressed the 'Shogun' in me!

Before long it got hot, sweaty, and wet!

Just before I came, I pulled-out for a short intermission. Rina, likewise, got up and retrieved some towels from the adjoining bathroom so we could dry ourselves. Less than a minute had elapsed before Rina forced me to recline onto the bed. When she climbed on top of my still-swollen penis, I was glad we weren't finished yet. Lying on my back, I watched her break another sweat riding me like a bucking bronco. As we gradually elevated toward the climactic level, I was taken aback by sights and sounds I had never witnessed in a porn video before. Phenomena such as squirting vaginal-fluid and pussy farts! In fact, this intrigue is what kept me from climaxing.

By the time Rina's moans were reaching a crescendo, I was also experiencing that dreamy feeling which precedes the intense pleasure of orgasm. Knowing I was only good for another stroke or two, I grabbed Rina's hips to lift her up. That was when she viciously dug her fingernails into my forearms.

"Ahhhh!" I yelled out.

Seconds after the pain arrested the energy building within me, Rina shrieked even louder before collapsing on top of me. For the next minute, neither of us moved. Lying there smothered under a blanket of wavy locks scented with the fragrance of Egyptian Musk, I was truly in heaven comfortably resting underneath—*and inside*—this Moorish princess.

My next memory is being awakened by the sound of a ringing telephone. At that time, Rina and I were still in sexual union. We later estimated we had dozed, as one, for about twenty minutes. When Rina finally answered the phone, I listened to her lie about a customer being in the living room before saying, 'extra crispy, mushrooms and onions.' After hanging up the receiver, she jumped back into bed and hugged me.

"Belkis and the kids are at Ricardo's Pizza," she said, beaming the same mischievous grin she had been flashing all afternoon. "We're lucky she called to get my order. They're coming home right after they buy the food, so we have about a half-hour before they get here." Following another kiss, we jumped in the shower together. After washing each other's backs and rinsing off, we hurriedly dressed and had just enough time to tidy up the apartment before Belkis and the kids arrived.

When Belkis opened the door, Rina and I were sitting at the dining-room table looking like diligent students. As a delicious aroma filled the room and everyone rushed to wash their hands, Rina reminded me about Dan's car, and my oath to be at the gas station at six o'clock sharp. Hearing this, I glanced at their grandfather clock. It was five-thirty-five.

"Tak, would you like a slice?" Belkis asked upon returning to the living room.

"Thanks, it smells delicious but I gotta go," I politely declined in spite of the rumbling sounds emanating from my stomach.

That day, Rina and I transcended the borders of a simple adventure. We had shed tears, dodged cops on multiple occasions, made love, and had two blissful slumbers—not to mention a Philly cheese steak! To me, this qualified as otherworldly.

Although Rina wanted to walk me to the car so we could sneak a last taste of each other's essence, I declined, thinking it would look suspicious. When I started the engine, it occurred to me I had forgotten to bust a nut. Oh well, I felt confident Rina had enjoyed her experience. And let's not front; so did I.

Chapter 6: Really just a Prankster

Although Rina and I had sex a few more times, the love affair soon fizzled out. Part of the reason for this was Belkis and I started spending more time together. The latter relationship was neither physical nor romantic; it was all about dollars and cents. Or should I say 'sense?'

"If it makes dollars, it makes a whole lot of sense!"

This was Belkis' favorite quote; you could say it was her Golden Rule. Her interest in drugs was strictly limited to the payday attached to them. In other words, I never saw Belkis get high. In my case, selling weed was a gimmick which enabled me to have a 'cool' standing in high-school society. It is important to note that without my street-hustle, I never could have afforded my cheeba habit nor my collection of 'fresh gear;' both of which were quintessential pieces to being black. In hindsight, sure I made a couple dollars, but for me, it was more about maintaining my 'rep.'

When Belkis caught wind of how frivolously I squandered my earnings, she shook her head and stated the obvious. "I guess opposites do attract because I'm all about making dough!" Be that as it may, she was impressed with the amount of business I brought her through my connections at Garfield and Eastern. Weeks later, she began compensating me with a modest commission for my contributions to her establishment. Since many brothers complained my sacks were too small and expensive, I ended up at her door several times-a-week for these low-budget misers. Due to the fact I never showed up without making a purchase, Belkis missed the tell-tale signs that Rina and I were sort of dating. This was a good thing because had she known the situation might have become a bit sticky. Fortunately, Belkis was focused on the money I handed her, having long ago stopped suspecting me and her niece were anything other than friends.

One Friday morning, in the middle of winter, Rina, Mike, and I sat in class silently hoping the snow that had begun falling was still coming down. Since our classroom was a science laboratory with no windows, it was impossible to become distracted by the wonders of nature. So we could only blindly wish.

"Tak, yo Tak wake up. The bell's about to ring."

After Mike lightly punched my arm, the public address system came to life. Following a couple seconds of static, I groggily raised my head and listened to the principal's voice.

"Ladies and gentlemen, please excuse the interruption. I have just been informed by the superintendent of schools that due to the possibility of freezing roads this afternoon, the remainder of today's classes have been canceled…"

Although Dr. Whitaker said some other things, the rest of his message got cut-off when the entire student-body spontaneously shouted, *"Hell yeah!"*

When Rina, Quinton, Mike, and I left the classroom, everyone in the hallway was charged with excitement by our unexpected reprieve from purgatory. Everyone, that is, except Rina. Recently, she had been quiet and somewhat distant in class. When I asked her about it, she said it was just jitters about her upcoming SAT examination.

"Tak, Rina, cool-out," said Quinton once we neared

the stairwell.

Quinton and Mike's homerooms were on the third floor, so they were leaving us.

"See y'all tomorrow," Mike added with a raised fist. "And Tak, don't fuck around outside with no snowballs…I know how you like to do!"

"Relax Mike, I don't participate in juvenile activities like snow ball fights," I stated in a high-falutin tone while sporting a sarcastic grin.

"Bye y'all," Rina said in a mellow voice.

As we neared Rina's homeroom, she mentioned Belkis wanted to see me today. Before I could ask her why, I saw Jo-Jo and his younger brother, Kalvin, exchanging pounds with some guys I didn't know. Then Jo-Jo looked in my direction.

"Yo Sev, playboy! Come talk to me man! Where you been?"

Rina, seeing the duo approaching, exhaled a sigh of disgust. "Go hang out with your friends!" she whined in an irritated tone before stomping away in anger.

I had no idea why she was upset. Her inexplicable grouchiness brought to mind comments by old-heads at the courts who claimed, 'All girls are bitches.' Although I did not think of Rina in this way, at that moment, I have to admit I was glad to get away from her.

"Trouble in paradise?" asked Kalvin after he arrived and gave me a pound.

"Yeah I guess so, huh?" I admitted my confusion. "What do they say about women? You can't live with 'em…"

"And you can't live without 'em!" Jo-Jo completed the popular saying. "I thought you said you and Rina were just friends?"

"We are…anyway, what's up with y'all?" I said to change the subject.

"You already know," Jo responded, "what we talked about before. But now I need a couple more grams for some other folks too."

"Cool," I replied, "let's be out."

Once Jo reminded me of the order he placed this morning, the three of us started walking. Prior to leaving, I glanced at Rina's still receding form. It was obvious she was frustrated about something other than the SAT. *But what?* I wondered to myself.

Jo-Jo rarely required the services of the Lady. And why should he? Without having to ask, I always gave him an extra bud and smoked with him as well. With his girlfriend acting as our chauffeur, we drove around town and got puffed before completing the transaction. By the time I got dropped off at Belkis' apartment, I felt guilty picturing Rina walking home alone; but what could I do? After all, she walked away from me.

When I entered the apartment, I realized Belkis was alone. Judging from the delicious aroma wafting-in from the kitchen, that plus her tired appearance, I surmised she had just finished washing the dishes after cooking that evening's dinner. Because Belkis only did this when she had an evening appointment, I wondered where she was going. Nevertheless I knew better than to pry into her private affairs so I didn't ask.

In the daytime, with everyone at school, the three-bedroom apartment had a different appeal. It was tranquil. When one of her customers showed up, I excused myself to the bathroom while she handled her business. As I returned to the living room, she was politely seeing the middle-aged, Latino man to the door. Once the guy I heard Belkis call

"Hector" was gone, I sat down in my favorite chair. After Belkis locked the bolt, she walked into the living room and handed me the twenty bucks she received from Hector.

"This is your latest commission," Belkis replied before I could ask a question. "Tak, since we're partners and you're hooking me up with customers, I want you to make more money too," Belkis explained. "So from now on, let's raise the bar a little. Whaddya think?"

"Sounds good to me," I coolly replied, eager for more details.

Hearing my response, Belkis produced a plastic baggie almost from thin air and placed it on the coffee table. After one look at the off-white chalky substance in the bag, I knew it was not cocaine.

"What is it?" I inquired.

"Crank," she answered. "This nasty, pasty stuff has guys literally bouncing off the walls."

"So it's an upper?" I asked, taking a stab in the dark. "Is it anything like coke?"

"Not really," Belkis then stopped to collect her thoughts. "True, cocaine charges you up too, but this is different. Coke gives you a party high, while crank is more like a 'working man's narcotic.' It's for students pulling all-nighters, or factory workers assigned to the graveyard shift." She then summed her words up into a cheap sales-pitch: "For anyone needing a boost to make it through their day, this blue-collar drug could be their magic bullet."

Listening to her explanation was okay on one level. However like any adventure in life, in order to truly understand, I believed it was necessary to 'become one' with it. The bottom line was: I was suffering from complexes which compelled me to hate myself. For this reason, a new drug translated into another possible avenue of escape. *I couldn't wait to get cranked up!*

"What do you want me to do with it?" I asked. Since I had never heard of the stuff before, I doubted there was any demand for it within my social circles.

"Do you think you could sell any?" Belkis asked.

"Nah," I responded, "but I'll ask around," I replied, hoping this was not the only reason she wanted to see me. Since she called me her 'partner,' I decided to see what other surprises might lie hidden within her bag of tricks. "Now if you had some coke or LSD, then we could make something happen," I uttered, rubbing the palms of my hands together. Although I was hoping for some good news, I was only half-serious. On the other hand, I also concluded if she was selling speed, she might have anything.

"Damn Tak, you deal with LSD too? You gotta be extra careful with that!" she warned.

Truthfully, I had done both drugs for the first time just a couple weeks before. It was during my sophomore year when drugs became a normal part of my routine. Let's just say the crowd I ran with was not into being 'high on life.' We got *zested* on illegal, and legal, stimulants as casually as many folks drink a cup of coffee in the morning. Aside from the constant threat of being arrested, we never considered the enormous risks we were taking.

When Belkis disappeared into her bedroom only to reappear, seconds later, holding a bag of cocaine in one hand and a 'happy face' sheet of LSD in the other, to say I was blown away is putting it lightly.

"Oh shit!" I exclaimed. "You got a top-notch candy shop going on here! And to think, all this time, I thought you were just a local, dime-bag distributor," I joked with her.

"Does Rina know about this?"

"Please! Are you kidding? I only keep weed here. My partner in North Philly has everything else over there," she explained before giving me a stern look. "And Tak, I want to keep it that way, okay? I'm telling you this because I think I can trust you."

"My lips are sealed," I assured her.

Hearing my smug response, Belkis relaxed. "I just received this shipment today, so I'm taking it into the city later."

Now I knew where her appointment was. At the mention of Rina's name, I became concerned about her. "By the way, where is Rina? Shouldn't she be here by now?"

"She called from the public library five minutes before you got here," Belkis replied, taking a seat on the sofa. After she placed the coke and LSD on the coffee table next to the crank, she spoke in an earnest tone. "Tak, there's something else I want to talk to you about."

"What's going on?" I inquired, giving her my attention.

Belkis went on to explain how her career as an accountant was not going well. This was why she had been tempted to expand her horizons beyond the Arizona brown. Listening to Belkis' frank explanation, I admired her integrity. She always seemed comfortable and in control of any situation. As she spoke, she seemed to be probing me for a response. Once I noticed this, I put on my best poker-face.

"Tak, I don't do drugs anymore," Belkis stated. "Besides an occasional glass of wine or maybe a puff or two on someone else's joint, I'm not into partying. For me, this is all about earning dollars…" Pausing here, she placed her index finger against her temple. "And making sense," she

107

completed her statement before pointing at me. "What about you?"

"Me? I smoke herb and drink forties, that's about it," I lied through my teeth. After I assured her I only tried other drugs to check out their potency, it seemed she did not quite believe me.

"All I'm saying is: be careful. I remember being at the experimental age myself. So I know when it comes to money and drugs, shit can get out of hand real-quick." We were interrupted by the phone ringing. Without a second thought, Belkis reached over and turned off the ringer. "The answering machine'll take it," she said before picking-up where she left off. "Tak, I like having you as a partner because you seem able to separate the business from the getting-high part. Most dealers can't get this simple principle straight."

"Don't get high on your own supply!" we chanted the well-known street slogan in unison.

"I gotcha Belkis," I replied, returning her serious expression. "Don't worry, I got it under control."

After negotiating a payment plan for the goods, Belkis forced me to choose between the coke and the LSD. "I can't front both of 'em to you," she explained.

"Okay," I said reaching for the bag of cocaine. As I picked it up, I abruptly changed my mind. Due to all the hoopla in the media about coke and crack, someone was constantly getting busted with it. Not to mention the numerous rumors of how good girls, even church girls, had been reduced to the type of whores who give ten-dollar-blow-jobs in public toilets. A few guys I knew actually pawned their parent's VCRs just to get another hit of the *snow white*. Thinking it best to steer clear of this type of drama, I put the coke down. "I'll take this," I said, pointing at the acid.

"Lemme get five sheets and a sample of the crank."

Even though everyone knew cocaine was a sure payday, I figured that LSD was a designer drug targeted at white customers with deep pockets. This prediction turned out to be accurate. I was delighted to find out whiteboys almost always wanted some herb whenever they bought *trips* from me. This was when I realized negotiating with Caucasians was a far cry from dealing with the tight-fisted folks in the hood. Over the next few weeks, my profits began to increase.

In my conversation with Belkis, I claimed I wanted to test the market for crank users. This was not true. The truth was I wanted to try it myself. So I headed to my friend, Charlie's house. Back in middle school, Charlie Willis was a basketball teammate two-years-in-a-row in our neighborhood Police Athletic League. In our second season, both of us got injured in the same game. For the next couple weeks, Charlie and I were on the bench laughing with our casts and crutches. We had no business having that much fun while our team suffered a three-game losing streak. Since we were also in the same reading class, we got to know each other quite well and became good friends. Even after going to different high schools, we remained tight by becoming weekend, substance-abuse partners in our freshmen year.

On my walk, I smiled reminiscing on some of our crazy experiences. I knew how hyped-up Charlie would be when he saw the surprise I had for TJ's party tonight. This would be a night to remember, I thought. *Man, did we get fucked up!*

"Here," I said passing Charlie a bottle of *Thunderbird*.
After Charlie took a sip, he handed it to the guy next to him.

I arrived at Charlie's early in the evening. Just like I expected, he got excited once he saw what I brought. After he made some phone calls, we went to one of his friend's houses because the guy's parents were out of town, not-to-mention he lived closer to TJ. Since Charlie and I were contributing the drugs, he assigned some other dudes to bring the liquor. Together, the five of us ingested the crank and got drunk. I cannot remember if we snorted the bitter chemical or ate it but there was no about doubt it, it had some serious kick because our hearts were racing!

"Y'all ready to roll over there?" asked Leslie, the host of our impromptu get-together.

"Word, let's jet," agreed Charlie after taking the last swig of his *Colt 45.*

Hearing this, everyone stood up.

On the way to the party we behaved just like you might imagine five teens under the influence would. We chased cats, threw stones at dogs, broke bottles, and slap-boxed. *We were bugging-out!* At some point, Leslie claimed his heart was beating so loudly he couldn't hear what we were saying anymore. Instead of thinking this was any cause for alarm, it only prompted us to crack jokes on him for the rest of the trip.

When we arrived at TJ's block, we saw about fifteen guys huddled-up together in the cold. They were standing a little distance from the party, so we figured they were waiting for someone. As our small group merged with the larger assembled unit, I glanced at the faces nearest to me. Not seeing anyone familiar, I remained quiet while Charlie and the others exchanged greetings with their Eastern classmates.

"Whaddy up, Jamaal? What's the deal?" Charlie asked the first guy we met. "Why y'all standing way over here?"

"It's a G-man party!" Jamaal complained without replying to the greeting. "The guy at the door ain't letting Eastern students in." Saying this, he nodded his head at me. "Your boy can probably get in though."

Although TJ attended my school, he lived in a section of town designated for students going to Eastern. As we contemplated the significance of Jamaal's words, a car drove around the corner and stopped in front of us. From all appearances, it seemed the driver thought he had arrived at the house holding the party. While I considered this possibility, two attractive females exited the rear doors of the black, Buick Regal.

Prior to the ladies' feet touching the ground, the brothers I was standing with gathered around the car to get a lustful look like a horde of barbarians. It took the girls a second to realize they were facing a bunch of strangers. Once they did, they stopped in their tracks, clearly frightened. Due to my poor vision, I was not sure who they were, but they resembled two girls in my English class. I took a chance and stepped forward.

"Hi Takuan," came the pleasant greeting from both my classmates as they smiled a look of recognition.

Hearing the familiar voices, I was relieved I had not made a fool of myself. Tanya and Petula were two sweet girls I was cool as hell with. "Wassup y'all?" I replied.

After they took turns giving me a hug and making me

promise to save them a dance, they pivoted and seductively stepped toward the party. Seconds after their figures faded into the darkness, every eye fell on me.

"*Damn!* Garfield got all the blazers!" a tall brother exclaimed, stepping forward from the back of the crowd. "What's up Tak?" he said, giving me a pound. "You know them fine honeys?"

I bumped fists with the long-legged guy but I didn't know who he was until he stepped under a street-light. "What up god!" I greeted him once he did. He was my friend, Nate.

Nathaniel Wagner was a kid who lived near me until last year when his family moved across town into a bigger house. In that time, Nate added three inches to his height, not to mention a moustache and goatee. Looking him up and down, I checked-out his new look and gave him another pound. Like Charlie and TJ, Nate was another old PAL of mine as well.

"Since you go to Garfield," Nate said, "the bouncer at the door will probably let you in. But the rest of us are stuck out here in the cold."

The forecasts that night called for strong winds with temperatures reaching the low-teens; it was terribly cold. In spite of the frigid conditions, since the five of us were filled with cheap wine and energized by the 'working man's drug,' no one in our entourage had commented about the weather so far.

"Tak, since you should be able to get in, why don't you go see what's up?" Nate pleaded. "See the guy standing at the top of the driveway, near the door? The dude with the white parka on? Now he's talking to one of the sistas that hugged you. You know him?" Repeating his question, Nate pointed at TJ's house.

"Come on cuz, you know damn well I can't see shit at night without my glasses," I replied. Squinting my eyes, I attempted to locate the bouncer. I figured if he went to Garfield I probably knew him.

I had been prescribed to wear glasses back in elementary school. At that time, my near-sightedness was relatively mild so I didn't wear them most of the time. Nevertheless after years of straining my eyes watching television, they gradually worsened.

Before long, everyone was encouraging me to go and speak to the sentry. They claimed I was their only chance to get in the party. "Okay, I'll see what I can do," I said agreeing to undertake the solo-mission. With that, I started walking away from Charlie and the others.

As I neared TJ's house, I squinted at the fuzzy images of people walking and talking.

"What's up Tak," said a familiar voice. "Earl and Quinton're inside lookin' for you."

"Thanks," is all I said, returning a pound to a friendly guy named Joey.

Joseph Hobson was the nicest kid anyone could ever meet. A clean-cut dude, I think it is fair to call him a 'cool nerd.' Joey was in my homeroom and he was also one my football teammates last year. This guy used to try to convince me to stop getting high. For this reason, I damn sure didn't want to talk to him now. "I'll check you out later," I said walking away from him.

The deejay was fading *Captain Rock,* on his "dip ship cruising at hyper speeds," in favor of *UTFO's 'Roxanne, Roxanne'* just as I reached the bottom of TJ's driveway. In the dark, I had difficulty negotiating the outline of the curb and stumbled badly. This was a hint to anyone watching I might be drunk; especially when I tried to play-it-off like it was a cool dip in my strut. Looking around, I hoped no one had seen me but of course someone had. The witness was staring from the top of the driveway. He was wearing a white coat with a furry hood. Although the silhouette was blurry, I was certain he was the guy Nate had pointed at. No matter how hard I squinted, I could not quite bring his face into focus but for some reason I felt like I knew him. And I was right—just not how I had expected.

"Yo ock!" I called out in an ill-mannered tone considering he might be a stranger. "What's up with entry rules to this joint?" Thinking I sounded cool, I continued. "It's cold as hell out here, and see my homies over there?" With that, I pointed at the forlorn distant group. "They're over there catching frostbite, cuz. So what's up? Can we go in, or what?" Having completed my macho presentation, I stood in my modified b-boy pose waiting for his reply.

"Takuan, *you* can go in…" Once the man opened his mouth, I was chilled to the bone. This had nothing to do with the low-temperatures. It was his voice, I had heard it before.

"Since this is TJ's birthday party, he continued, "all his classmates from Garfield are welcome. But I'm afraid those other gentlemen will have to warm their feet elsewhere tonight."

Some voices are unforgettable. Even now, if I heard the voice of my 6th grade teacher, Mr. Davis, I bet it would still sound familiar. As the only black male teacher in our school, he had made a huge impression on me. In his class, even the coolest kids wanted to do well to please him; so I too directed extra energy toward my studies. I can recall how disappointed Mr. Davis was when I rejected my induction into the Program for Academically Talented Students. This was our school's version of the Honor Society. He was almost teary-eyed when he confronted me in private. "Takuan, you have an obligation to use your god-given talent!" he shouted, pointing at me before diving into a rant which detailed some of the sacrifices our people made during the Civil Rights Movement. "Do you know how many folks suffered so you could have this opportunity?" Following his speech, he asked why I was snubbing the newly-formed PATS group. Seeing him in such an emotional state, I was too embarrassed to explain Earl's theory on black and white activities. Therefore I agreed to join the geeky group.

"Takuan," my former teacher continued, "how are you *feeling* tonight? How's your father doing these days?"

"Hey Mr. Davis," I responded in a sullen voice, trying to evade the intended barbs embedded in the word 'feeling,' and by mentioning my father. Now that it was too late, I recalled Mr. Davis telling me, years ago, that TJ was his nephew.

"Maybe," Mr. Davis added, "it would be a good idea for you to go home and get some sleep." Glaring at his prized pupil from four years ago, the very one he had repeated the same edict to over-and-over again: *"Son, don't waste your ability!"* he then folded his arms and ended on a cordial note. "Good night, Tak. Please tell your parents and Kay that I said 'hello'."

"I will sir," I replied realizing Mr. Davis knew I was wasted. The last thing I was going to do was add insult to injury by trying to con him. By this point, I just wanted to disappear into the night. "And yes, maybe I will go home," I resumed. "Good night, Mr. Davis."

When I noticed Mr. Davis was talking to someone else before I completed my sentence, I knew my effort to demonstrate my former straight-A personality had had little effect. If Charlie, Lester, Nate, and the rest of the Eastern High posse had not been awaiting my report, I surely would have run off into the darkness and bawled at the moon to release my anguish.

"What happened cuz, can we go in?" Nate asked sounding optimistic.

"Nah, it ain't gonna happen," I reported the moment I walked up to them. "Fuck TJ!" Saying this, I started walking away. "It's cold as hell out here! Charlie, let's be out. What you gonna do Nate?"

"I'm rolling with y'all." Nate replied as he followed me toward the corner. "Yo, I heard there's another house-jam in Millbrook. You know a girl named 'Margot'? She goes to Garfield too."

"Nah," I replied.

Even though Margot was in two of my classes, I lied because I didn't want to talk to him or anyone at that moment. My main concern was staying in front of everybody to conceal the tears stinging my face. Since I was leading the pack, I figured I would just walk toward her house. This was the first time I felt a hint of disgust for who I was becoming. Suddenly I felt cold...*very cold indeed.*

A Genuine Menace

After diversifying my narcotics portfolio as a salesman for the Lady, the resentment I harbored for not being accepted as a super-jock, G-man resurfaced. That being said, I was still proud to be acknowledged as a 'somebody' amongst my peers. So long as I was not linked to anything corny or 'white,' being recognized as a hoodlum, drug addict, or dealer was okay. Reflecting on this now, I realize this was not a conscious thought process. It was more like being stuck on stupid. Allow me to clarify because it was around this time when I began to devolve from a relatively harmless deviant into a genuine menace to high school society.

To anyone who is paying attention, it should be obvious I was just a confused boy picking up the wrong signals. It was not a question of being good, bad, lucky, or unlucky. Nor were my parents or the neighborhood where I lived to blame. A big part of my problem was my need to judge everyone and everything by a set of irrational standards which I had accepted as truth. *Had I not learnt how to be 'black' while paying my dues as a Jap?* Even Ant called me 'youngboy.' So in my own illogical way, I was trying to balance the scales.

Nonetheless, by my junior year things had certainly changed. Having mastered my street persona, seldom did anyone question my blackness these days. If any inquiries were made, it was only to ask if I was Latino or Native American. Whether in the hallway or on the street, even known thugs acknowledged me with respect; I had developed a reputation. At this point, I should have been happy because more than basketball, girls, or even clockin' dollars, my priority was being 'Down by Law.' This was our slogan-expression for having respect in the streets before 'Keepin' it Real' eclipsed it in the '90s.

How many prison cells and coffins contain the remains of such similarly misguided souls?

The '80s taught its youth that drugs were the 'in-thing.' Perhaps nothing sums this analysis up more than the launching of the hit-television series, *Miami Vice*. This weekly, police-drama introduced the idea that cocaine and being cool were one concept. Detective James "Sonny" Crockett and Detective Ricardo "Rico" Tubbs, dressed in Armani suits and driving Ferraris, demonstrated that fast cars, loose women, and automatic weapons were the definition of manhood. All this, mind you, on a cop's paycheck. *Come on, who's zoomin' who?*

When you consider I actually believed Ant and Chauncey had lived some sort of 'Tony Montana from *Scarface*' lifestyle while collecting All-State honors and scholarships, this helps to shed light on my particular brand of ignorance. In other words, I was trying to repeat the plan that appeared successful. Now that I had become one of the guys younger girls were chasing after, this was evidence enough my strategy was working.

Chapter 7: An Unlikely Partnership

The lingering images of Patrice swapping candy and kisses with Justin stung my memory as I sat at a round table in the lunchroom. Lost in my own thoughts, I barely noticed the other students sitting nearby. I had become the definition of anti-social. Since school started three months prior, I had purposely sat by myself. If anyone approached *my* table, I sent them to eat elsewhere with very direct, "Get the fuck outta here!" fiery edicts. In fact, my sole interest in attending school had become to peddle my merchandise.

Separated from the others, I imagined what it was like to go clubbing; or to just travel beyond my normal Philly – Trenton drug circuit. As I fantasized about making love to exotic women in faraway lands, believe it or not, I also spent a considerable amount of time mulling over my Japanese heritage. I was inspired by a book entitled *Shibumi.* It was a novel which incorporated the game *Go* to create the perfect assassin. My search for novels about Japan led me to another author named James Clavell. I ended-up reading most of his Asian series, and was relieved to discover Caucasian protagonists who transcended the outdated 'John Wayne types' I had become accustomed to. Even though the heroes in these novels won everything in the end—just like those other whiteboys—compared to Charlton Heston or Clint Eastwood, they at least had personalities I could relate to. So unless a passage made reference to their European ancestry, I could forget they were white because they didn't 'act white.'

"Hey Tak, long-time-no-see. What's going on man?"

The Caucasian intruder's words startled me. After the uninvited, male student interrupted my solitude, he took a seat at my table. In spite of my preference to eat alone, I grinned when I looked at him.

"Speak of the devil! What's up Jeff?" Considering the timing of the pun, I smiled to suppress my laughter.

Although I often saw Jeff around school, we *never* acknowledged each other. Both of us, having bought into the white-versus-black dichotomy, believed we were inherent enemies.

Following my greeting, I could hear murmurs from the surrounding students who were observing this lunchtime irregularity. I was curious to see what wind of chance had blown this nerd into my presence so I patiently waited while Jeff glanced both ways suspiciously before pushing his school-boy styled glasses up onto the bridge of his long Pinocchio-like nose. Appearing satisfied no one could hear him, he then mumbled something incoherent.

"What?" I snapped almost yelling at him. "Yo man this is the lunchroom. It's noisy as hell in here and we're the only two people at this table. Speak up!" Even though Jeff was older than me, I addressed him like a youngboy.

"A-hem," Jeff cleared his throat before speaking again. This time in a louder tone. "I heard you got some trips man. Me and my friends wanna cop some, if that's okay."

Sitting there looking at Jeff in his *Metallica* t-shirt, I was pleased because everyone knew the kids who called themselves "thrashers" were big acid-heads. I crossed my fingers, hoping this was an opportunity to enter the largest drug market. Not to mention I needed new customers. Truth be told, my only sales recently had been to friends who I ended up tripping with. *Way too much getting high on my own supply!*

"Yeah Jeff, you heard right," I replied following a lengthy pause. Then I hit him with the standard sales pitch. "I got the high-quality shit. What can I do you for?"

"I dunno exactly…at least four." Saying this nervously, he counted and recounted using the fingers of both hands. "Maybe six…I'm n-not sure."

When Jeff started stuttering, it irked me. "Well, when will you know? 'Cause I don't like carrying shit around with me," I lied.

The truth was I had weed and trips in my pocket even as we spoke because I *never* put the goods in my hall locker. The reason for this was, about twice a month, the police brought their drug-sniffing canines to Garfield. On their random visits, they consistently made a couple arrests. Three weeks prior, they busted two of my friends. Only once when I absolutely needed to stash it somewhere did I dare to use my smelly gym locker, but never my hall locker. If I wanted to shoot baskets or play dodge ball, I would ask a friend to hold it in their book bag. Otherwise it was on me at all times.

"Tell you what J," I said abbreviating his first name, "I'll meet you at your house after school. We can discuss the details then. Cool?" Seeing he lacked the confidence to express himself, I started sympathizing with the shy boy. After all, I had suffered from a similarly social awkwardness not long ago, I reflected.

Jeff finally found the words to respond to my offer. "Cool Tak, I'll see ya later." With a grin on his face, he stood up and disappeared.

And with that, I slouched down in my seat, closed my

eyes, and returned to my daytime fantasies amidst the rumbling activity in the lunchroom.

Later that afternoon, I put most of the LSD, some high-grade bud, and a few dimes in my pocket and walked out the door. Minutes later, I was approaching Jeff's street. Near the corner, I spotted a kid named Tyler standing on his driveway with his dog. Jeff lived behind me and next to Tyler, so all of three of us were neighbors. Once I confirmed Ty had not seen me, I dropped down behind a parked car out of sight. With a sly grin, I shaped a soggy snowball in my gloveless hands. Just as the stinging became too much to bear, I cocked my arm back and took aim but before I could release the snowball Ty's father stepped out from behind a tree which had been concealing him.

"Damn!" I vented under my breath once I dropped the snowball and wiped my smarting hands on my coat. Then I watched Ty turn in my direction; he looked angry.

"Tak!" he yelled, running toward me with his golden Labrador.

We convened about ten yards from where his father remained standing.

"What's going on, youngboy?" I said, trying to impose Ant's nickname for me onto him. Somehow the effect was lost. As we exchanged a pound, I noticed his father was searching the sky for something.

"What's your pop doing? I asked. "Bird watching?"

Ty and Jeff lived on the street behind mine. This was within the area I considered 'my turf.' Once Ant stopped hanging out on our block, he left a gaping hole in the sports contests. Being Ant's heir-apparent, I had developed a sort of following amongst the younger guys. Tyler Felton was one such dude. Ty, who was still in middle school, was a light-skinned 'pretty boy.' A huge Michael Jackson fan, I used to tease him when he dressed up in his *Thriller* jacket and other MJ accessories. Although I liked Ty, it seemed everyone else liked to pick on him.

Ignoring my question, Tyler started talking about something else. "Am I glad to see you!" he said looking relieved. "I told you Jeff wasn't done fucking around. He's at it again! That fool always thinks people got time to play with him! Please kick his ass!" Ty appealed to me as if I were the district henchman.

At this point, the only thing I knew for certain was he was angry at Jeff. I soon realized Ty was referencing an incident he already told me about but I had completely forgotten. Since he appeared upset, I did not want to admit this unless I had no other choice. Knowing how talkative Ty was, I figured if I remained silent he would eventually explain everything I needed to know.

While I listened to him, the unmistakable sound of tiny metal objects striking the garbage cans Ty's father was carrying caught my attention. His father, appearing petrified, dropped the cans on the driveway. Then, for the next couple seconds, I watched Mr. Felton contort his body in a series of strange poses. When his bizarre movements stopped, I almost thought I had imagined the whole thing. Not knowing what to say, I decided to simply greet him.

"How ya doing Mr. Felton?" I said in a loud voice to ensure my words traveled the distance to where he was standing.

"Hey Tak," came his calm response. Oddly, his words

were in contrast to his worried countenance.

Mr. Felton was staring at the sky so he never looked in my direction. For five seconds, none of us moved. I had no idea what I was waiting for but I felt compelled to remain quiet and watch. Finally, Mr. Felton grabbed the garbage cans and started walking up the driveway one more time. Just as I was about to say something to Ty, he started the psychotic dance step again.

In spite of being several years before the *Vogue* would become popular in NYC gay-clubs, Mr. Felton appeared to be doing a schizophrenic version of it. Once I got a second chance to witness his bizarre two-step, I recalled something Ty told me last week. Every evening, Ty stopped by my bedroom window for a nightly chat. During my house-arrest days, I really came to appreciate his visits. Last week, just after a heavy snowfall, he had arrived with a scowl on his face.

"Tak, can you do me a favor?" he had inquired.

"Yes of course, for a small handling fee," I joked in response.

Ignoring my satire, Ty bent down and rolled up his right pant-leg. "That muthafucka Jeff shot me with his BB gun!" he griped revealing a black-and-blue welt on his calf. "He thinks that shit's funny!"

After inspecting his injury, I promised to avenge him. Nevertheless I had forgotten about the incident until this very moment.

By the time Mr. Felton went into round three of his convulsions, I knew I had to do something. Looking at Jeff's house, I spotted a silhouette on the roof crouching behind the chimney. The person was holding a long object which appeared to be a rifle. *Unbelievable!* I thought to myself.

What had seemed disrespectful and trifling a week ago somehow had a different appeal now that it was happening in front of me. Standing there watching Mr. Felton, I did everything in my power to keep from busting out laughing. At the next cease-fire, when Ty's father again stared at the clouds waiting for an explanation from the heavens, I almost shouted 'Hey, what the hell do you think is hitting your body?'

"Hey Mr. Felton, let us to do that," I said instead. "Come on Ty, stop loafing!" I kidded with him in a loud voice. I did this to ensure the sniper was alerted to hold his fire. When Jeff vanished, probably to re-load, I placed myself between Mr. Felton and Jeff's house.

If I hear even a single BB whiz by, I'm gonna knock Jeff's teeth out!

Ty and I carried the tin receptacles to the backyard and released the dog. With his mission accomplished, Mr. Felton allowed us to escort him inside. By the time we walked next door to Jeff's, the marksman had put his assassin's kit away and come down from the roof. Moreover he had opened his garage door and was kicking a heavy-bag dangling from the ceiling by thick chains.

As mentioned earlier, Jeff was the weird kid in the neighborhood. Using my fingers and toes, I couldn't come close to accounting for half the times I had seen 'glass-jaw' Jeff take a healthy ass whooping. And that doesn't include my own personal beat-downs. The strangest thing about Jeff was, more often than not, he 'asked for it' by insulting people with high-handed, sarcastic remarks. In an attempt to end his trend of 'getting jacked' after school, Jeff's mother had insisted he take karate lessons. Unfortunately they did little to alleviate the situation.

Ty and I walked up Jeff's driveway and stopped.

125

During the tense pause, I watched Ty glare at Jeff while Jeff looked at me with the countenance of a condemned prisoner on death row. He seemed ready to accept his grim fate. In which direction this gathering would proceed was still in question.

"*Hahahahahaha!*" I couldn't hold the suppressed emotion in the pit of my belly any longer.

Following my two-minute cachinnation, I eventually regained control of my body. Looking around, I realized Ty was nowhere to be found and Jeff was now seated Indian-style in his training area. On his face was a smug expression. Walking through his garage door, I wiped the tears coursing down my face with my sleeve.

"Jeff, what the fuck are you doing?" I began. "You're sick as hell shooting Ty's pop like that!" Saying this, I was still erupting in pockets of laughter here and there. "Yo, he's gonna call the cops on your behind!"

"No he won't," Jeff arrogantly replied. "He's too stupid to even figure out what's going on, let alone have the courage to contact the authorities. That's why I chose him as my target. He ain't the brightest bunny in the forest, if you know what I mean."

Although I had witnessed it with my own eyes, it still seemed strange Mr. Felton did not realize whom and what was assaulting him. Despite this, and the fact I had gotten a good chuckle out of it, there was no way I could allow my friend's father to be pummeled like that.

"Yo Jeff, I gotta admit that was funny but seriously man, you gotta cut-it-out," I started in slowly at first.

"Why?" he complained. "I always aim for the trashcans. Don't worry about it, he'll be okay."

"*Jeff!*" I snapped. "You're shooting BB's at Ty's step-pop! That shit's dangerous and you know it!"

Because I was still smiling, Jeff did not take me seriously. Even though I realized this, I couldn't stop myself because that shit was funny! To end this moot conversation, I knew it was necessary to pull my street ace. "For your information," I added once I was able to keep a straight-face, "last week, Ty came to me crying about how you had shot him—not no trashcan! Jeff," I continued, "after he showed me the bruise, I promised him I'd kick your ass but I forgot about it."

Seeing the stubborn look on his face, I cut to the ultimatum.

"Okay Jeff, what's it gonna be? We gonna do some business this afternoon like we planned? Or do we have to expose that fake-ass karate class again? You make the call, tough-guy."

Having let loose this macho spiel, my adrenaline began to flow. Seizing the moment, I warmed-up for the potential clash by imitating Jo-Jo's pre-fight routine. I wondered if I looked even half as intimidating as when the master did it himself.

"Okay, okay!" Jeff conceded. *"Fuckin-aye!* If you're going to make such a big deal out of it, it's not even fun anymore! I'll stop, are you happy now?"

With his face flushed-red, Jeff projected the frustration of a child who can't have his way. Due to his stereotypical, whiteboy response, I was at my wits end and barely able to avert another round of gut-wrenching laughter. Taking a deep breath, I clapped my hands together to suppress my emotion. I was determined to get the business out of the way before any other distractions surfaced.

"So, did you decide what you want?"

In my experience, selling drugs to Europeans was easier than dealing with my own people. Once they were interested, they never tried to nickel and dime—or rob me. In fact, whenever white dudes agreed to do business, they always knew exactly what goodies I possessed in detail before I even met them. As the connoisseurs of pharmacopoeia, often times, my Caucasian customers taught me things I didn't know about my own products. Jeff was no exception to this rule.

"We're told LSD was accidentally synthesized back in the 1930s by an inept chemist named Albert Hofmann, and made famous in the '60s by the Harvard fag, Timothy Leary. But the real deal is this shit was created by the Nazis." When I was slow to respond, he continued speaking. "They were experimenting on Jews to develop a truth serum," he revealed. "Man, you know those evil bastards fucked-up thousands of minds in those underground labs! I dunno if they ever got the serum they wanted, but they did end up creating LSD. The reason I like acid is because it doesn't turn you into a fiend like ready-rock."

By the mid-1980s, crack was sweeping the nation. Firmly entrenched in the streets, the demon seed had crept into some rap lyrics too. It was still over a year before University of Maryland star, Len Bias, would overdose celebrating his multi-million dollar contract with the NBA Champion, Boston Celtics. On the streets of Camden, Trenton, and Philly, 'crackheads' themselves called the crystalline freebase-form of cocaine, "Ready-Rock."

"Tak, the world is my oyster! And it could be yours, too."

"So how much you looking to cop?" I inquired after Jeff mumbled something incomprehensible. By repeating my question, I made it clear I wanted to get down to business.

"Where's your patience?" Jeff complained. "I thought you were supposed to be Japanese!"

I had no idea why Jeff was upset; nor did I care. "Listen Confucius," I said removing the LSD from my pocket. "Save the Chinese parables for one of your karate classmates. I got shit to do and people to see."

However, Jeff did not give up and before I could steer the conversation to the business at hand, he jumped back in. "I just want to encourage you to use your common sense, that's all."

Feeling my anxiety growing, I almost smacked him in the mouth before remembering how much I needed this sale. After grounding myself by taking a deep breath, I decided to chill-out and relax. Once I did, I got the surprise of my life. Not only was Jeff's conversation interesting, he was actually *dropping knowledge* on a range of topics. Although he made many noteworthy comments that evening, perhaps it was his analysis of how black kids sold drugs which caught my attention the most.

"Tak, why are you following a sure-path to incarceration? If you're walking around saying 'I got that sess' to strangers, or hanging-out on a corner that's known for selling drugs, you're bound to get busted any day now," he said shaking his head. "I guess you're so personally involved you just can't see what's obvious."

"See what? What's so obvious?"

Smiling benevolently with a pompous air, Jeff grinned before resuming his theory. "It's obvious that people on the low end of society have been tricked into getting themselves locked-up," he stated.

"Whaddya mean?"

129

An Unlikely Partnership

"Okay, take you for instance," he resumed pushing his glasses up with his finger. "Like I said, if you're selling to strangers you'll definitely be caught sooner than later. Why do you think the Lady has you on such a long leash? She's much too intelligent to risk her freedom by selling to an undercover cop. Even though you know the Lady personally, you haven't learned anything from her."

The logic in his words stung!

Having assumed the esteemed position of teacher, he proceeded to bring the lecture full-circle. "Don't get mad at her!" Jeff said laughing once he sensed my emotion. "You were determined to become a jailbird long before she met you. She's an opportunist that's all…and good for her! She probably figured she might as well get paid before you start paying your debt back to society." Shrugging his shoulders, he added another snooty comment. "Look at the bright side and see it as charity. Tak, you're a really nice guy!"

Before I could reply, he switched topics.

"Didn't you get arrested a couple years ago?"

"That didn't have anything to do with drugs," I shot-back in a defensive tone.

"So what! Aren't you listening? Tak, they've tricked you into becoming a convict. Every time you get popped for fighting or some other petty crime it gets added to your juvenile record. If you get a drug charge, the prosecutor can show the judge evidence that you're progressively getting worse, not better. Once this happens, you're outta here amigo!" Rubbing his chin, he summed his statements up with a crooked grin. "So you say they've already gotten you to commit your first strike on the path to social-suicide, huh?"

Prior to this night, I never viewed Jeff with anything other than contempt or pity. Aside from his lecture on drug-

130

selling, I was blown back he knew so much about my relationship with Belkis. This alone forced me to respect his words.

"Exactly what're you trying to say?" I said taking a seat in a lawn chair near the door. "You have a better idea for clockin' dollars with this stuff? If so, now would be a good time to speak up." Although I possessed little in the way of leverage for this type of swagger, it was the only way I knew how to communicate.

"Yes I do," Jeff stated with confidence. "As a matter of fact, it's such a sure-shot deal, I'll tell you what the catch is upfront: you can't pull it off without me."

Once Jeff revealed his real intention for wanting to meet this afternoon, I stood up and acted like I was about to leave. Seeing me rise to my feet, Jeff came to the point.

"Let me work for you," he said before adding, "we should only sell to white kids from now on because they have way more cash to burn." He explained this wearing a stern expression. "But most of them are scared to deal with blacks because they always get ripped off."

He definitely had a point there. I had witnessed brothers snatch money right out of the hands of unsuspecting whiteboys on more than a few occasions. To make matters worse, if any of the victims tried to retaliate or complain, they were sucker-punched and mercilessly stomped into the ground. Because we only understood immediate gratification, it never occurred to us these petty thefts were bad for business in the long-run. *What the hell did 'long-run' even mean?*

"Hold up," I broke in. "If you sell to the white crowd, I gotta pay you, right? So I guess you got clientele up and down the East Coast, huh playa?"

131

"No. But I have access to over a hundred kids who trip constantly. Oh, and by the way, most of them are filthy rich."

Jeff sealed the deal right there, however, I had been schooled to never reveal my hand; therefore, I pretended like I had ten other options I could roll with. "That sounds great and all, but how much of a cut are you looking for?"

"Tak, you may turn out to be a good businessman after all," Jeff commented with a chuckle. "Tell you what, gimme whatever you feel I've earned. To be honest, I just want to get high free-of-charge."

Whaddya know, a whiteboy after my own heart! Hearing Jeff's words, I realized he was expressing exactly how I felt when I met Belkis just over a year ago.

I listened to his proposition with interest as the moon and the stars became visible in the sky. With absolutely nothing to lose, I agreed to Jeff's terms and became partners with the most unlikely character in our school. Even if he got busted, I pondered, no one would ever link us together. It was an ingenious plan!

Following a handshake, I rolled a joint to cement our deal. While I did this, Jeff called a few of his synogogue buddies to announce he had a new connection for party favorites. The brilliance of his plan revealed itself right away when he took four orders totaling almost two hundred dollars. He accomplished all this on the telephone before I even sparked the joint. Seeing this, I canceled my scheduled trip to the courts. I was in no mood to haggle with homeboys over the price of a dovesack. Jeff and I ended up talking until late into the night. During this time, three more guys called to place orders.

After we finished discussing business, Jeff started

breaking down the history of the martial arts. I was impressed with his wide field of knowledge. He was the first person I ever heard link Nubia with ancient cultures in modern-day India, China, or even Tibet. He read way more than I did. When he mentioned *Daruma*, which is a name well-known in Nippon folklore, he surprised me by claiming he was Dravidian, not Japanese; and that his real name was *Bodhidharma*. I already knew Bodhidharma was the master who taught the Asian fighting-systems to the legendary Shaolin monks because back in 6th grade, to commemorate Black History Month, Mr. Davis played a recording of a speech on the origin of Kung-fu, Gung-fu, and Wushu from the Pan-African griot, Baba Kwame Ishangi.

By the time I left Jeff's garage that night, I had a different opinion of him. I was shocked to discover we had some things in common. This led me to wonder how much losing his father at a young age had contributed to his lack of social graces. He seemed to be a different guy when he was relaxed. Even though we had a great time cooling out together, I was glad we established a strict business relationship. With no mention of anything else, since I had already given him most of the LSD, I figured I'd wait a week before arranging another meeting. Nevertheless it seemed Jeff had other ideas.

Chapter 8: Friends...How many of us have them?

Glancing at the clock, I knew had to leave in the next couple minutes if I was going to meet Jo-Jo before school. Running into the bathroom, I rushed to brush my teeth and pick a zit, careful not to overdo it like in my frosh days.

"Anta itsumo okureruno...hayaku shinasai! Ano hito mou tsuita-yo!" yelled a perplexed voice from the hallway.

Because my sister had graduated the previous year, I knew my mother was yelling at me. Hearing her say somebody was at the door, I figured it was someone in Jo-Jo's crew. Rushing back to my room, I started grabbing the items I needed for today's classes: Jo's quarter-ounce, fifteen dime-bags, some rolled joints, a bottle of Visine, a pack of gum, a lighter, some rolling papers, and a pint of Bacardi 151. After stuffing everything into my jacket pockets, I ran down the hallway and almost collided with my mother when she exited the kitchen.

"Oka-san, who is it?" I asked her.

"It's Jeffrey," she replied, looking pleased.

Since I knew a couple guys named Jeff, I did not jump to the conclusion it was my neighbor. At first, I thought it was Jeff Conrad, one of my ex-football teammates who liked to 'get his groove on' but I had to scratch our left-tackle from the list because my mother never met him. With this in mind, I tested my growing suspicion. "Jeff who?" I asked.

135

After arriving home the previous night, I made sure to tell my mother where I had been. I did this because she thought Jeff was a nice boy. It amazed me how white kids involved in all kinds of dirt could still maintain a positive reputation.

"Tonari-no Jeff," she replied still beaming.

"What?" After confirming it was indeed 'next door Jeff,' I was horrified. My mother, seeing the expression on my face, knew what was coming next. This explains why she immediately turned around and hurried back into the kitchen. "Tell him I already left!"

Being a habitual liar, I thought nothing of asking my own mother to do it too. *Talk about a son with no morals!* When she ignored my request, I knew my options were narrowed to dissin' him or feeling sorry for him.

"Damn! What am I gonna do now?" Mumbling this under my breath, I tiptoed toward the door and looked through the peep hole. For over a minute, I stood there watching him while I considered various escape scenarios.

A couple years ago, when crack took over as the 'great white dope' in the neighborhood, whiteboys stopped getting jumped. Therefore I wasn't fearful of any violent repercussions for walking with him. It was my reputation. I didn't want to jeopardize my 'down by law' status after working so hard to earn that title. Although some blacks and whites in our town hung-out together, whenever I examined any of these cardboard set-ups, I found that one of the pair— *usually the black kid*—was required to turn a blind-eye to his own culture. In return, these sell-outs were given 'mascot membership' into another ethnic group's circle of activities. I felt then, and still do to this day, this type of phoniness is just the flip-side of the same racist coin. However it was the

136

absence of this hypocrisy which allowed Jeff and me to become friends.

Charlie summed it up best: "Cuz, I thought you done lost it the first time you brought that whiteboy around here. But the thing about Jeff is: he never tries to 'act black,' nah I mean? He doesn't say 'yo' and 'bro' in every other sentence. If you think about it, he's still the same goofy-ass whiteboy he always was, except now he's cool."

Following my lengthy deliberation, I closed my eyes to make a decision. When I opened the door, I hoped Jeff had gotten the hint and left on his own accord. But of course, he was still standing there. Wearing the same tired burgundy sweat-suit from the previous evening, he was gazing at the ground with a brown book bag draped over his shoulder. On his face was a solemn expression.

"What up man?" I said with a grin. "If you rollin' with me, we gotta move 'cause I'm meeting Jo-Jo and Quinton before homeroom." Speaking my words as a matter-of-fact, just as I had expected, Jeff appeared intimidated when he heard Jo's name. I pretended not to notice his uneasiness, figuring if this whiteboy wanted to be down, he was going to have to toughen-up quick-fast-and-in-a-hurry! It was not about being a great brawler who could knock everyone out. However if someone dissed you, it was a done deal. You were required to inflict as much damage on your adversary as possible. In our hood, a person was judged on how he or she reacted to being challenged to a fight. Once folks believed you were about defending yours, the problems with *hard rocks* 'requesting' your lunch money, your sneakers, or even your coat, faded from the radar. As the last generation of 'knuckle-up kids,' we became teens just before crack and gangsta-rap hit the market.

As to be expected, Jeff got his first opportunity to 'defend his' the very next day. We were walking home together following a detention when I heard my friend Marcus calling my name from behind. After Marcus caught up with us, he only greeted me. Then with a scowl on his face, he looked at Jeff and used his thumb like a hitchhiker.

"A-ight whiteboy, you know the deal," he calmly stated, "hit the road Jack." When Jeff did not move fast enough, Marcus viciously shoved him out of the way. "Get the fuck outta here!"

With the space next to me cleared, without another word, we started walking again.

Jeff did not leave but since the pavement was only wide enough for two people to walk side-by-side, he had been demoted to the back row. If Jeff continued trailing behind us, I knew before long Marcus would get angry. *And I was dying to see how Jeff was going to handle himself!* With no other kids around to stomp on Jeff if Marcus dropped him, this was the ideal setting for Jeff's heart to get tested. Sure enough, after a couple minutes, Marcus stopped and turned around.

"Why the fuck are you still here?" Following another two-handed push, Marcus then punched Jeff in the chest. When Jeff again failed to respond, he looked like the same old punk everyone knew. Seeing exactly what I saw, Marcus dropped his ultimatum. "Jeff, you got ten seconds to get outta my face!" Then he started counting backward. "Ten, nine, eight…"

When Jeff glanced at me, I felt embarrassed for him but I was also vexed. Regardless of my feelings, I knew Jeff had to defend his own cause so I didn't say anything. By the time Jeff realized Marcus was collecting stones he tried to run but it was too late.

"Three, two, one…blast off!" With this emphatic declaration, Marcus started firing.

Jeff was barely fifteen feet ahead of us when a large rock struck him on the back of his neck. *"Ouch!"* he yelled, falling forward onto his hands and knees.

Then Marcus, showing no mercy, hit Jeff two more times before he could regain his feet. For a split second, I almost grabbed Marcus' arm. Then I remembered Mr. Felton and the BB gun. Once Jeff resumed running, I smiled thinking how this story was going to make Ty happy when he dropped by later.

Karma, it seems, has quite a sense of humor.

By the time Jeff ran out of range, Marcus had put on quite a shooting display. Hurling about twenty stones in all, he pegged Jeff at least eight or nine times. What made Marcus's target-practice especially amusing to watch was he did it while he bragged about his recent, bedroom conquests with his new girlfriend. Even though I laughed at his sexually-explicit tales, inwardly I was disgusted watching Jeff sprint, skip, and scuttle down the block. *What a coward!*

A half-hour later, Marcus and I arrived at his street.

"A-ight Tak, peace," Marcus said giving me a pound.

"Cool out Marc," I replied.

"Oh, and tell that pussy that lives behind you I ain't done with him yet!" After pointing ahead at Jeff's barely visible image, Marcus reached into his jacket pockets. Pulling out the remaining rocks, he dropped them onto the pavement.

"Okay I will," I said with a grin as Marcus turned the corner.

After Marcus was gone I yelled ahead but Jeff did not respond. Putting on my glasses, I saw him listening to his *Walkman* so I broke into a jog. I was bristling with anger thinking about how Marcus had chumped him like a little girl. When I got within fifteen yards, I yelled again but he still could not hear me. With a sly grin, I picked up a stone and threw it near him just to get his attention; however it bounced off the street and grazed his leg.

Jeff, thinking Marcus had resumed pursuing him, ran and hid behind a parked car. Several seconds elapsed before he dared to peek over the hood. Once he confirmed Marcus was nowhere in sight, he stood up with his headphones resting around his neck.

"What a bitch-ass coward!" I vented, pointing at him. "Are you so frightened of Marcus that you'll let him treat you like that?" Without allowing him to respond, I berated his unsatisfactory hood ethics. My point was clear: Jeff had to learn to stand-up for himself.

In spite of my harsh critique, I understood Jeff's fear quite well. A couple years ago I endured my own trials to overcome this phobia. My training had come in the form of body-boxing, playing the dozens, and real fights against my peers. *Not to mention those brutal one-on-one's against the whirling dervish, Jo-Jo.* Plus, let me not front, I got my 'heart took' a couple times too. Again, my life changed the day Jo said, "Don't let any of those muthafuckas call you Jap anymore!" That marked my unofficial graduation. It became official the following day when two would-be comedians tried cracking some *Ultra-man* jokes. I knocked both of them jokers out.

Now Jeff had to earn his stripes so I made this easy for him to understand. "Jeff, if you get punked, it makes me look like a pussy too…for hanging-out with your punk-ass! So when you go to bed tonight, think about that because if you ever get chumped in front of me like that again, word is bond, I will beat that ass myself!" Then I ended the tongue-lashing with a challenge: "If you ain't ready to run with the big dawgs, stay on the porch. Don't bring your cowardly lion-ass to my house tomorrow morning!"

"Tak—"

Being at the corner where we separated, I crossed the street before Jeff could apologize. That night, I fell asleep wondering if I had poured the 'tough love' act on too strong. For this reason, I smiled the next morning when my mother said "Next-door-Jeff's here."

After my friend, Wayne, moved across town, I started hanging out with Jeff a lot more. Jeff represented a portal to a different world, so this relationship caused significant changes in my life. At first, I was nervous about other peoples' opinions until I realized this was just another level of cowardice. Besides, considering I despised everything about Garfield anyway, whose opinion was I worrying about? Not only did this simple realization liberate me, it provided an opportunity for both of us to expand our horizons. *And make some cash!*

On 'white days,' if Jeff and I were not tripping on mescaline listening to *Peter Gabriel* or *The Doors,* we were selling weed at a keg party. On 'black days,' I took Jeff around the hood to places he dare not tread alone. Again, to sell dimes. There, Jeff saw first-hand how disenfranchised people walked, talked, and thought. Socially, both of us were introduced to ideas and opinions which reshaped the way we viewed the world.

I was astonished at how easily I could strike up a conversation with the sons and daughters of upper-class, Caucasian families in the Delaware Valley. Then I wondered if it was only due to the drugs. Wayne and I would laugh whenever they expressed envy that Jeff could attend Hip Hop events like the *Fresh Fest* without catching a beat-down. Although Jeff later revealed some of his synagogue buddies labeled him a 'nigger lover,' I never heard any racist epithets on our visits.

While life had not completely changed, my opinion of it was severely altered—that along with my income. By opening-up shop at both black and white events, my regular customers had more than doubled. When Belkis inquired about my expanded list of clients, I told her some of my cultural revelations. Hearing my explanation, she began shaking her head like I was strange. For a split second, I felt discouraged. Then Belkis clarified her assessment.

"Don't get me wrong," Belkis began, "in order to understand the world, you gotta discover the 'white side' of things sooner or later. And you and this boy are making quite a pretty penny together. Remember Takuan, whenever in doubt, always reference the first commandment…"

As I watched Belkis declare this with her index-finger raised, for a hot second, I thought she was going to spit out something biblical.

"If it makes dollars, it's gotta make good sense!"

Listening to Belkis rehash yet another variation of her Golden Rule, I imagined she had over a thousand versions of this extremely secular proverb,.

"Tak, do your thing, it's all good," she continued with a smile. "Just don't bring that whiteboy anywhere near my apartment." Chuckling, she then added another amusing

142

comment. "And don't lemme hear about you dating no white girls either!"

"Oh, no doubt," I said despite knowing Jeff was outside waiting in his mother's car.

But I did stay away from the white girls!

At this point, we had money to burn and everything was rolling smoothly. It was undeniable: Jeff and I made a good team. My fresh gear steadily increased to the point I became a walking, talking, brand-name billboard. While Jeff, on the other hand, decided to combine his earnings with his bar-mitzvah savings and buy a '67 Mustang Fastback. His mother, thinking his only priority at seventeen-years-of-age should be his education, absolutely hated the car. Over the next two years, Jeff and I shared many adventures in that classic Ford.

In spite of my increase in material goods, by midway through my junior year, I became disenchanted with life in general. Jeff and I were constantly walking the ledge under the influence of drugs and alcohol. It had gotten to the point we started welcoming high-risks so long as they were fun. Long overdue for a reality check, by testing the limits of the social order, we came across a slew of hypocrites disguised as teachers, police officers, and other adults in official positions. In fact, many of these 'respected people' became our most loyal customers.

One weekend, Jeff returned from his synagogue service brimming with excitement. "Tak, I met a blazin' girl named 'Sandra' at our temple tonight."

"Word," I responded. "Does she go to Garfield?"

"No, she's a sophomore at Eastern. She said she knows Charlie. They're in the same gym class," Jeff added.

A year younger than me, not only did Sandy turn out

143

to be attractive, she was a cool girl to hang out with. To be honest, I was surprised she was attracted to Jeff. In the coming weeks, Jeff would go to great lengths to impress his Jewish American Princess. Ironically, it was his extra effort to prove his manliness which ended up sabotaging the relationship.

With his new girlfriend, car, and status amongst the melanin-rich community, Jeff gained a lot of self-confidence. While this was a good thing, it also had the effect of bringing out some ill qualities in his personality. Perhaps Jeff wanted to take revenge on a world which, up until recently, he had been very much afraid of. Whatever the reason, in many instances, Jeff just didn't give a damn whose toes he stepped on. Serving as a sort of comical prodigal-son, I doubt anyone else could get caught out there as much as Jeff did *and* never be tossed into jail or the ICU. It seemed whenever Jeff came upon someone he felt he could intimidate, he turned into a complete asshole. This became such a common occurrence that Charlie, Wayne, and whoever else was with us learned to step aside in order to allow Jeff's insulted victims a chance to fight him.

"Yes, that's right," Wayne would say to these pissed-off strangers. "He might be our friend but we understand he can be a dickhead. So if you wanna fuck him up, don't worry about us jumping in. Actually, you'd be doing us a favor."

Then we would sit down and smoke while Jeff slugged-it-out with his opponent. Most of these altercations amounted to nothing more than a long-winded argument, but a couple episodes actually escalated to the physical stage.

Although Jeff's ego constantly set him up to get knocked down, similar to the prodigal son in the bible, he was always sorry in the end. It seemed every time I hung out with

Jeff another lesson on humility was being imparted. Back then, I never considered fate had provided me a front-row seat to these classes on virtue for reasons much deeper than mere entertainment. Had I heeded these lessons, perhaps I could have avoided some painful moments which occurred later in my life.

Chapter 9: The Slap Heard Round the World!

On the way to pick up the new sunshine in Jeff's life, we made a brief pit stop in Indian Creek Park to smoke some strong smelling *skunk* weed. The previous afternoon, Charlie and I made a trip into Camden to purchase the putrid herb especially for tonight's game. Billed as the 'G-men versus the E-men,' even though the contest was held at Garfield, on that particular night, the G-men were the visiting team because Eastern and Garfield shared Garfield's stadium. With Jeff's beloved Mustang in the shop, he had insisted on driving us in his mother's Subaru hatchback rather than sit in the back of Charlie's beat-up Ford Torino with his date. Once we caught a whiff of the overwhelming stench, the three of us agreed to puff before going to Sandra's.

"Hey Charlie, you know a kid named Pete Meyers?" Jeff asked after he turned down the music and opened his window.

"Nah, am I supposed to?" Charlie replied between tokes.

"He's some dude that gets his rocks off by intimidating defenseless girls," Jeff explained as he received the joint from Charlie. "Last week, Sandy complained about this guy three times."

"Word? So what're you gonna do?" Charlie asked after coughing out a mouthful of smoke and spitting out the

147

window.

"I want to confront this punk tonight but I don't know what he looks like. Since he goes to Eastern, I wanted you to help me find him." Having finished his statement, Jeff took his first puff.

"You said this guy's harassing her? What's he doing? Squeezing her ass?" I became intrigued enough to ask a question.

"I ain't sure—" Jeff abruptly started coughing.

Once the vapors stuck to Jeff's lungs, it took him almost a full minute to recover.

"Damn pussy, stop coughing!" Charlie teased from the back seat as I patted Jeff on the back like I was burping a baby.

As soon as Jeff regained control over his senses, he resumed his narrative.

"I dunno exactly what he did but whatever it was it made Sandy upset. Tak, take this," he said handing me the stogie. "I just want to make sure you guys have my back because I might have to kick his ass."

"You know that!" Charlie immediately replied.

'Might have to kick his ass?' Reflecting on what Jeff said, I almost started laughing. *Damn!* I guess times done changed from a year ago when he was dodging rocks.

Although Jeff had earned some cool points a week ago by holding his own in a fight, that marked the first time we didn't have to pull one of his opponents off him. Nevertheless he had demonstrated the proper attitude after the guy spit on him and that's all that mattered. Since then however, Jeff had become quite cocky. I knew he was head-over-heels in love, so I rationalized his recent behavior was only a phase. After all, everyone goes through changes. That said, as I listened to him talk about beating-up some guy he had never seen before, moreover, for something he could not even explain, I started having second thoughts.

"I'm sensing an upset in the making tonight!" Charlie expressed his optimism about Eastern's chances to win the game.

Hearing this ridiculous prediction, I knew it was not the proper time to address Jeff's delusions of grandeur. "Yeah right!" I sarcastically replied, exhaling my *buddah-blast*. Thanks to Jeff's coughing incident, I was careful not to inhale too much smoke. "We're gonna stomp a manhole in Eastern's ass!"

Although the #2 ranked G-men were expected to blow the game wide open, with so many family members and friends in attendance, everyone knew anything could happen.

In the final seconds of the first half, my homie Marv made a spectacular one-handed grab in the end zone. Being the third G-man to score in the offensive clinic put on by Garfield, the crowd was electrified into a frenzy. Due to the low temperatures that evening, I was ready to visit the concession stand to sip on some hot chocolate. *Not to mention hit the designated smoking area for a stinky minute!* Following a quick glance at the scoreboard to ensure the shut-out remained intact, I poked Charlie on the arm.

"Pardon monsieur, in the car you mentioned something about an upset?"

"Fuck you!" Charlie exclaimed with a bashful grin. "And fuck Eric, Ed, Calvin and the rest of those non-football-playin' scrubs!" he said pointing toward the field. "I knew I

149

should've joined the squad this year. I can't wait to talk shit to them on Monday 'cause they're sorry as hell!" Having finished his rant, Charlie's frown flipped upside down into a grin. "Come on, let's go get blazed!"

Standing up, we saw Jeff waving for us to come over. In order to give the lovebirds some privacy, Charlie and I had moved down the bleachers shortly after the kick-off. While we shuffled over to where Jeff and Sandra were standing in a loving embrace, I cringed at Charlie's next comment.

"What's up with Jeff?" he asked sounding vexed.

"Whaddya mean?"

"You know what I mean…he's not just being an asshole to *other* people tonight."

"Yeah I do," I replied with disdain. "And I dunno what's up him. He's been trippin' ever since he bought that car and got with Sandy." At that moment had we not been approaching them, I would have vented some more. Clearly, I knew something had to be done.

Arriving next to Sandy, I wanted to take their order so Charlie and I could be on our way. That's why Jeff startled me when he began barking out instructions like he was one of the coaches in the locker rooms.

"Okay fellas, when we find Petey, you two drop back unless his buddies want some trouble too. Remember, you guys are only there for backup. I don't want people saying I jumped him with my friends."

Still caught up in the action of the first half, it took Charlie and me a second to register what Jeff was talking about. Before either of us could respond, Jeff pecked Sandra on her lips.

"Doll baby, I'll be right back. You stay here okay?"

"But Jay-Jay, I wanna see the look on Petey's face

when you put him in his place!"

"Just a second," Jeff said reaching into his backpack. "Here," he said after pulling out a pair of shiny binoculars. "These are for you." Then he handed them to her. "You can watch the action from here."

Upon receiving the field glasses from her boyfriend, Sandra tested them by looking at the halftime show. Satisfied she had a birds-eye view of the home bleachers, she literally jumped in the air ever-so-slightly. "Oh Jeff!" she cried out, "you're so brave and wonderful!"

"Oh my god!" Charlie whispered, "this corny shit's way *too white* for me!"

Listening to him, I stifled back a chuckle.

Following a second, much more dramatic kiss, Jeff strode off with the pompous air of a Roman senator. Charlie and I also started descending the bleacher steps but we trailed far behind Jeff. Along the way, I greeted some of my friends while Charlie kept a wary eye on Jeff.

"Yo Sev, you rolling to the jam later?" This is how my friend Scottie greeted me before whispering in my ear. "I need two of those."

"A-ight, meet me in the parking lot later after the game," I responded. "Yo, what about Keith? Does he want one?"

"Yeah, one of them is for him," replied Scottie. "And I know B, T-Rex, and Sam want one too."

"Cool, tell them the same thing." Following another pound, I resumed descending the bleachers.

While I considered if it was necessary to stop at Belkis' apartment before heading to the party, I noticed Jeff was looking back at us. He looked frustrated. His behavior was amusing because I did not understand why he was in such a big hurry. Then Charlie reminded me Sandra was watching us through those binoculars.

Arriving at the refreshment stand, luckily Earl was at the head of the long line, so we gave him our money. As Earl was placing our order, I waved over at Jeff but he ignored me. Even if he hadn't wanted anything himself, I thought he would at least chill for a minute to let us get our grub on. When he remained standing far away, Charlie and I looked at each other.

"Guess that means he don't want nothing," commented Charlie as he received his hot chocolate and pretzel. Then seeing I was already munching on mine, he chuckled. "Yo Tak, what about your boy?"

"What about him?" I responded with a quizzical look.

Fortunately Jeff's math instructor, I believe his name was Mr. Goldstein, approached him and started talking. This allowed me and Charlie to eat in peace. By the time Jeff weaseled himself out of the conversation and backtracked to where we were, Charlie and I were throwing the remains of our snacks into a garbage can. Jeff looked upset.

"Come on Tak, let's go find this guy," Charlie said after tapping me on the shoulder.

Once we were moving again, Jeff calmed down and settled back into his mission. Upon reaching the home-side of the stadium, I was surprised at how dead Eastern's crowd was. When some kids approached Charlie, I took a second to scope-out my surroundings. It seemed Marv's breathtaking catch had broken their spirit. I made a mental note to mention this later when I teased Charlie. Unlike me, Charlie kept his conversations brief by telling his friends he'd catch up with them at the jam. Like Jeff, he seemed interested in playing this drama out to the end.

With scores of people moving to and from the toilets, the refreshment stand, and the smoking area, it took us several minutes to reach the bleachers. During this slow migration, my attention was fixed on the sexy ladies in the stands. "Who was the fool who said 'all the blazers' go to Garfield?" I whispered to Charlie in a low voice.

"Hi Takuan!"

Looking in the direction of the female voice, I recognized a classmate of mine from middle school. "Ay wassup Vicky," I replied, returning her smile.

Before long, I spotted several girls I had not seen in years. Returning their waves, I was astounded at how their bodies had filled-out. *Mother Nature is something!*

When Jeff stopped climbing the stairs to enter the area designated for the marching band, I figured he probably saw a former classmate too. Perhaps his old buddy could help us find Pete Meyers. In any event, since we were searching for a 'tough guy,' I never considered we might find him here. While we waited, Charlie pointed out Patrice's main rival for my attention back in 8th grade. I was surprised to find Aisha on the field performing. Then I recalled hearing she was Eastern's head-cheerleader.

Oh my god, what a beautiful pair of legs!

Charlie interrupted my mental masturbation by tapping my shoulder. "What?" I griped, reluctant to peel my eyes away from Aisha. When I looked to where he was now pointing, I saw Jeff shouting at a pimply-faced kid with freckles. This was no friendly conversation.

"Are you Pete Meyers? Are you Pete Meyers?" Jeff repeated the question over-and-over in a threatening tone.

The boy being questioned never uttered a word. With Jeff towering over him, almost in his lap, he just sat there trembling behind his huge brass horn. After a couple seconds, he started crying.

At first, the nearest spectators were confused. Perhaps they thought Jeff and Pete were joking around. All that changed when Pete began shedding tears. Then his band mates and other bystanders came to his aid.

"Hey! What's going on here?" asked a middle-aged man sitting two rows from the action.

"Who do you think you are?" a band member chimed in.

"You hoodlums, get the hell outta here!" yelled another man.

It was only after several people stepped forward to defend Pete, that Charlie and I drew the obvious conclusion that this ninety-eight-pound weakling in the marching band uniform was the target of our search and destroy mission. In our skunked daze, it took us longer than it should have to understand what was obvious to everyone else. What added to our confusion were two other factors: not only did Jeff know exactly where to find this guy, he also seemed aware that 'big bad Pete' was really a little runt with thick glasses. Once Charlie and I comprehended the situation, to say we were embarrassed is an understatement. However due to the intermission log-jam, we could not get far when we tried to flee the area.

For close to five minutes, we remained stuck at the scene.

Even in the intense cold, I was perspiring due to all the indignant comments and stares being hurled at us. At one point, Charlie and I spotted an elderly woman glaring at Jeff while he poked Pete in the chest. Being only a few feet away from Jeff, I wanted to tell him to stop but I was too busy pretending I didn't know him. The old lady, seeming to read my thoughts, turned her head to make eye-contact with me. In spite of any racial differences, it was obvious the three of us were together.

"You bullies leave that poor boy alone!" the old lady shrieked in a voice way too loud for someone as frail as she appeared to be. Once she expressed her contempt, so many people began threatening us, I honestly thought we might have to defend ourselves.

"You guys are a bunch of jerks!" yelled an elementary-school-aged boy before his father likewise vented his opinion.

"If you punks are looking for a problem tonight, fight me!"

Glancing over at the real bully, who was now standing next to me, Jeff seemed to be enjoying his 'bad boy' moment. In spite of everything going on around us, he started bragging like he had done something cool.

"Did you see Pete's face?" he said in a snickering tone once the crowd began moving forward. "He started crying!"

Neither of us responded. As soon as the space in front of us cleared, Charlie and I treated Jeff like the plague. We took off and refrained from looking back until we had ditched him. When we finally stopped to rest, Charlie voiced something I already feared to be true.

"Damn!" he whined. "I left the skunk in his car."

"Oh Jeff, you were great!" Sandra screamed before turning toward the back seat. She appeared ready to melt. "All three of you were!"

155

Since the football game was a sold-out event, the parking lot was swamped with traffic. It was total gridlock. This extended the time Charlie and I were forced to listen to Jeff and Sandra's theatrical nonsense. To avoid the ridiculous scene we found ourselves in, I had argued it was better to walk but Charlie would hear none of it. Since receiving his Ford Torino for a birthday gift a couple months back, Charlie never walked anywhere. Besides, he always complained about the cold more than any of my other friends.

Sitting there, I couldn't believe Jeff and Sandra were gloating about scaring a little boy with a tuba. The only consolation I could think of was maybe Jeff might get some pussy. At the park, Jeff said his grandparents were out of town this weekend and after the game he and Sandy were headed over to their house for a romantic evening together. I hoped a dash of *trim* would bring him back to his senses.

Glancing out the window, I noticed many of my friends had driven their parent's cars to the game. *We can just hitch a ride to the jam with one of them!* With this realization, I was confident if Charlie and I walked around, we could find a more agreeable mode of transportation. At any rate, I wanted out. Because the Subaru had no rear doors besides the hatchback, I felt trapped next to Charlie. Being directly behind the driver, I kicked Jeff's seat with my knee to get his attention.

"I just saw Keith and Scottie," I said pointing behind us. "I got two dove sacks with their names on 'em. Lemme out here."

One of the fringe benefits of dealing cheeba was I always had an excuse to spontaneously go anywhere or do anything.

"Yeah I saw them too," Jeff replied in a nonchalant

tone like a father addressing his son. "You can just meet them later at the jam."

Hold up!? Did Jeff just deny my request to leave?

Before I had the chance to respond, the car lunged forward, snapping my head back. After the Subaru rocked violently from left-to-right, I realized Jeff had chosen an alternate route to the bumper-to-bumper traffic.

My friends and I did a lot of stupid shit back then but in my opinion speeding on the front lawn of our school—*with weed and beer in the car*—was right at the head of the list of ill-advised activities.

With *MC Shan's 'The Bridge'* reverberating out the windows, I glanced at dozens of school officials, parents, and students staring back at me. When Sandra, in a total panic, turned down the music, I recalled the overwhelming police presence I witnessed inside the game.

"Jeff, what the fuck are you doing? Look!" Charlie yelled. Then he punched Jeff on the arm.

"Ouch!" Jeff complained. "I see it!"

Everyone was scared shitless when the flashing lights of a police siren came into view.

"Turn back into the parking lot *now!*" I yelled.

Jeff veered toward the pavement and awkwardly flopped the Subaru over the curb. Fortunately for us, the lights we had seen were only a reflection from a squad car parked around the corner. As Jeff reentered the parking lot, the Subaru grazed another vehicle's bumper.

"Move the fuck out the way, dumb-ass!" Jeff chewed-out the teen and his female passenger through the open windows. Having successfully *bogarted* his way into the parking lot, he continued his verbal assault. "Bitch, I saw you speed up! You were trying to block me, weren't you?"

157

For the next several minutes, the traffic stopped moving several times. Jeff used this time to ram into the same car's rear bumper again and again. Although none of the collisions was hard enough to create a dent, we definitely felt the jolts. Just before we reached the main road, the traffic again trickled to a halt.

"Hey fag!" Jeff screamed out the window. "I see your Garfield bumper sticker, and I'll be paying you a visit at school next week!"

The young man and his date remained silent; they were clearly afraid. Likewise Charlie, Sandra, and I had said very little, not knowing what this hothead was capable of next. A couple seconds later, Jeff looked at us and smiled. With the Subaru back on the pavement, we now resembled every other law-abiding vehicle. Appearing smug and relaxed, Jeff reached down to turn up the music. This was when another man's voice was heard outside the window.

"Hey kid, is that how your father taught you how to drive?"

Much deeper than the high-pitched vocals of the teenager, I turned in the direction of the baritone voice. Standing on the corner was an elderly white man and his wife. The man was pointing at Jeff with a scowl on his face. Considering the couple was walking along the roadside, I surmised they had not attended the game and Jeff's antics were ruining their evening stroll.

"Yeah, yeah, whatever old man," Jeff waved his hand and yawned, barely acknowledging the man's existence.

Jeff's rude response made me too embarrassed to watch. I mean damn, the man was like eighty years old. After I looked away, all of a sudden everything got dark because something blocked the glare of the street lamp. Before I could turn my head back around to see what happened, a deafening sound caused me to flinch.

Smack!!!

"You better learn some respect boy!" threatened the incensed elder-statesman.

The open handed slap in the face sounded much more like a 'punch' sound effect in a martial arts movie.

"No dear, stop!" his wife pleaded pulling her husband away from the Subaru.

Following a nervous pause, Charlie leaned on his street instincts. "Jeff, open the door. Let's get out!" Having been programmed whenever someone hits you, you fight back, this was Charlie's automated response.

"No…no, that won't be necessary," Jeff replied in a solemn tone while the grizzled warrior was being led away by other bystanders.

For the next thirty seconds, there was a hush that lingered not only in our car but amongst the other vehicles as well. While I did not actually witness the blow, I did see Jeff's glasses ricochet off the windshield and fly out the passenger-side window. As people began to whisper about the unlikely scene which had just transpired, I was waiting for Jeff to get out of the car to retrieve his glasses because his vision was worse than mine so I knew he could not drive without them.

"I'm not sure," an unknown voice broke the silence, "maybe that was his grandfather."

When Jeff put the Subaru into gear and started driving, I was shocked and remained so until we turned onto the main road. There, we continued crawling at a snail's pace along the right shoulder. Before long, the occupants of many of the cars driving passed the slowly moving hatchback began

159

to yell jeering remarks.

"That old guy fucked you up! Hahahaha!"

"You got what you deserved, asshole!"

At our pathetically slow rate of speed, I knew it would take at least thirty minutes to reach Jeff's house. I felt sorry for my friend. If only I could've asked Sandra to turn the music up, I might've been able to ignore Charlie's rumbling laughter. Clenching my teeth, I was afraid if I opened my mouth, my own emotion would likewise erupt from my esophagus. Not knowing what else to do, I started elbowing Charlie to keep him from leaning on me. To no avail, he grew louder by the second and his chortling became contagious. Just before I lost control, Jeff slammed both hands onto the steering wheel and shouted. Although I don't believe he intended it to be funny, his one liner said it all.

"I can't believe it...I fuckin' got slapped in the face by an old man!"

That was it. From that moment, the dam holding back a month's worth of frustration gave way. Once the floodgates opened, I thought the laughter would never cease. It got so bad I had to remind myself of the need to inhale oxygen.

By the time we arrived at Jeff's house neither Charlie nor I could look at Jeff, let alone think about speaking to him. The second we were released from the laugh-pit, otherwise known as the back seat of the Subaru, considering the only sounds we could emit were laughter, we tried to leave without making a fuss. Standing shoulder to shoulder, Charlie and I glided by Ty's driveway in an attempt to distance ourselves from Jeff and Sandra. We urgently needed to release this *tsunami* of explosive energy before we ruptured a spleen. Just as we were realizing our escape, Jeff called our names.

"Tak, Charlie...wait a minute."

160

Jeff's voice had lost all traces of the overbearing arrogance which had been its main feature an hour ago; he almost sounded castrated. If it is possible to be overcome with laughter and simultaneously infuriated, this describes how I felt. Jeff had to realize we wanted to laugh in peace. Had we let loose in front of Sandy, it would have added serious insult to an already fractured ego. Plus, since he had plans to be with his girlfriend anyway, it's not like we were abandoning him. By the following day I would be okay to face him but not tonight.

When Jeff finally waddled over to the corner in front of Tyler's house, he was wearing a confused, diffident expression. After a few seconds to search his thoughts, he stammered something in a barely audible tone. "Umm, umm, nothing." Then he feebly turned around and returned to where Sandra stood waiting.

Once Charlie and I disappeared around the corner, we broke down in laughter. "Come on," I said after a few seconds, "no one's at my house."

Arriving at my home, I was thankful my father was working the graveyard shift and my mother and sister were out for the evening. It was the perfect place to vent our emotions. There are really no words to describe how hard we laughed that night. I was sprawled out on my bed while Charlie cackled in a nearby sofa chair. Both of us were using towels to wipe our tears.

Twenty minutes later, we heard someone knock on the front door. At that time, we were still in stitches. "Come to the door with me," I said, dying to share the humorous news with whoever it was. On our way down the hall, we were not shy with our remarks, never considering the visitor might be Jeff.

"That old man smacked his glasses like thirty feet into the grass!" I exaggerated.

"Did you hear people asking if the old guy was his dad?" Charlie said in reply.

"No, they thought he was Jeff's grandfather," I corrected my friend and we again erupted in laughter.

Then before I could say it, Charlie recalled the funniest comment of the evening.

"What did that fat girl say when she walked passed our car? 'Kelloggs Sugar…'" Pausing here, Charlie then clapped his hands together to make a 'smacking' sound just like the chubby student had done. And right-on-cue after the smack, I replied *"Dig 'em!"* in a deep-voice exactly like the frog does in the commercial.

With tears streaming down my face, I had difficulty seeing through the peephole so I gave up. "Who is it?" I asked. Not hearing a response, I wiped my eyes and looked again. "Oh shit, you gotta be kidding!" I exclaimed in a low voice once I recognized the same downcast pose he struck on the first morning he came to walk to school. "It's Jeff!"

Hearing this, Charlie started heading back to my room.

"No!" I said grabbing his arm. "You gotta help me. I'm gonna laugh in his face if you're not here," I said between chuckles.

"Me too, I can't do it! This is your house so you gotta answer the door," Charlie replied.

I was so determined to have Charlie present when I opened the door, I grappled with him for an additional ten seconds until he twisted out of my grasp.

"Ouch!" I complained rubbing my mildly sprained wrist.

Once Charlie scampered down the hallway, I took a deep breath and unlocked the door. Needless to say, Jeff's new love had already become his old flame.

After the Smack Reflections

Ironically it was Jeff, not Pete, who got put in his place that evening. Even though I realized the embarrassment had been traumatizing for my friend, since getting high, having fun, becoming depressed, and then growing frustrated again was our normal cycle, besides laughing about it, I did not think much about the incident the following day.

I was raised in a society which uses brain-dead concepts like 'scarcity,' and foolish phrases like 'survival of the fittest' or 'Columbus discovered America,' to augment its divide and conquer agenda. By the age of sixteen, I had been thoroughly indoctrinated into believing I was a minority—which is just a code word for second-class citizen. Accordingly, this is the stage of the programming where the dehumanization is escalated.

I wish I had been wise enough to learn from Jeff's lesson. It took over twenty years but fate demanded I too experience my own smack-back-to-reality check. Like my heartbroken friend, I was shocked and depressed to find how far I had strayed from reality. Even though my self-realization moment was not a public spectacle, it was just as humiliating. Definitely karma.

Chapter 10: Trying to Graduate

In the spring of my junior year, my rebellious spirit collided with the brick wall called society. This prompted me to make a change, so I ran away from home. But not right away. It took a week to make the arrangements because I planned to visit my friend, Donovan Dean. What makes this interesting is Don had moved to Gainesville, Florida back in 6th grade. As you can probably imagine, when I arrived at his doorstep holding two suitcases, I shocked everyone in his family. Although my vacation got cut short when Mr. Dean realized my refugee status, I was there long enough to hatch two crazy memories.

The first involved duck-taping a couple ounces of marijuana to my legs before leaving for the airport. Since Don and I used talk on the telephone every now and then, I knew he was a big weed-head. The other one took place on the last of my three days in Florida. It occurred at a pool party after this *bama* challenged me to an emcee battle.

"Even down south, makin' sucka emcees tremble, like that of a cat on the mic I'm nimble..."

Since I knew the radio stations down-south would not play *LL Cool Jay's 'I Need a Beat'* for at least another month, I dared to *bite* the tall, young, legend-in-leather's lyrics and mix them into my own free-style. Once 'Kidd-Money,' which was the emcee-moniker I created on the spot, finished spitting his bars, no one else dared to touch the microphone. While

Don and I were celebrating my victory, we spotted his father amongst the teens congregated around the pool. After one look at his face, I knew the party was over.

"Takuan, you lied to me!" Mr. Dean yelled, making a scene. Then he grabbed my arm and pushed me toward the exit. "Let's go!"

On the way to the airport, he screamed about how my father said he was going to break my neck if I did not return today. "And I don't blame him!" Mr. Dean added.

To my surprise, I was happy on my flight back to Jersey. Even though I had fallen in love with the Florida weather, I missed my friends. Not much was said by my parents about the incident. My mother mostly shook her head and looked disappointed while my father summed up his feelings in one phrase: "Boy, if you ever pull another stunt like that again, don't come back!" At school, everyone cracked-up at my story about biting *Cool Jay's* lines. Two of my classmates laughed so much they had to serve detentions for their continual disruptions. Every day, until summer vacation, someone brought up how Kidd Money had dismantled the bama-boy emcee.

By June, everyone was eager for the annual 'bullshit and party' season to commence. This year was special because Jeff had his own car so we were able to venture into New York City. Like all Jewish kids, it seems, Jeff had a rich uncle who lived on the upper-east side of Manhattan. This provided us with a home-base to work from. Getting our first taste of 'the City,' we couldn't believe how fast life moved.

Every summer, from mid-July to mid-August, Jeff's uncle took his family to Hawaii. This year, the generous man was kind enough to leave his nephew a spare key to 'house-sit.' This is when things really got out of hand.

At first, many of our friends wanted to go until they found out our trips usually turned into a two-or-three-day event. As the stakes continued to rise, no one had the sense to advise putting on the brakes. For this reason, on the first day of school, my classmates were surprised to see me there on-time and sober. Wearing a friendly grin, I walked in and politely greeted my homeroom teacher. When I took a seat, everyone was staring at me. It was obvious something had changed my attitude but no one guessed I had been *scared straight*.

The day before Jeff's uncle returned, we cleaned up the house. Since most of our partying had occurred in clubs and other peoples' homes, it was just a matter of throwing away the bottles, pizza boxes, and other trash which had accumulated. That was a good thing because both of us had been up all night. On the ride back, I dozed off somewhere along the Westside Highway. Shortly after exiting the Holland Tunnel, an unmarked police car got behind us and flashed its lights.

"Oh shit!" exclaimed Jeff looking in his rearview mirror. "It's the cops!"

After pulling us over, the detectives ordered us to get out of the car. Once they found the cocaine Jeff had hidden under the seat—not to mention his mother's revolver in the glove compartment—we were handcuffed and thrown into the back of a brown Oldsmobile.

"For this much coke and weed, plus possession of an unlawful weapon, you two are gonna face felony charges!" screamed a solidly-built detective who was about the same age, height, and complexion as my sire. When a squad car arrived, the plainclothesmen took our IDs and went to confer with the officers.

With our heads drooped in our laps, Jeff and I watched three of them chit-chat while one cop radioed the station from inside the vehicle. About forty five minutes later, the detectives returned and opened both rear doors.

"Get out!" the white one commanded.

As soon as Jeff and I were standing next to each other on the sidewalk, the detectives waved at the patrol car as it drove away. Then the same guy started talking again.

"Not only do neither of you have a rap sheet, *youse* ain't even from around here," he began before his partner expressed a hunch.

"My guess is: you two don't do this very often, do you?"

"That's right!" Jeff almost screamed. "Actually, this is our first time experimenting with drugs, and we swear we'll never do it again! Right Tak?"

"Ahh…yeah, that's right." Caught off guard by Jeff's question, I almost blew his cover.

Unbelievably, the same detectives who were threatening us an hour ago now seemed to have had a change of heart. They almost sounded friendly. Sensing this, I started to believe Jeff's crying act was working. With this in mind, I did my part by gazing downward and poking out my lips. I knew Jeff would pour it on from here and he did not disappoint; the boy was definitely on his game that afternoon.

Capitalizing on the moment, he expressed how devastated his mother would be if he lost his scholarship to Seton Hall. "My father died when I was five-years-old, officer…" Pausing here to sob, he resumed after taking a deep

GAIKOKUJIN - The Story

breath. "My mother is a single woman raising three kids, so she could never afford to send me to college without this financial assistance."

"So that's your excuse for breaking the law?" asked the melanin-rich detective whose name was Billups. "Because your old man kicked the bucket?"

"No sir, I'm just trying to explain we were only celebrating my scholarship, that's all. Then these other guys showed up with the drugs…we didn't even know them!"

Jeff, being a Jewish kid with a long nose, and me, appearing much younger than my seventeen years, we were not exactly your stereotypical, drug-dealing tandem. When Detective Billups' next comment reflected how proud he was his son had played football for Seton Hall a couple years back, I knew we were good-to-go.

"Even though the team was terrible," said the detective with a chuckle before he pointed at his partner. "I took Roger to a couple of their games."

"Yeah," snickered the short guy with dirty-blond hair, "if that's what you wanna call 'em. They were more like football clinics sponsored by the visiting teams, if you ask me. The Pirates got blown-out every time! It's no wonder the football program got cut."

Jeff used this opportunity to compare me to Detective Billups' son by saying that I wanted to play football too but our high school coach would not allow seniors to try-out for the team. In his final remarks, Jeff laid it on thick by describing us as two good kids who had been tricked by some street-thugs who made a living from exploiting college students.

"If we let you go, do you promise to stop using drugs?"

169

I couldn't believe my ears!

Following our sworn oaths of abstinence, the detective who favored my father made me promise to try-out for the G-men. "I know Coach Belmont personally," he said. "I'll give him a call. He'll let you try-out as a favor to me. If you get cut, at least you know you tried."

"Yessir," is all I said. There was no way to get out of it.

Then for the next several minutes, both detectives took turns giving us a paternal lecture. It was the same old story. They described drugs as the gateway to becoming losers in life. After nodding our heads in agreement to everything they said, we were un-cuffed. When they took off our handcuffs, words cannot describe the depth of gratitude I felt.

Barely dodging a major bullet, images of sitting in that musty Oldsmobile wreaked havoc on my nerves well into my senior year. Even after Jeff left for college, not only did I ace Trigonometry that fall, I made the team and practiced with the #1 ranked G-men every afternoon, just as I had promised. The only bad thing was I never cracked the starting lineup so my playing time consisted of stretching-out my hamstrings running down the field on special-teams coverage.

This incident frightened me so much I got through a couple months of my senior year without a hitch. My new attitude raised some eyebrows amongst the school faculty. During that state championship season, Detective Billups showed up twice to ensure I kept my end of the bargain. So my sudden switch to model student-athlete had a less than genuine origin. Despite counting my blessings and trying to remain positive, I started showing signs of buckling under the pressure even before the season ended. The second marking period revealed a slip in my grades and after winter recess I found it difficult to return to school at all.

By the time 1986 rolled around, 'senioritis' was in full-effect all around me. While my classmates announced their acceptance letters to universities, or discussed color combinations for the prom, I was busy creating a well-crafted scheme to avoid school altogether.

I recalled what Ant and Chauncey told me about their recruiting visits to colleges. This led to researching our school district's attendance policy. My investigation revealed that official academic trips qualified as excused absences. That said, I never imagined we would exploit the information to the extent we did. By the time the weather started warming up, the Attendance Scam was perfected and ready to be implemented.

Jeff and I took turns telephoning colleges on my behalf. We committed identity theft by impersonating teachers, coaches, counselors, and even vice-principals in order to schedule trips to their universities. Of course we had to 'exaggerate' certain details about my academic and athletic credentials. Since Jeff's uncle was the rabbi of the fifth largest synagogue in the Tri-State area, Jeff was accustomed to hobnobbing with white-collar Caucasians.

While lying could never be described as honorable, in the beginning, our intentions were just to get me a week of vacation. Although in our youthful exuberance, we did harbor some optimism our efforts might somehow create an opportunity for us to chill together the following fall, more importantly, since my father had mandated I must leave 'his house' after my graduation, I realized the need to investigate my options. Even though no scholarships were awarded, my experiences small talking about tuition fees and meal plans paid dividends years later when I applied to Rutgers. Therefore our scheming did not go to waste.

Jeff and I spent the majority of my 'excused absences' chilling at Seton Hall. While Jeff attended his morning classes, I walked around scoping-out college chicks. I never imagined a university campus was such an exciting place. The biggest thrill of the day occurred each afternoon when the ballers played pick-up games in the main gymnasium. I stumbled upon these games by chance one day on my way back to Jeff's dorm from the library. After a couple days of getting schooled, I found out everyone playing was either a member of the varsity team, or planning to try-out in the summer. As I steadily improved, it was cool swishing my 'money jump-shot' over guys I had seen playing on television.

Strangely, the best memories of my senior year occurred during the time I was absent. Or should I say officially excused. On the day before I left, one of the coaches encouraged me to try-out for the team in the summer. "Thanks Coach, I'll think about it," I replied with a grin. Whether or not I would have made the team is debatable but I was just flattered he thought I was a student at 'the Hall.'

By the beginning of May, even the most die-hard party animals in Jeff's dorm were studying for exams, so I decided it was time to leave. Once I packed my stuff, I took a bus to the train station. During my ride home, I reminisced about my great adventure. In addition to the fine women I met, just thinking about how I had played ball all day and partied all night caused me to grin. And there had been other benefits as well.

One evening following our games, I invited a Jamaican ball player to Jeff's room to puff with us. After one toke, Andre was so disgusted by Belkis' *babbit* he refused to smoke anymore. The next day, he drove me across the George Washington Bridge to meet a ganja dealer, uptown in Harlem.

Once Dre parked his white Toyota Corolla near the corner of 145th & St. Nick, we walked a couple blocks to meet a Rastaman who took us to his apartment. By the way Dre was speaking to him in their native patois, I suspected they were related. We followed the herbman into a raggedy, tenement building and climbed four flights of stairs. The dimly-lit stairwell was covered in decades of graffiti, and the halls were strewn with cigarette butts, bottles, and other trash. Due to these deplorable conditions, I was surprised at how nicely his home was furnished.

In contrast to the beat up conditions just outside his door, the Rastaman's apartment was fit for a king. It featured earth-toned leather furniture and a wide-screen television. However, what I admired most was the colossal painting of Haile Selassie I center-piecing the living room. Seated on a majestic black stallion, the Emperor of Ethiopia had a red, yellow, and green flag draped over his shoulders. On either side of his majesty, a regal lion stood on-guard.

After Dre declined on something to drink, he introduced us. "Tak, this is my uncle. His name is Binghi."

With a friendly smile, the dreadlocked Rasta walked toward me and extended his hand. *"Breddah,"* he said in his thick accent. *"Frah wha pawt yuh deh?"*

"Jersey," I replied understanding he was asking where I'm from.

"Takkie, sit down," Dre said before Binghi could ask

another question. After everybody took a seat, he handed his uncle a lighter. "How about a sample spliff?"

Right on cue, Binghi reached into a drawer next to his couch and pulled out a gigantic cone-shaped joint. "Here *bredren*," he said handing it to me along with the lighter.

It was rolled so neatly, I almost did not want to smoke it. Once I did, I got so high it was difficult to count my money.

Arriving at Philly's 30th Street Station, I was glad Quinton and Earl were there on time. As we walked across the parking lot, they complained there had been no cheeba around lately. Hearing this, I pretended I didn't have any; I wanted them to sweat for a couple minutes. Once we got in the car, I reached into my bag. "But," I declared proudly, "I do have a quarter-pound of the bud Rastas call 'Kali'." Saying this, I pulled out it out.

Talking about looks of astonishment!

Even more astounded than my pot-head clientele were the faces of my guidance counselor and assistant principal at the hearing for my excessive absences. This surprised me because I submitted my documents a week in advance, as per my counselor's instructions. Once the session began, it was obvious none of the school officials present were prepared to debate the validity of my claim. Following the meeting, the adults had a short deliberation before announcing I would be allowed to graduate on time.

It was episodes like this which convinced me society placed little priority on morals or ethics. There I was sitting in front of five school officials. Not only was I obviously lying, I was also committing numerous counts of fraud. Nonetheless because I possessed letterhead from respected universities inscribed with dean's signatures, everyone was too embarrassed to take any action. Together they threw their hands up in exasperation exclaiming, "There's nothing we can do!"

When the student no one had seen for weeks appeared at the dress-rehearsal for graduation, a collective hush encompassed the crowd. Walking in, I issued my trademark wink and smile; especially to the non-believers who had insisted the scam would never work. This was the first of many graduation ceremonies where I was the recipient of similarly perplexed looks.

In our final week, my homeroom teacher asked to speak with me in private. Ms. McAfee was liked by most students. She was known for extending herself to help kids in bad situations. Rina told me she slept at Ms. McAfee's house one time. In fact, Ms. McAfee was the person who informed Belkis about the abusive situation in Rina's home.

After we walked into the hallway, the melanin-rich woman expressed a maternal concern for my well-being. "Takuan, you have so much going for you. I don't understand why you're not more concerned about your future."

Having made this declaration, she stared at me like I had lost my mind. And I looked back at her like she had lost hers. I was screaming for help at that moment but the only thing Ms. McAfee wanted to discuss was some godforsaken future. To be honest, I didn't understand how she expected me to think about tomorrow if I couldn't even deal with what was going on today.

Now that my varsity basketball fantasies were a thing of the past, as far as goals were concerned, I was left out in the cold. From the beginning, my sole focus had been to become an All-Star G-man, like Ant and Chauncey. In my mind, there were no other options. How many similarly misled brothers and sisters believe their opportunities are restricted to athletics and entertainment? Even beyond this, what about the kids who lack passion for either of these pursuits? Due to the influence of the media, Caucasians are quick to compare all of us to Eddie Murphy, Kobe Bryant, or Beyonce. Could this explain why some children who find mathematics or science interesting keep it a secret? Have we been tricked into being embarrassed about our non-entertainment-related talents?

This is what Jeff had to say on the topic: "Tak, we're both way too intelligent to take this fucking 'society shit' seriously! We're destined to do great things in life, and it starts with us hanging-out together next year. We can't allow a few rules get in our way because remember, they're only in place for suckers. Anybody who's 'somebody' knows rules were made to be broken. But only by those who are qualified to do so."

Jeff and I couldn't believe the world was so caught up on racism. To us, this was just another indication we were indeed living in an era of mediocrity. Having transcended the black – white divide, we thought we had devised an angle on life no one else had yet conceived.

Foreword to the Asia Saga

Along the path of life, I've had the privilege of calling eleven ladies 'my girlfriend' at one point or another. What a blessing indeed! This is not to be confused with sexual partners. Some people are prone to mistake an erotically pleasurable experience for a reason to go shopping for a house with a white picket-fence. In such a bizarre world as this, if a man and woman can manage to love-and-laugh in each other's graces for even a relatively short period of time, who can stand in judgment of such a divine pairing?

Of my significant relationships, three of them blew my mind for different reasons. My '1986 Summer Love' qualifies as the first of this distinguished trio. The brevity of this 'forbidden affair' contributed to the drama. Lasting only a few months, the relationship climaxed as I was leaving for boot camp before quickly dissolving afterwards. Nonetheless for two young fools in love, sometimes Father Time can be persuaded to extend ninety days into what seems like an eternity.

In order to unravel the details of this complicated saga, we must flashback to the summer of 1983.

Chapter 11: A Typical Day around my Way

Around my way, the brothers with the 'most game' gathered at the courts every evening for a supreme test of skills. One night, after several hours of balling, Wayne and I, along with the usual suspects, were chugging some forties of *Ol' E* we had won. Aside from liquor, we also bet money to make these games more interesting. Anyone who has seen the sensationalized blockbuster movie, *White Man Can't Jump*, may have some understanding of this urban ritual.

On this particular evening, it was thanks to my homie, June-bug, that Wayne, Mann, Brian, and I had the privilege of bragging rights at the post-game, 'libations pouring' ceremony. June, being a deft ball-handler, was known for performing *Globetrotterish* dribbling antics before passing the rock to Don, Pat, or one of the other sky-walkers who patterned their thunderous two-hand jams after *Dr. Dunkenstein* himself. June, on the other hand, standing a paltry five-foot-three-inches if he wore six pairs of socks inside his sneakers—which he actually did—was the set-up man.

On game point, June executed a cross-over dribble just before half-court that would've made Tim Hardaway and Allen Iverson exchange a pound. After breaking his own brother's ankles so badly that Kevin fell down in a heap, he used his sibling's unwittingly-created screen on Quinton to

179

beat the double-team and penetrate the tiring defense.

This game had gone on far too long. More than fifteen minutes had elapsed since everyone agreed the next basket would decide the winner of our best-of-seven series. The teams were so evenly matched these nail-biting contests had gone back-and-forth all evening with neither squad able to establish a consistent advantage. Therefore once *Kev* and Quinton fell down, everyone knew this was the game-breaker.

With me and Wayne flanking June's left and right wings, we advanced unchallenged into enemy territory. Once the three remaining defenders, Terrance, Scottie, and Earl, identified their predicament, they backed closer to the basket to prevent an uncontested dunk from deciding the overtime thriller. Despite being outnumbered, and forced to huddle close to their own goal, the thought of giving-up never entered their minds.

Everyone knew I possessed a reputation for never missing near the 3-point arc. For this reason, whoever was guarding me normally picked me up around midcourt. However, at this juncture of the evening, my legs were shot. After miscalculating on sinking the game-winner two times in-a-row, Wayne had also shown symptoms of the rubbery-leg syndrome by tossing up a brick of his own. But this time, our squad was so close to ascending the winner's circle, where the forty-ounce bottles of 'champagne' were awaiting our victory celebration, we could taste the bitter malt-liquor quenching our thirst as well as our pride. It was rare to find myself this wide-open near the foul line so of course I wanted to take the shot.

"Damn June, what're you doing?" I whined.

With both hands on my head, I watched June slash across the lane from right-to-left and leap into the air. I

180

complained because he was doing precisely what he used to scold me about; he was playing into the defense's strength instead of probing for their weakness. As June floated toward the baseline, the *Extra Terrestrial* shot-blocking-machine launched his wiry six-foot-five-inch, aero-dynamic frame into the stratosphere. Once Earl intercepted the streaking point-guard, I was so sure June was doomed to be *ET's* next victim, I sprinted to where I thought Earl might smack the ball. For this reason, my mouth fell wide-open after June's left-handed hook shot (by the way, June was right-handed) barely grazed ET's outstretched wing before floating *back over the backboard* and splashing through the chain!

It was such a perfect shot we almost came to blows when our opponents claimed it was an air-ball that grazed the chain on its way down. Following some minor squabbling, our opponents finally surrendered and the post-game festivities got underway. While claiming the spoils of the evening, we celebrated with numerous high-fives and loud recaps of the highlights. An hour later, everyone decided it was time to go home. Since Wayne lived on the same street as Jeff and Ty, we left together. On our way home he confided he had a surprise.

"Check-it-out," Wayne said with a bright-eyed grin, "a new flygirl just moved in around the corner from us."

"Word? You know her?"

"Yeah, she was in my homeroom."

"Oh, she goes to Eastern?" I inquired surprised to hear this.

"She did last year before her family moved," Wayne replied. "But she told me she's gonna transfer to Garfield this fall."

"So what's up? You trying to get-with girlie, or

what?" I asked suspiciously. "And don't front because I don't wanna hear no jealous bullshit if I kick it to her!"

"Naw, do your thang cuz. Isis is just my homegirl."

"Cool, I wanna meet her. Let's go check her out." Considering I had been confined to my bedroom on house-arrest for most of the year, there was no way I wanted to go home yet. "Yo, did you say her name was 'Isis'?"

I met Isis in the summer following my turbulent freshman campaign. She and Wayne, having just completed their sophomore year, were both older than me.

"Who is it?" asked a girl from behind the door.

"Ay Isis, it's Wayne," he said recognizing her voice.

After Isis opened the door, Wayne greeted her before gesturing my way. "This is the guy I told you about that lives around the corner."

"Hi Takuan," she said in a cheerful voice before turning around to report to an unseen person who sounded like her mother. "It's for me." Then she came outside onto the porch and closed the door.

"Nice meeting you Isis," I replied politely, pleased she knew my name. *Damn, she's blazin'!* I thought to myself, taking a look at my new neighbor.

Isis was almost as tall as me. Endowed with a copper-toned complexion, she was a bit on the lanky side. At first glance, her slim frame did not seem adequate to support her achingly-swollen breasts which were pressing against her sleeveless white camisole like a pair of ripe nectarines. Her shoulder-length, curly hair was tinted brown and flawlessly swept to the side. In spite of her physical allure, I ended-up being more attracted to her warm, down-to-earth personality and crazy sense of humor.

Ten minutes after we sat down in the porch, Isis'

mother and little sister, Asia, came outside to meet us too. Once everyone had been introduced, Ms. Kalif told Asia to go inside and take a shower while she shared a few words with the teenagers. When Isis' little sister expressed her desire to remain on the porch with us, her mother in humorous fashion pointed-out she was not yet a teenager.

"Little girl, the number 'twelve-teen' does not exist."

"Maybe next year!" teased her elder sister as the frustrated child stomped inside the house.

Forty minutes later, while her hair was still wet, Asia found an excuse to return to the porch. All teeth and dimples, she glided outside pretending to search for an imaginary book she had allegedly left there. Although Wayne and I found it amusing how annoyed Isis was at her intrusion, this was merely the tip of the iceberg. From that day onward, their rivalry was epic in my mind because these sisters literally rumbled in the jungle.

POW! BLAM! BOOM!

Objects crashing against walls, bodies colliding with those same walls, wailing shrieks, you name it, we heard it. Wayne and I were never allowed to enter the house, so we listened intently from the porch. This lack of visual footage had the effect of magnifying the sounds of the skirmish a hundred-fold. Even though no captions were visible, I was reminded of the old Batman series with the animated phrases superimposed on the television screen. Years later, I remember laughing with Asia while giving her a play-by-play of a typical visit to her home.

Even before arriving at their one-story rancher, the war cries of the combating *sorors* were audible from the street. Most times, their cat-fights escalated into physical violence. The amazing thing was, whenever Wayne or I pushed the doorbell, the melodic chime completely silenced any hint of anarchy. Standing on the porch, we suppressed our laughter imagining the girls repairing their battered appearances. Seconds later when the door swung open, Asia's innocent smile was usually revealed first. Nevertheless shortly after her greeting, she would get rudely snatched from behind the door like a second-rate comedian being yanked off-stage by a long invisible cane. At that time, Wayne and I would sit down for round two.

In spite of her four-year handicap, Asia was taking no prisoners. Yet, in the end, Isis always vanquished the poor girl before triumphantly appearing in the doorway flashing her comely smile. Amazingly, on most occasions, she appeared unruffled. After a few days of being entertained by this audio broadcast, Wayne and I would get gassed-up for another exciting slugfest whenever Ms. Kalif's Buick Skylark was not parked in the driveway.

Isis and I became good friends during my sophomore year. Nothing physical nor romantic, just a healthy dose of teenagers *chillin' and buggin' out!* Since the queendom was conveniently located on the way home from the courts, it became a favorite hangout-spot for Wayne and me. Even at my young age, I noticed families lacking a male presence tended to yield girls who were a bit 'boy crazy.' Accordingly Isis, being popular in two schools, had more male than female friends. This notwithstanding, I never heard any deprecating 'hoe rumors' about her. Since Wayne and I sometimes ran into her guy-friends on our visits, I assumed the precious dimples Asia displayed were not for me alone.

Like Isis, Wayne ended up moving across town soon afterward. I never understood these cross-town relocations but many of my friend's families did it. Some kids even moved more than once. The greater distance did not stop the three of us from hanging-out on Isis's porch whenever Wayne was in the area. It was the place to be!

In my junior year, the middle schools were closed due to budget cuts. This had the effect of keeping the seventh graders in elementary school and pushing the eighth graders into high school a year early. Thus, when Asia entered eighth grade, I often-times bumped into one or both of the sisters on the way home from school. Since they lived nearby, this seemed normal enough.

But I ran into Asia every day.

Considering I never observed any after-school pattern due to having detentions or just hanging-out, I should've noticed something was strange; especially after my friends started accusing me of 'rocking the cradle.' Despite their allegations and the fact that Asia, like her mother and sister, had been blessed with the stunning qualities which have intoxicated men since time immemorial, to me, she was just Isis' little-sister and nothing more. My feelings did not change even after I saw Asia sitting on a fence alongside the road one afternoon. She appeared to be waiting for someone.

"I told you man!" Jeff exclaimed as we passed her in the Mustang. "She's out there every day waiting for you. Two weeks ago, I saw her sitting in the rain with an umbrella!"

"And I know your wack-ass tried to pick her up, didn't you?"

Jeff laughed along but never denied the charge. Since Asia didn't seem to notice us, I refrained from waving to get her attention.

After Isis graduated in '85, she began attending community college and working part-time in Philly. While seeing much less of her, I ran into her sister even more than

185

before. Only now, I was a superior senior. So accordingly, I had less time to spend with the 'youngster.' However since I knew she was fond of me, I always greeted her with a simple 'Ssup' before moving on. I assumed her crush was a phase and expected her to grow out of it the same way I had stopped doting on Kay's friends. My opinion changed altogether one sunny morning in April. I will never forget viewing that inaugural 'Asian' cherry-blossom-season.

Sakura in the Springtime

When people think of New Jersey, they usually envision urban areas like Newark, Jersey City, or Trenton. However in the southern regions of the Garden State, outside of Camden, most towns are surrounded by farms and expansive countryside. Due to the harsh winters, April was a month everyone looked forward to. Seeing stubborn patches of ice and snow melting away, the vibrant sunshine even inspired *Grinches* like my father to crack a smile and utter a good word to celebrate the coming of *Akitu.*

As colorful and refreshing as spring is, this phenomenon cannot compare to the type of blossoming which occurs once-in-a-lifetime. After all, the seasons change every year. Images of a colt struggling to its feet, or that of a bud unfolding into a magnificent rose, these are indeed intimate treasures to behold. Nevertheless, in my opinion, they too fall short of the artistry, charm, and grace of a young lady who is blooming in *her* season. Particularly if the princess is determined to use her newly acquired attributes to enchant a prince. And especially if the lucky guy happens to be you.

"Who dat?" I asked in a grumpy tone, unaware Ant

was home for spring break. It was way too early on Saturday morning for someone to be banging on my windowpane. Not hearing a response, I sat up and rubbed my eyes.

Having returned three hours prior from my usual Friday night of partying, the only thing I was certain of was the person outside was not Wayne. As I drowsily pushed aside the curtains, a burst of sunshine invaded my room, causing me to shield my dilated pupils.

"Wake up youngboy!" said a familiar voice. "And get on this early-morning, get-high session!"

It took me a couple seconds to recognize the short guy greeting me. Opening my eyes, I spied a mischievous smile etched across Ant's *Kayumanggi* features. In his hand was a Philly blunt which perfectly matched his skin-tone.

We smoked in Ant's backyard. As we puffed, he revealed his reason for waking me up so early. He wanted me to help him wash his family's three cars: his and both his parents' vehicles. Of course I was thrilled to assist the old-head.

"Tak, you want something to eat or drink before we get started," Ant hospitably offered on his way inside the house as I remained seated on his back patio.

"Yeah, lemme get some orange juice if you got any," I responded with a yawn.

After I drank the juice and he downed a bowl of yogurt, we walked around front.

While we washed, Ant schooled me on the ins and outs of college chicks. In high school, Ant always dated more than one girl so I wondered if he was able to maintain his gigolo-lifestyle at the university level. As if reading my mind, Ant more than satisfied my curiosity by telling me what happened to him in a Miami nightclub a few weekends ago.

In a charismatic style all his own, Ant described a scene where *both* of his girlfriends met each other at the bar while he was on the dance floor with a third girl.

"And I still got some pussy that night!" he bragged.

Hearing this, I cracked-up. This was the type of stand-up performance Ant was legendary for. He was about to say something else when he stopped talking to stare wide-eyed at something behind me.

Since Ant was a certified 'don,' I was accustomed to taking a back-seat whenever flygirls stopped by. Once I recognized that familiar lustful look in his eyes, I yawned realizing how sleepy I still felt. When I turned around to see who it was, I was unprepared for the scene which materialized.

"Hi Takuan."

"Ssup," I lazily responded before glancing back at Ant's dumbfounded expression and yawning again. I was disturbed to find it was just little ol' Asia who had the superstar-pimp's tongue tied in a knot. I must stress this confusion lasted for only a couple seconds.

Our street was one of the two thoroughfares leading to a shopping center, so plenty of pedestrian traffic flowed passed every day. Asia's mother, being an old-fashioned homemaker, preferred to cook her family's meals whenever her schedule would allow. For this reason, she sent her daughter to the store several times a week. However Ant left for college a month before the Kalif's moved around the corner, so he had never met Isis or Asia. Of course this information was escaping me at the moment.

When Asia bent-down to tie her shoelace, Ant almost went into a trance. With nothing else to do, I resumed talking to Asia. "Are you gonna help your mom cook dinner

GAIKOKUJIN - The Story

tonight?" I said just to pass the time.

"No, not unless you're coming over to eat with us," Asia replied in a flirtatious tone I never heard before. This caused me to take a good look at her.

Asia was now standing with one hand on her hip to illustrate her curves. Showing a full-set of teeth, her seductive smile was riveted on me as she all but ignored Ant.

Oh my god! I thought, studying the contours of her hip-hugging jeans. No longer sleepy, I was astounded at how her legs, breasts, and buttocks had developed into a woman's figure. After she left, I was speechless but Ant wasn't.

"You better get on that, youngboy," he advised.

Reflecting on what I'd just seen, I could not have agreed more. Nevertheless, it took a couple weeks for the opportunity to present itself. This occurred at an event simply known as the Cut Party.

Herb's Cut Party

We were busted!

On this occasion, I am beginning with the conclusion of the story because I feel the police crashing the party was a good thing—especially since I got away. In addition, I ended up with some decent earnings that day even though I had to fight a dude the following week when he demanded a refund. *Yeah right!* As great as it was to escape unscathed and make dough, for me and Asia, the half-hour we spent together was the crème de la crème of the event. This was the first time we spoke to one another in an intimate way; so I guess it was a sort of 'coming out' party for us. So that's what happened in a nutshell. But to miss the details of this escapade would be like

189

eating ice cream intravenously and believing you had an appreciation for vanilla fudge.

Herbert Huxtable was another youngboy who resided within my area of influence. A year younger than me, Herb lived around the corner in a big yellow colonial. One Friday morning, this house became the venue for a crazy congregation of teens that, believe it or not, innocently began when Herb and three of his friends decided to cut school. At first, I was not interested in their party. My reason for being there was to sell some dimes before speeding off to school in the Pontiac, Firebird I had borrowed from Jeff.

Jeff was home that weekend for his sister's Bat Mitzvah. Ms. Chason had rented the sports car for him to drive to the ceremony because the Mustang was not in running condition. When things at Herb's began getting interesting, I called Jeff and woke him up.

"Bring some weed and get over here fast!" I said once he answered the telephone.

"Why? I mean, what's going on?" Jeff asked, his voice sounding froggy.

"Herb's having a cut-party."

At times, word about an event can travel fast. In spite of this, when I heard Herb's friend, Gary, on the phone inviting girls over, I never imagined *all* of them would show up. Another unexpected surprise was the artist we called 'J-Ski,' taking it upon himself to draw a funky-fresh flyer which detailed the event.

After J-Ski smoked and bought a dime, he complained how he couldn't afford to miss an Algebra test. Then he grabbed his book bag and left for school. Arriving there early, J sat in his homeroom and sketched a *Wild Style* scene of b-boys and b-girls partying in Herb's living room. Having penciled-in the finishing touches, he then snuck into an office to print a hundred copies of the Ernie Barnes-like masterpiece. Once he, along with his brother and some friends, distributed the advertisements in the hallway, things started spinning out of control.

It was no secret I liked to cut school if the opportunity presented itself. Because I did this regularly, I had a system to obtain beer and liquor on-demand. In other words, I had access to several twenty-one-year-old sponsors and a car. Although many kids did not smoke or drink, wherever a party was happening, somebody wanted party-favorites. Feeling the growing vibe, I soon recognized my favorite combination: the chance to have fun and make dough at the same time. There was no way I was going to homeroom.

It was cool in the beginning. We sat in the living room watching sports highlights and listening to music. When six girls arrived, they said their friends were on the way over too. Well, it's easy to get guys to come if they believe girls are lined-up waiting for them. At this point, we suspected something big was brewing but the confirmation came after kids started calling from a payphone at school. Once Herb and Gary verified the rumors, droves of students ditched school to get their grooves on.

By ten o'clock, half the people at Herb's door clutching graffiti-laden flyers were complete strangers. However we could not risk any of them getting caught by the cops, so we let them in. This proved insignificant in the end because many of these dummies had attended homeroom and their first class. You can probably imagine, once seventy students disappeared by 3rd period, somebody was bound to notice something.

According to many, the snitch was a gym teacher named Ms. Gaines. When she noticed four of her students had vanished midway through a softball game, she thought they had snuck-off to a nearby 7-Eleven. On her walk to the convenience store, she found several discarded flyers on the ground. After she failed to track-down the missing students, she interrogated the party-goers' friends. That was the beginning of the end.

Around the same time I imagine Ms. Gaines was conferring with school officials, Jeff and I were making a run to the liquor store. On our way out the door, we counted twenty people in the kitchen and living room. "There's way too much wood in here!" Jeff complained using 'wood' as a metaphor for a penis. In the car, we discussed which guys should be kicked out. Nonetheless upon our return, we had to shrug our shoulders once we noticed the crowd had tripled in size.

"Who wants a brew?" I yelled after putting a bottle in both of the inside-pockets of my Lee jacket and popping open a third one. Those pockets were the perfect size to store beers. Once Jeff likewise stocked two in his Guess jacket, we started passing-out the beer and wine coolers.

What started as a handful of teens taking a break from school had morphed into complete chaos. With separate parties going-on in the bedrooms upstairs, this gathering had ballooned into a standing-room-only shindig. After the brews were distributed, kids were getting royally fucked-up all over the house.

With my errand finished, I sauntered into the living room with a joint in one hand and a beer in the other. Leaning

GAIKOKUJIN - The Story

against the wall, I watched couples groove to the sounds of Mr. Magic and Marley Marl from one of my mix-tapes. There was plenty of laughing, joking, kissing, handshaking, and hugging going-on in that party. Just when I thought it couldn't get any better, I glanced across the smoky room and there she was sitting alone on the sofa.

I know it sounds corny but she was actually sitting across a smoky room by herself.

Taking a final drag of my spliff, I handed it to my boy, Steve, before stepping through the crowd toward Asia. For the next thirty minutes, amidst the hustle-bustle of blunts and bottles being passed, there were two youngsters in that blown-out bash experiencing a tranquil, *Just the Two of Us,* moment. From that day onward, Asia was no longer Isis' little sister.

Once the idea of Asia being my girlfriend crystallized, sizzling poetic-verse spewed from my lips like molten-lava pulsating from the mouth of a volcano. Matching my affections tit-for-tat, Asia added some uniquely feminine sentiments to seal our solemn pact before I leaned forward for our first kiss. Upon locking lips with my betrothed, a tremendous wave of ecstasy overcame me. This natural blast catapulted my senses higher than the Colombian Gold in my possession ever could. The reason for this might have been because my so-called 'Columbian Gold' was nothing more than Belkis' regular, ol' babbit.

Sheeit, those suckers didn't know the difference!

"Yo Tak."

Hearing my name snapped me out of my daze. Looking up, I saw Herb and Gary standing in front of me. "Y'all look zested!" I said pointing at them and laughing.

Asia did not drink or smoke so she was amused

watching the two of them as they struggled to keep their balance.

"Cuz, you're weed is blazing!" Gary replied with a grin.

"Thanks," I stated as I rose to my feet. I was determined to get rid of these two drunkards before they ruined the romantic moment. "Fellas, check-it-out—"

"This is for you," Herb said placing a stack of dollar-bills in my hand. "We took up another collection."

Then I noticed Gary was holding two handfuls of change.

"Yo Jeff, commere!" I bellowed into the dining room.

Within seconds, Jeff arrived with two unlit joints behind both ears like pencils. "Here," he said handing one to Herb and one to me. "What's going on?"

"We gotta make another run," I said, looking down at Gary's hands.

Once Jeff followed my eyes, he cupped his hands together.

"This time get some hard stuff too. Some rum or vodka," Gary emphasized as he poured the quarters, dimes, and nickels into Jeff's hands.

Jeff and I glanced at each other, pleased to receive this unexpected payday. After assuring Herb and Gary we had their order memorized, we put the money in our pockets.

"Fire-up them doobies!" Jeff barked-out, sounding like *Spikolie* from the movie, *'Fast Times at Ridgemont High.'*

Following one hit, I sat back down next to Asia. "I don't want no more," I said waving them away with my hand. "Ay do me a favor, go in the kitchen with that." Saying this, I looked at Jeff. "I'll meet you there in five...cool?"

"Alright lover-man!" Jeff teased as the three of them walked away laughing.

Before they could exit the living room, the doorbell rang again. Surveying the swelled masses, I yelled to Herb not to let our newest visitor in. Nonetheless when T-Rex looked through the peephole and shouted right after I did, nobody was concerned with what I had to say.

"Oh shit, it's the man!" T-Rex screamed.

With that declaration, the scene became mad hysteria as the police stormed-in waving their pistols causing a stampede. It was a crazy escape. Hordes of intoxicated teens followed me, Asia, and Jeff out the back windows. Some of them tripped crossing the road behind Herb's house. In an effort to avoid running them over, three drivers skidded into a minor fender-bender.

The next day, we laughed at Herb's post-party analysis.

"I'm suing those cops for police brutality!" Herb claimed. "Plus, I got seventy witnesses who know they didn't have a search warrant."

"Correction, sixty-nine," I said subtracting myself from his list.

"Sixty-eight," voiced Jeff right before a 'sixty-seven' and then a 'sixty-six' was heard from two other guys who had also escaped.

Following a couple seconds of laughter, I encouraged Herb to resume his story. "So what happened after we left?"

"The police were all over the house so we hid in the attic."

Hearing this, I could not understand why these fools did not leave but I refrained from making my feelings known.

"There were about fifteen kids up there with me,"

Herb continued. "I guess it was one person too many because the ceiling collapsed."

"Oh shit!" Wayne exclaimed and we all laughed.

"I fell right on top of a fat white cop," Herb reported with a frown. "After he stood back up—"

"You knocked him down?" I asked still laughing.

"Yeah and you know he was pissed-off. After we both got up, he grabbed me and threw me back on the ground," Herb said, showing us the remnants of his torn t-shirt as evidence.

Needless to say, everyone got taken into custody. In spite of this, I still believe the police showing up was a good thing. Simply put, the party was escalating into an orgy. For Asia and me, the romance was put on-hold as the Attendance Scam went into operation. During my stay at Seton Hall, I never doubted Asia and I were meant to be. It was just a matter of when.

On the evening prior to leaving for South Orange, Charlie and I were pumping weights in his garage. When an instant-song-request went out to a 'sexy guy who lives around the corner,' I thought the voice between the giggles sounded like Asia. I almost mentioned this to Charlie before becoming embarrassed for entertaining such a ridiculous notion. The caller referred to herself as the guy's 'secret admirer' before asking the DJ to play *Silly of Me,* by Denise Williams. In case you are not familiar with this classic, it's about a love-stricken girl who is enamored with a guy she is convinced hasn't noticed her. It wasn't until September, with my departure to Ft. Leonard Wood looming in three days, when Asia revealed it was indeed her who had made that call back in April.

"After the cut-party, I was desperate to get your

attention," Asia said wrapping her arms around my neck. "Do you know why?"

"No, why?" I asked.

"Because I was already in-love with you," she almost whispered.

"I love you too," I replied, melting under the spell of those precious dimples.

Chapter 12: Young Love in the Summertime

Similar to many first love scenarios, my nose was wide-open. The clear evidence of this was I got *zero* pussy. Nonetheless I could not get enough of Asia's amorous aroma, her seductive smile, her touch, and let's not front, she had a phat ass too!

Like many females, by the time Asia was fourteen, she was maturing into her adult body. Believe me, I was not the only person who had taken notice. Asia's mother was an over-protective woman in her mid-thirties who was still good-looking in her own right. She had spawned two beautiful princesses by different men; therefore it is fair to say there was a good mix in her gene pool.

Having lived the life of a dime-piece in West Philly, Ms. Kalif realized her daughters possessed the goods men craved. Far from naïve, she was doggedly determined to protect them from unsavory characters. As a result, her presence was felt in every move Asia and I made. On most days, it was difficult to catch even a fleeting glimpse of my girlfriend. Even when her mother went to work, Asia was not permitted to leave her house alone. She was kept busy doing chores under the watchful eye of her sister and cousins. Unless she was sent to the store, it was almost impossible to see her.

Fortunately, Asia went to the grocery store almost

every day. On our way to the *Shop 'n Bag,* we were elevated into seventh-heaven just walking-and-talking amidst hugs-and-kisses. This is what young love is all about. Those forty-five-minute errands lent us a feeling of eternity while simultaneously seeming to end in a split-second. Being young and flamboyant, it was not long before I started sneaking to her bedroom window at night. However due to the constant flow of family members in and out of her room, it was too dangerous to enter so we were forced to content ourselves with hushed whispers through a screen window. Sometimes I'd hear Asia arguing with Isis while I waited for her to return from the kitchen.

Even though Isis was attractive and had a warm sense of humor, she came to symbolize the old ruler at the cusp of a fresh new era. With an upstart prodigy making her way up the ranks, the elder queen seemed determined to squelch this 'changing of the guard,' thereby extending her reign on the throne. It was obvious a great deal of love existed between the fiery sisters. Nevertheless it was equally apparent the absence of the *Yang* principle within the Kalif household turned their overabundance of *Yin* energy on its head at times. Despite their imperfections, for a person starving for familial affection like me, the Kalif's might as well have been the *Cosby Show.*

On some nights, it was so hectic in their house, after an hour of sitting in the dark getting bitten by mosquitoes, I'd go home without ever speaking to Asia. I soon became frustrated and pleaded with Asia to tell her mother the truth; or allow me to. There were several reasons why this was not a feasible plan.

The obvious one was the age difference. Had we began dating while I was still in high school, perhaps the three-year gap could have been overlooked. As things stood, with Asia just starting 10th grade, for her to announce that her boyfriend was leaving for boot camp in a few months was out of the question. Moreover since Ms. Kalif already identified me as Isis' friend, it was a no-no any way you sliced it.

Eventually, we decided it was better for Asia to come over my house after her mother fell asleep. This set-up was great for me. My heart would leap in my chest around midnight when I detected a faint tapping-sound against the windowpane. Once in each other's arms, Asia and I elevated to a world where feelings of bliss were absolute.

As the clock struck twelve, *DJ Tony Brown* kept it brown until dawn with his *Extra Sensory Connection;* this was the ultimate slow-jam program. To say our grind sessions were intense is putting it lightly. By the time the sun's rays were peeking through my curtains at dawn, we'd be fast asleep in a lover's embrace, completely exhausted. Even in my dreams, Asia was the great light in my life.

In July, I started working a gig on weekdays from seven in the morning to four in the afternoon. Being a recent high school graduate with no work experience, I had to settle for a minimum wage, field-negro position. Taxed with loading heavy crates into trucks for eight long hours, despite my physically exhausting job, the energy of our all-nighters was never dampened in the least. I wonder if this was because Asia never allowed me to go 'all the way.' Although my alarm sometimes rang following as little as forty minutes of sleep, those mornings were purely euphoric. Yearning for my Asian Goddess, she had become my sole inspiration for rising each day. The personification of beauty, her appeal was all the more apparent upon awakening. Even with her disheveled hair and wrinkled clothing, just inhaling her divine scent dazzled and energized me like the sun.

"Young, dumb, and full of cum!"

Years later, this is how a Green Beret named Major Steven Brackett described me after I revealed my plan to attend university—thereby rebuking his attempt to get me to sign-up for Officer Candidate School. Although a somewhat vulgar statement, perhaps no phrase better expresses that 'urge to merge' within adolescent men and women.

Reminiscing on that summer more than two decades later, I realize the innocence was the best part. In my humble opinion, women generally give up 'the goods' far too early simply because they don't realize the value of what they possess. Had Asia given it up like many of the girls I knew, I wonder how much faster the in-love varnish would have worn off. To borrow a phrase from a different girlfriend's father: "Why buy the cow if you can get the milk for free?"

Running Out of Time

Weekends were the only time Asia could have company or go outside. Since the only person I could visit at the Kalif residence was Isis, Asia and I started meeting at Herb's while Ms. Huxtable was at work. Obviously, Asia could not tell her mother where she was going so to create a believable story, she solicited the assistance of her friend, Tricia. *Trish* was the ideal alibi because she was the only friend Asia had that Ms. Kalif liked. With two girls to entertain, of course, I asked Herb to distract Trisha so I could maximize my time with Asia. I was skeptical until Herb's eyes lit-up at the prospect of spending time with Trisha. Before long, Herb and Trish started dating too. Since Asia and

I always met at Herb's house, this turned out to be a perfect situation.

On those afternoons, the four of us chilled in Herb's den watching a movie or just talking. After a couple hours, Asia and I would go upstairs until the inevitable, "Okay that's enough, stop!" signal sounded to crush my hopes of using one of the condoms Herb kept stashed in his guest room.

As July ripened into August, our passion heated-up right along with the temperature. I doubt ten minutes of any day went by without me thinking about Asia. Young love is so intense…so amazing! Before Asia and I started dating, I told my friends I wanted go far away from Jersey after graduation. Around mid-July, my change of heart became apparent. It comes as no surprise this coincided with the arrival of my orders for basic training.

I was smiling when the recruiter stated I had been ordered to report to Ft. Leonard Wood, Missouri on September 9, 1986. Upon hearing this, I inquired about the possibility of changing the location to nearby Ft. Dix. This likewise brought a grin to Sgt. Thompson's features.

"What's her name?" he asked.

"Asia," I replied with a dreamy grin.

"Pretty name," he said before adding, "Hell no!"

Overhearing our exchange, the other recruiters in the office started laughing.

"My man," Sgt. Thompson continued, "these orders are cut in stone!"

In spite of Sgt. Thompson being a dark-skinned guy from Baltimore, he seemed out of place using terminology like 'my man.' Yet, seconds later, when he cited a military catch-phrase, he appeared much more at home.

"Jody's about to get your girl and be gone!"

Once again, the others began to chuckle. When I asked who Jody was, everyone really started laughing hard. By mid-September, not only did I know this Jody-character all-too-well, I wanted to beat his ass!

The official countdown to basic had begun.

Following my high school graduation, I had to promise to maintain a full-time job if I wanted to remain at home until my departure to boot camp. Truth be told, I made more money selling reefer to co-workers that summer than from my slave wages. However, even had I quit my job, I still would not have been able to see Asia on the weekdays, so I persevered.

Each afternoon, at the sounding of the four o'clock bell, I rushed home on my bicycle. After a quick shower and a bite to eat, I went to either Herb's or Jeff's. At some point, Asia usually showed up on her way to the shopping center. The first sensuous kiss of the day was by far the best one. Although we held hands on our way to the store, we never touched on the way back, fearful that Isis or her mother might catch us. At precisely forty-five-minutes after we met, we would part with a kiss and a promise to meet later that night. I always felt lonely watching Asia walk away from me.

I spent every day of that summer with Asia, Herb, and Jeff. Being into the moment like most young folks are, I did not appreciate how my circumstances were catered to fit my needs. With the people in my social circle living within walking distance from my house, we took full advantage of our close proximity. We spent our time joking, smoking, laughing, kissing, dancing, drinking, boxing, rapping, and deejaying. This is what we called *cold lamping!* Aside from this, we had philosophical discussions about life the way open-minded youth are supposed to. In spite of the imperfections, it was a positive vibe and indeed a blessing.

Please don't misunderstand me, I am not promoting 'smoking and drinking'‡ as constructive activities for teens. Instead I am describing the reality of our world. We did not create it; but rather, we were its victims. And you cannot blame the devil's victims for being creative enough to have fun in hell.

A Sunday drive to the Moshulu

At the beginning of August, Herb and I wanted to do something special with our ladies. After Herb declared a 'Last Supper' was in order prior to my departure for boot camp, I suggested we combine it with his birthday celebration to create a festive, *Sayonara* party. Considering the magnitude of the occasion, we agreed it had to be a five-star venue.

Following a short discussion about every soul-food restaurant, greasy spoon, and pizza joint we frequented, Herb and I had to admit neither of us knew much about fine dining. Just as frustration was settling in, Herb uttered something unrecognizable. At first, I thought he was trying to speak Japanese.

"Mo-shoo-loo," he pronounced, deliberately moving his finger in-sync with each syllable of this unfamiliar word.

Locking onto the stilled image of my friend, my mind struggled to decipher his code. Herb, seeing the blank expression on my face, realized more information was necessary.

"You know what I'm talking about," he explained.

---

‡ Note: Aside from the cut party, girls usually did not get intoxicated with us

"Whenever we ride the 9A bus into Philly, we see that old ship that was turned into a fancy restaurant. Remember?"

His explanation caused the foggy landscape in my mind to be replaced with an image of four sharply dressed teens dining on the poop deck.

"Oh yeah," I blurted out. "I can't believe I forgot about my dream spot! You're talking about the Richie-Rich joint anchored over at Penn's Landing, right?" In my excitement, I resumed speaking without allowing Herb a chance to respond. "Yo, did you know that bad boy was in the first *Rocky* movie? Or maybe it was the second one, I forget."

On our trips across the bridge into Philly, we never failed to check-out the historic four-masted ship docked in the Delaware Bay. Formerly a battle ship, this floating relic had been refurbished into an upscale restaurant. For some reason, the thought resonated with us that patronizing the *Moshulu* was the definition of success. So naturally, we believed our younger, female companions would be impressed as well.

For the next couple weeks, I hustled more shrewdly and cut down on spending money. Since my entire world revolved on the three streets nearest my house, this was not difficult to accomplish. Ironically, our extra efforts accounted for little because on the evening of our 'reservation for four at a private table under the skylight,' everything that could go wrong did.

Asia and Tricia, knowing nothing about our haphazard plan, failed to fabricate the existence of a skating or slumber party. Herb and I forgot that the girls needed to concoct a believable story to convince their mothers to allow them outside that night. Besides this, the only vehicle I could get my hands on belonged to Jeff. And his car was in sad condition.

Since first-year students at Seton Hall were not permitted to park on campus, the Mustang had remained in his mother's driveway in total neglect. Sporting an expired inspection sticker, it was neither registered nor insured. Although the engine turned over, it had a host of minor problems which required immediate repair. In a nutshell, along with the car's brakes being suspect and the emergency brake being broken, it had one blown headlight, no wiper blades, and the horn wasn't working. We also cannot forget I did not have a driver's license. Yet again displaying the recklessness later described by my drill sergeants as "a total disregard for authority"—*particularly considering the girls never showed up*—Herb and I went to Philly anyway.

Shortly after setting off, we stopped at a Cinnaminson package store to buy some beer. While sitting in the parking lot, we decided to visit Herb's aunt in West Philly. We hoped one of his cousins would steer us toward a party going on that night. In the event there was nothing happening, there were so many flygirls in the area, we figured it would still be fun. On the other hand, if we were lucky, we might get to check-out *Schooly D, Steady B, Jazzy Jeff*, or even the master of the scratch himself, *DJ Cash Money*, at a live event.

By the time we reached Camden, the brakes felt soft and squishy but Herb was so busy playing with the radio he failed to notice I was using the automatic transmission to slow down. When we arrived at his aunt's house we were having such a great time, I decided to hold-off breaking the bad news. The most surprising thing about our trip was we didn't do anything special. After Herb's cousin told us there were no parties that night, we walked down the street to see if any girls we knew were sitting on their porches. Once this plan likewise failed to yield results, we returned to Herb's aunt's. Following a couple boring hours of watching television with his cousins, we left.

Any rational person would have thanked god for bringing them that far and parked the car until it was repaired. Well, we were anything but rational. I knew if the beat-up Mustang was left on the street 'Philly's finest' would have it towed away. Therefore the stage was set for a memorable ride; one which defied logic on many levels.

Walking out of the house at eleven-thirty, being the driver and the person responsible for the car, I felt *hmmm,* let's see…not worried. Too immature to be worried and too stupid to be afraid, I was looking forward to this risky adventure, imagining we were on a mission like the agents in my Robert Ludlum novels. Since I knew I had to return the defective vehicle to Jeff's house no matter what, perhaps the best word to describe my feelings is 'anxious.'

"Before we jet, there's something I should tell you," I said once we were inside the car.

"Okay," Herb replied. "Let's roll a joint for the ride."

"Herb," I said putting my hand on his shoulder to get his attention. "We don't have any brakes."

Herb looked at me and chuckled, thinking I was joking. Once I convinced him this was not the case, his eyes opened wide.

"What!" Herb yelled. "No brakes! How the fuck are you gonna stop the car?" Then he sat back and started laughing.

"I'm gonna downshift with this," I said pointing at the gear shaft.

"You think that's gonna work?" Herb asked, not quite understanding what 'downshifting' was all about. Not only did Herb never discourage me, he popped a warm brew and lit the first spliff. "Fuck it," he said with a grin. "Let's get ghost!"

As traffic slowed near the Ben Franklin Bridge, I pushed the brake and felt no resistance whatsoever. Realizing we lost whatever was left screeching to a halt ten minutes ago at a traffic signal, I resorted to downshifting. When I detected a burning metallic odor and saw clouds of black smoke billowing from underneath the Mustang, I got scared. With the transmission being abused so badly, I feared it might drop out of the car any second. I was about to pull-over until I glanced at Herb and saw how much he was enjoying himself in the passenger seat.

Interstate 130 has traffic lights positioned every couple hundred yards to regulate its numerous intersections. It is said if a driver can time the lights right and maintain a high speed, it is possible to pass through many green lights in succession. Well, for the next sixteen miles, we put this theory to the test as *DJ Chuck Chillout* was announced as the author of the next hour's master-mix.

"Turn it up," I barked out.

When Chuck mixed-in *Just Ice* and *Mantronix*, I floored the accelerator because just like them, Herb and I were *'Cold Gettin' Dumb!'* Once the wicked scratches incensed our eardrums, Herb and I entered a cheeba-filled, malt-liquor trance. Passing through consecutive intersections, at times, Rt. 130's three lanes proved insufficient to keep our topsy-turvy ride in motion so we slashed into one of the shoulders.

"Watch out!" Herb screamed pointing in all directions. With a lit joint protruding from his lips and a quart of Colt 45 between his legs, Herb was laughing and yelling at the same time.

At our high rate of speed, we reached our exit in the blink-of-an-eye. However, even after leaving the freeway, we continued screeching around corners in the suburban district.

"How you gonna stop the car?" Herb asked after adjusting the music's volume.

"Muthafucka, does it look like I know?" I scolded, racking my brain with the same question. Each time I downshifted to a reasonable velocity, I had to speed back up to make it through a traffic signal. "Gimme me some ideas," I implored.

It soon became evident the only reply forthcoming from Herb was hysterical laughter. Ignoring him, I somehow navigated to our elementary school and skidded into the parking lot. Veering the steering wheel hard to the left, I drove toward the same baseball field where I used to whiff batters, thinking the un-mowed grass would help to slow us down.

Bang!

When the wheels slammed into the curb, the collision was so loud I thought something exploded underneath us. But the car finally stopped. Jumping out, I checked the wheels for damage fearing one of them might have fallen off. I was relieved to find the Mustang was okay. By this time Herb was exiting from the passenger side; he was laughing so hard he could barely stand.

"Get back in!" I roared with a grin, opening the driver's door. In celebration, I floored the gas pedal and we skidded in circles to create 'doughnuts' on the grass. On our fourth spin, I lost control of the steering wheel and we swerved into a sign. "Oh shit! I didn't see that sign, did you?" Getting out a second time, I grimaced at the laid-out sign before inspecting the Mustang again. I was pleasantly surprised the classic Ford almost looked untouched. Come to think of it, I don't think Jeff ever noticed the small nick left on his hood.

This time Herb and I decided to call it quits. After I slowly drove to Jeff's and parked in his driveway, we crept away and blazed our final joint on Herb's roof. While we puffed, the fact we were in one piece—and not in jail—did not particularly impress us. A perfect example of the irrationality of youth, that night epitomized the phrase: God takes care of old folks and fools. In this case, two fools to be exact.

Chapter 13: The Calm before the Storm

With my departure date breathing down my neck, Labor Day felt much colder than usual. Every day, one of my homies told me I was crazy for leaving a budding beauty like Asia behind. A few guys even became jealous she was my girlfriend.

"Sev, you got the flyest babe in the borough, cuz!" This is what Malik yelled out the window when his car pulled up next to me. "Youngboy, where you been?" Chris asked from the passenger seat before both old-heads exited the car to give me a half hug-half handshake. "I thought we were supposed to hang out together over the summer?"

"Oh yeah, my bad on that," I admitted before looking ahead to the weekend. "What're y'all doing Saturday?" I asked. "Let's link-up then."

"We won't be here," declared Malik. "We already started our fall semester. We just came back to pick up a few things from the *crib*. We're rolling back to Long Branch tomorrow."

Chris and Malik were both seniors at Monmouth University.

"Did Brian tell you we're sharing an apartment this year?" asked Chris. "You gonna visit us before we graduate, right?"

"Thanks for the invite but I'm outta here too. I gotta

213

report to Fort Leonard Wood on the ninth for boot camp," I stated with pride.

"Get the fuck outta here!" Malik replied in astonishment. "I never thought you'd join the service!"

After Chris agreed, he suggested we hold a parting celebration at Malik's house. "You bring the weed and we'll buy a case of brews—" he proposed before Malik cut him off.

"And some *Everclear!*"

I laughed, thinking they were joking until I noticed them waiting for my reply. "Are you serious?" I asked, looking at Malik. "What about your folks?"

"They took my little brothers to a musical on Broadway," replied Malik. "That means they won't get back from my aunt's house in Brooklyn until tomorrow evening."

"A-ight then, let's do it," I said before adding, "is it cool to invite Herb and Jeff?"

Being five years older than me, they thought Herb was still a child; and Jeff, well he had earned a dubious reputation over the years. After they rebuked my proposal to include my friends, I wondered why they wanted to hang-out with me.

"Why am I so special?" I inquired in earnest.

Hearing my question, they looked at each other like I asked something stupid. "'Cause you got the weed," they responded in unison.

While I laughed at their brutal honesty, we jumped in Malik's old brown Lincoln Continental. My snickering continued when Malik started the engine and his favorite song blared from the speakers.

"Hungry...hungry for your love!"

"Yo *Leek* turn it down a little," said Chris.

"No, turn that bullshit off!" I proclaimed from the back seat. "I mean damn, I like club music too but this is the only song you ever play. What the hell is this? The extended 'Hungry for your Love' sucka re-mix?"

This set off a round of dozens which lasted until we were at Malik's house mixing the moonshine with fruit juice. Although Chris added juice until we could barely taste any alcohol, it was still strong as shit!

An hour later, the Spirits had taken control of our gathering. By this time I was tired of Chris calling me 'youngboy.' After all, Ant was the only guy who got away with that. In retaliation, I dubbed him and Malik, the 'Over-the-Hill Gang.' While I was cracking a series of 'senior citizen' jokes, Chris lost his cool and punched me in the chest. This caused me to start laughing hysterically. For some reason, I couldn't take Chris seriously so I walked out the front door onto the porch.

"Where do you think you're going, youngboy?" Chris asked following in hot pursuit.

At the age of eighteen, I had not yet reached the pinnacle of my physical maturation but I was probably in better shape than these two, having spent my afternoons the past year chasing wide receivers and swishing 3's.

"See the problem is," I addressed them once they joined me on the porch, "y'all remember me when I was like twelve. Wake up old-timers, it's 1986 and things done changed!"

"Shut the fuck up!" Teeing off again, Chris hit me squarely in the chest with his best shot.

When all it did was cause me to laugh harder that should have warned him to stop. But it didn't. Feeling invulnerable, I grinned as Chris hit me again and again. Following a series of rights and lefts, he pummeled me into a corner with Malik cheering him on.

215

"Come on grandpa…please tell me this ain't all you got!" I teased him.

In a frenzy, Chris reared back and launched several behemoth blows to my arms and chest. By this point, he was breaking a mean sweat.

"You disappoint me, old man," I resumed my over-the-hill humor. When Malik realized I was still clowning he started laughing.

"Malik, watch and learn," I said in a joking manner, blocking most of Chris's blows. "There's an art to defending yourself."

Eventually I began to feel a stinging sensation. Once I was able to stop laughing and catch my breath, I spoke in a serious tone. "A-ight Chris, chill out that's enough."

"Nah, you was talkin' shit a minute ago. What's up now youngboy?" Chris replied taking another couple whacks at me.

"Chris, for real, chill out!" I warned.

Ignoring my pleas, Chris landed another series of strikes. Malik, seeing I had stopped laughing, tried to step between us but Chris angrily pushed him out of the way. At this point, I sensed Chris wasn't playing around.

"I ain't done with you yet!" Chris growled, shoving me back into the corner.

Even though I was tired of playing, I never thought of fighting back. It was just that a voice in my head commanded me to attack. So I did.

"Captain Caaavemaaan!" I yelled this cockamamie war-cry from my snarled lips and went on the offensive by stepping through his next two punches and landing three superhuman blows of my own. This sent Chris into a sloppy backpedal until he reached the railing separating the porch

from the bushes in the front yard. In less than a second our circumstances had been reversed. With his back against the railing, I had little trouble dispatching him into the bushes with my final left-hook.

"Goddamn Tak!" Malik roared pointing at his buddy sprawling in the shrubs. "I didn't know you were hittin' that hard!"

Neither did I. As I contemplated my Jo-Jo type demonstration, Malik helped Chris out of the bushes. Incidentally, I never spoke to Chris again after that night. Well not really.

Following his graduation, he entered the Police Academy. Six months after becoming a State Trooper, Chris stopped a Mercedes with a blown tail-light on the Turnpike. Due to the misdemeanor nature of the offense, neither he nor his partner suspected the well-dressed travelers might be wanted drug traffickers. When they approached the car they were taken by surprise and shot by a .357 Desert Eagle. Chris's partner took two slugs in the chest and one in the face; he died instantly. Chris only got hit once but it was in the head. Although he managed to survive the gruesome incident, he had to undergo brain surgery to remove the bullet.

Years later, I accompanied Malik, Brian, Keith, and Scottie on a visit to Chris's parent's house. I was relieved to see Chris's face did not appear damaged. In fact, besides having gained a couple pounds, he looked the same. This notwithstanding, even before shaking his hand, I was aware he was a shell of his former self. It was eerie watching him stare into my face, search his memory, and draw nothing but a blank; all this while understanding he was supposed to know me. Sadly, many of Chris's memories were dashed forever.

By the third hour of our farewell-party, the

atmosphere had given way to a mood of melancholy and it culminated in a drunken, farewell hug. The three of us wished each other good luck while insisting we'd all have 'shit on lock' by October. It was now passed midnight. With my departure date lurking a week away, my emotions were stirred to the point I had to leave.

On my way to the place Wayne and I used to call 'Isis' house,' I staggered passed Herb's and Ty's homes. With every step in the humid night, the liquor flushed through my arteries. Upon my arrival, I stumbled up to Asia's window and banged on it, forgetting the need for caution. The events at Malik's had me feeling depressed; therefore I was in dire need of love and affection from the only person who mattered to me.

Asia pulled back her curtains with a finger pressed to her lips. She was looking at me like I was crazy. *"Shhh!* What're you trying to do? My mom's still awake!"

Seeing her face, I felt a sense of relief. "Open the screen," I coaxed in a soft voice.

"Why? My mother—"

"Just do it," I insisted in a firmer tone.

Once she did, I leaned forward and kissed her. Before I could relish the sweetness of Asia's lips, she became aware of my overwhelmingly reeking condition. I was out of it!

"Yuk!" she blurted, jerking her head back. "What did you do? Fall into a bathtub of liquor?"

After Asia wiped her mouth with a tissue, she laughed for a few seconds before insisting I wait in the backyard until her mother went to bed. Following her directive, I walked behind her house and instantly passed out. I wish Asia would have allowed me to remain there until morning but that was not my karma. And like everyone my karma had to be played out.

I woke up hearing Asia laughing in a hushed voice. She was kicking me. Asia later confided I was sleeping so soundly she thought I was dead. Maybe I was. By this time, even with Asia's assistance, I could barely walk. Leaning against her, we staggered down the street like two drunk and disorderly bums. Zig-zagging into the street and back onto the sidewalk, we stopped to rest three times before finally arriving at my window. Luckily, it was late and no one was outside.

Once we were in my bedroom, not only was I unable to stop my hands from fondling her breasts, I found it impossible to keep my voice down in my inebriated state. I felt nothing was more important than convincing Asia how much I loved her. Put another way, I was too drunk to give a damn about my father being home. At one point, Kay came to my door complaining we were "way too loud." However with me drunk off my ass and Asia under the influence of my unpretentious show of affection, we forgot about my sister's warning minutes after she left. It was not long before my father heard the racket too.

Smash!

Once our chocolate paradise was invaded any quiet storm that had been brewing inside my room was canceled. In addition to the crashing sound, Asia and I were startled by a bright light from the hallway. After my father flung the door into the metal closet behind it, we watched him clumsily fumble with the light switch. Seeing this, I imagined he was stoned on stimulants of his own choice. As soon as the lamp was illuminated, it became clear we had exited the eye of the typhoon and were now facing the most forceful winds of the tempest.

219

"Get that whore out of my house!" hissed the Serpent as he glared at the two semi-naked bodies reeking of liquor.

Asia scrambled to make herself decent as I donned a pair of shorts and a t-shirt. I never uttered a word. Normally whenever my father yelled at me, my mother would intervene but on that night she was out singing *karaoke* with her friends.

When Asia appeared ready, I nodded at her.

"Okay, I'm ready" she replied, clearly afraid.

While I walked Asia home my embarrassment plus the liquor pierced my Emotional Pain Body containing nearly two decades of fear and frustration. With tears of pent-up rage coursing down my cheeks, I heard the challenge loud and clear: *you gonna let him get away with calling Asia a whore?*

In an effort to psyche myself up, my drunk ego decided it was a good idea to break something. Stepping into the yard of a vacant house, I walked up to a medium-sized hickory tree and grabbed a limb at just below my eye level. Having underestimated the suppleness of the bough, I tried to snap it with my bare hands. Once I proved unworthy of the task, I decided to use my body weight. Soon, I was completely absorbed in this irrelevant activity.

Following twenty seconds of hanging on it and pulling with all my might, the branch, along with my body, came crashing down to the ground. Had Asia not been crying, surely she would have laughed at the buffoonery being presented to her. I was way too fucked-up to care how foolish I looked. Staggering to my feet, I picked up the long leafy trophy and carried it to her house.

Once we arrived, I watched her climbed through the window.

"Promise me you won't do anything stupid," Asia

pleaded once she was inside. "Promise!"

Asia waited until I nodded, then she wiped her tears and kissed me on the cheek. After she closed the window, I stalked away from her house with my wooden *bokuto* in hand, imagining I was a fearless knight sent to defend his queen's honor.

Five minutes later, however, I discarded the branch and contemplated my next move. Anyone familiar with the dynamics of my family knew I was terrified of my father. Even in his mid-fifties, the man was still cock-diesel. Since my childhood he had been a model warrior. Not only did he strike fear in my heart, likewise, my sire intimidated our neighbors too. This had been both a source of pride and apprehension growing up.

With Asia at home, the incentive for my macho-man performance dissipated. For this reason, common sense should have directed me back to Malik's, or even to Herb's. But it didn't. I was sick and tired of being afraid of my father. *Was I a man or not?* This question was being repeatedly whispered in my ear. Perhaps my mind was playing tricks on me; or maybe it was nothing more than the alcohol. Whatever the reason, I was insane to go home.

Chapter 14: The Serpent versus the Beast

I regretted my decision the minute I stepped through the door and saw the Serpent standing on his feet with both hands on his hips. It seemed he had been waiting for me; he was practically licking his chops.

"Who the fuck do you think you are?" he yelled, wasting no time before picking-up where he had left off. "The man of this house? Back there smoking reefer, drinking liquor, and fucking sluts like you're some kind of man…you ain't shit!"

Standing there, I stared at the reason why I did not believe drugs were as bad for the human body as reported in the media. My father got stoned on a daily basis but was as strong as ever. After getting a closer look, I was certain he was soaring on a cocaine-beer high. In an attempt to ignore his venomous assault, I did the only thing I could do: walk away. This made him even angrier.

"Don't turn your back on me!" he screamed in a rage, interpreting my actions as disrespect.

When I walked down the hallway toward my bedroom, I was unaware my father was pursuing me. In other words, I only wanted to go in my room and shut the door. I didn't mean to slam it in his face; it just looked that way.

Smash! The Serpent flung the door back open, sending it crashing into the closet again. This was the uncouth manner in which the Serpent always entered my room. "Muthafucka, I will kick your ass!" he threatened.

A couple days prior, my father confirmed his suspicion that I had been dipping into his cheeba supply. At that time, my mother was barely able to step between us long enough for me to escape to the courts. As this resonated in my mind, the Serpent sprang forward and released an over-hand right. The punch, striking me flush in the mouth, caused me to stagger back two steps. Even though I could taste my own blood, for some reason, I did not believe I was in a fight. Perhaps I was waiting for my mother to protect me. My father, knowing I was scared of him, thrived on that knowledge. In this sense he was a bully. I was still standing there wearing a bewildered expression when he stepped forward to taunt me. Although his point was clear, he stated it anyway.

"Look atcha…" he spouted with both hands down by his sides. "You ain't gonna do shit! Just like I thought, nothing but a fuckin' pussy!"

My father seemed determined to push me over the edge. Well, he succeeded. I barely remember throwing the punch which landed squarely on his nose but I have a vivid memory of the tyrant stumbling backward and crashing through the closet door.

Smash! After creating that awful sound for the third time that night, the Serpent landed on a cardboard box. By the time Keiko ran into the midst of the melee, I had both hands raised above my head like Cassius Clay did after he knocked out Sonny Liston.

"Look Kay!" I shouted, "I dropped him! I dropped the Serpent!"

From her vantage point, my sister was unable to see

what I was pointing at inside the closet. Once she walked next to me and turned around, she gasped.

"Oh my god! Dad, are you all right?" she uttered before grabbing my shoulder. "Tak, what did you do?"

"I shook up the world! I shook up the world!" I screamed in my badly-slurred pronunciation. Following this declaration, I proceeded to dance around in a circle, demonstrating the drunken version of the 'Ali-shuffle.'

For the next forty seconds, Kay and I watched this demon disguised as our father struggle to free himself. The Serpent had sunk to the bottom of a half-cut, refrigerator box containing old toys. With his face and knees nearly touching, only his head, hands, and feet were visible. His two-hundred-pounds of scaly muscle had easily crushed the board games, jigsaw puzzles, and Star Wars action-figures in the box beneath him. The more he struggled, the more entangled he became in my shirts and jackets, and the lower he sank.

The Serpent looked ridiculous.

"Hahahahahaha!" I cracked-up pointing at the fallen Goliath, recalling all the times he had terrorized us since childhood. Only the Almighty knew how many times I had prayed to witness the scene now before me. Once Kay likewise began laughing, the Serpent became even more furious and resembled a child throwing a temper tantrum. He eventually destroyed the box and sprang to his feet.

"Run!" Kay yelled, shoving my still-laughing form toward the door. But it was too late.

The Serpent pounced on me and grabbed my arms.

"Get off him!" my sister screamed on my behalf.

After my father bulldozed me across the room, we both fell onto my bed. Several seconds of struggle followed. It took all of my strength—plus Kay's assistance—to wrench

225

myself free from his grasp. Once I did, I stood up and so did he. I was exhausted from my effort but the Serpent was too coked-up to get tired.

Before I could catch my breath, the Serpent uncorked a wicked haymaker which landed on my left temple. The force of the blow ejected my body from the room like a stone from a slingshot. Only after ricocheting off both sides of the hallway did I collapse on the floor somewhere near the living room. The Serpent, being a true predator, was uninterested in gloating like I had done. Wasting no time, he slithered-in for the kill.

Kay's scream jolted me back to consciousness. When I opened my eyes, I was already fighting—perhaps by instinct. Laying on my back with the Serpent on top of me, I thrashed and kicked while Kay pulled the Serpent from behind. With his knee pinning my chest down, I couldn't get his hands off of my neck despite our collective efforts. There was nothing I could do. As the scene faded into darkness, I glared at the snarling face snuffing oxygen from my lungs. Before long, the only thing I could hear was Kay's shrieks. "Get off him! Get off him!" she screamed again and again.

Once drawn into the essence, everything was pitch black and quiet. It felt like I was levitating in total blackness. The only thing I could think of was the concept of 'triple staged darkness' that *Rakim* mentions in one of his raps. It was peaceful. Before I got used to my new surroundings however, a sound barely became audible in the distance. Faint at first, the chilling voice seemed to be gaining momentum. "I hate you! I hate you! I hate you!"

Kay was kneeling on the floor hugging my body when I began to stir. "Thank God you're alive!" she blurted out between sobs. "I thought you were dead!"

After Kay released me, I sat up and looked around. The Serpent was nowhere to be found. With my mind on auto-pilot, I jumped to my feet and ran to my bedroom. I was still chanting "I hate you!" when I entered my room and grabbed the aluminum bat Ant gave me years ago. I kept the bat next to my bed in case of a Serpent attack. How many times had I cried myself to sleep listening to the rage and frustration of a black man in America? In those moments I had gripped this green bat in my hands scared-to-death. Holding it now, I no longer felt afraid. In fact, I wanted to kill him!

Running outside, still hazy with the effects of alcohol and hatred, I actually expected my enemy to be waiting for me. "Where the fuck you at? Who's a pussy now?" I screamed at the starless night sky. Unable to find my target, I unleashed my wrath by swinging the bat at anything near me. It only took a couple seconds for me to realize that hitting the bushes would never release my anguish. That's when I went inside the house to break anything that reminded me of the Serpent.

The Beast destroyed the living room.

At some point, my sister telephoned for help. By the time Ken and a close friend of the family appeared on the scene, I was back outside hurling verbal thunderbolts again.

"Tak, calm down," a soothing voice came from midway down the driveway. "It's me, Mr. Clark."

"And your brother, Ken."

I never noticed them until they were within fifteen feet of me. Having announced their presence, they cautiously approached.

"It's over," resumed Mr. Clark. "He's not here anymore. Gimme the bat, okay?"

Even though I was surprised to see Mr. Clark and Ken, it did nothing to pacify the Beast. When the two men combined their efforts and tried to take the bat, it was no contest. I easily overpowered both the six-foot-four, two-hundred-fifty-pound man and my brother. After I snatched the bat back into my sole possession, I stared at them. *At that point I felt indomitable!*

The Beast never sought to harm these two. After all, Mr. Clark was like an uncle to me. That said, it was equally evident the warlike deity was not ready to return to its bottle yet.

"Baka ya rou!" Ready or not, once my mother appeared, the Beast vanished. Then, with a fearless expression, she approached and snatched the bloody bat from my grasp before commanding me to go inside.

Ken drove me and Mr. Clark to the hospital. While he parked the car, Mr. Clark helped me into the emergency ward. When people in the waiting room shrunk away in fear, I was confused until I remembered I was drenched in blood. Although my mother and Mr. Clark attempted to stem the crimson flow with bandages back at the house, blood was seeping from underneath the adhesive strips.

About an hour later, I was escorted by a nurse into an examining room.

"You're sure you don't want to press charges against anyone?" the doctor confirmed for the third time as he finished stitching-up my hands and lip.

"Yes sir, I'm sure," were the only words I responded with.

Shaking his head in disgust, the physician behaved as if treating battered teens in the wee hours of the morning had become an unwelcome part of his routine. Nevertheless, once

228

his duties were completed, he released me without any further questions.

We left the hospital at six-thirty. After refusing Mr. Clark's offer to stay at his house, I asked Ken to drop me off at Herb's knowing his mother had already left for work. At that point, the only thing I wanted to do was get high.

"Who is it?" came a drowsy voice from inside. Before I could respond, Herb opened the door. When he saw my face, his eyes opened wide. "Damn!" he exclaimed. "What happened to you?"

After waving good bye to Ken and Mr. Clark, I walked inside, almost ignoring my host. Climbing the stairs, I entered Herb's room and procured a joint from his drawer. "You smoking?" I asked in a sullen tone when he entered.

"Yeah."

Once Herb opened his window, we crawled out onto the roof of his garage. Following a couple tokes, I relaxed enough to give Herb a summary of the previous night's events.

"That's fucked up!" Herb showed his sympathy. "Is there anything I can do?"

"Yeah," I responded. "I need a shower and a place to stay tonight."

Hearing my request, Herb took his last hit and went inside. "I'll get some towels."

"Thanks cuz."

I fell asleep after taking a shower and eating half of Herb's *Egg McMuffin* set. Hours later, I woke up to a painful sensation. Not only was my body throbbing, I had a terrible headache.

"I was about to wake you up, it's almost two," Herb stated while he flipped through the cable stations with a remote control. He was lying on a bean-bag chair propped in front of the television.

"Check it out," I said after yawning and sitting up on the sofa. "I gotta get some clothes at my house before my father comes home from work. Can you help me bring some of my shit over here?"

"Let's be out," Herb responded, eager to assist anyway he could.

Arriving at my former residence, my friend was speechless. The first viewable attractions were a shattered mirror, an annihilated stereo system, and blood staining the walls. The living room bore an uncanny resemblance to a ghastly murder scene; the only thing missing was the white chalk outlining the positions of the corpses. When my mother saw Herb, she began to chuckle at our family's misfortune. She did this to preserve her dignity because Japanese believe a smile conceals one's true intentions.

Due to my shame, I found it difficult to look at my mother. Passing by without speaking, I went into my bedroom with Herb following closely behind. After grabbing my money and stuffing some clothes into two bags, I handed one to Herb. Then I realized the weed and the trips were gone.

"Damn!" I complained with a disgusted frown.

"What?" Herb asked staring into my desk drawer with me.

"Nothing, let's go." Saying this, I lead Herb to the living room. Before I could leave, my mother stepped in my path.

"Takuan," she said, staring at me with a worried expression.

"*Hai,*" I replied, looking at the ceiling to avoid eye contact.

"Where are you going to stay?" my mother asked.

"At Herb's."

"Do you want me to see you off when you leave for basic training?"

"No, that won't be necessary."

"Wakkata," my mother replied in a somber tone. As I pivoted to leave, my mother grabbed my wrist. "Takuan…"

Turning my head toward Herb, I told him to go ahead. "I'll catch up with you," I said before looking back at my mother.

"Kio-tsukete," she uttered. With Herb walking down the driveway, she allowed a tear to escape. Using her hand to wipe her face, she repeated her wish for me to be careful. *"Kio-tsukete-ne."*

Too Close to Homeless

My week of exile prompted me to visit friends I had not seen in months. Although it was great saying good bye to my homies, since everyone wanted to party before I shipped off, I was high for consecutive days on end. With no weed to sell, I became desperate once my money was gone. A bundle of nerves, I thought nothing of stealing whatever I needed from convenience stores. Even in my severely intoxicated state, I knew there was nothing clever about my thieving approach. How I avoided getting arrested, injured, or into any type of embarrassing incident only the Spirit can explain.

Charlie's mother insisted I stay at their house on my final day. I arrived at my friend's door on the morning of the eighth of September, which was the eve of my departure. By this time, I was broke and had barely slept the past couple

231

days. That afternoon, I fell into a deep dreamless slumber. Four hours later, I woke up feeling refreshed and without a care in the world. I was surprised at my surging optimism concerning my upcoming life in the Army. Perhaps I did dream something after all. Whatever it was, it convinced me there was no way I could lose. Still, the thought of eating lunch in Missouri the following day seemed so surreal.

I remained completely still lying in the tranquil darkness of Charlie's bedroom. With the blinds drawn and the air-conditioner humming softly, the atmosphere was so peaceful I wanted to stretch this moment for as long as possible. Curled on my side in the fetal position, I overheard Charlie laughing with his mother, sister, and niece while they set the table for dinner. Having spent many weekends at Charlie's over the years, I was more comfortable here than in my own house. As I eavesdropped on the downstairs conversation, I realized how talkative Charlie had become since his father passed away two-and-a-half years ago. With his elder brothers living far away, Charlie had been thrust into the 'man of the house' role much sooner than most of my friends.

Although I had greeted Mr. Willis many times, being a man of few words, I cannot say I knew him well. Despite this, I mourned after he lost his battle with lung cancer. Having no ties to my own family, this was my only brush with death, albeit second hand. In addition to sympathizing with my friend's loss, the stark reality that everyone inevitably had to die was unsettling. On the day Charlie announced the sullen news, I was impressed at how strong he appeared. With this in mind, I excused myself to the bathroom to shed some tears in private.

A year later, Charlie and I were in his car tripping on

mushrooms. When I began to vent my unbridled hatred for the Serpent, his suppressed feelings erupted.

"Shut up!" he snapped before speaking in a calmer tone. "Tak, I got something to say and you ain't gonna like it."

"What?" I asked, taken aback by his show of emotion.

"You gotta make peace with your dad," Charlie simply replied.

"What're you talking about?" I scoffed. "That muthafucka threw a bottle at me this morning!"

"I didn't say it was gonna be easy. But you gotta make the first move."

I chose to not reply, believing his cognitive abilities were deluded under the hallucinogenic spell.

"Cuz, I used to think I hated my father too. Then he got sick..." All of a sudden my friend was choked with tears. He had to catch his breath to keep from sobbing.

"It's okay, I understand, say no more," I said placing a hand on his shoulder. I was astonished to see Charlie so shook up.

"Nah hold up," he replied, wiping his face. "When my dad came back from the hospital, the doctor told us he was dying but I refused to accept it. Tak, that was most I've ever prayed in my life. On some nights I prayed for hours, but he died anyway. That's fucked up!"

"Ay!" I interjected in an attempt to change the subject. "We're supposed to be having a good time, right? That's enough of this conversation. Yo let's call Mike. I heard he got some blazin' indica bud. He was bragging about it yester—"

"Tak!" Charlie scolded. "This is important, lemme finish."

It was apparent Charlie was going to make his point

so I sat back and relaxed. His painful words—*plus the psilocybin*—soon beamed me telepathically to those morbid moments in 10th grade.

Charlie and I were so tight, on a few occasions I accompanied his family when they visited Mr. Willis at the hospital. Although I remained in the waiting room, I shared their emotional burden on the ride back to their house.

Suddenly, the thumping sounds of feet climbing the staircase interrupted my daydream. I glanced toward the door, anticipating Charlie walking into the room. Noticing it was barely ajar, I caught a glimpse of his niece, Ruby, scampering by on her way to the bathroom. This image again teleported me back to my sophomore year—to the first time I noticed Charlie's doorknob was broken. It was a memory I wanted to forget.

Three days after Mr. Willis returned from the hospital, I ate dinner at Charlie's house. Following the delicious feast prepared by Mrs. Willis, Charlie told me to wait in his room while he took care of something. After climbing the stairs, I entered his bedroom and swung the door shut. However, since the door was lacking its bolting mechanism, it bounced off the frame and re-opened slightly—*just like it was now.*

As I walked back to shut the door properly, I saw something not meant for my eyes. Charlie was transferring his father upstairs from the living room to his bedroom. The former six-foot-two, one-hundred-ninety-five pound man now resembled a limp ragdoll in his arms. Mr. Willis' body had shrunk to half its normal size. When his yellow-glazed, sunken eyeballs met mine, I stared into a mask portraying the hideous face of death and I knew the *Grim Reaper* was lurking in the shadows.

"Like I was saying," Charlie continued that night in

his car. "When my father came back from the hospital, everything changed. The cancer had eaten up his lungs and it was working on his brain. Even though I was praying hard, after a few days I knew he wasn't gonna make it. Tak, I had a week. A whole fuckin' week to tell him."

"Tell him what?"

"To tell him…" Charlie again paused to keep himself from crying. "To tell him I loved him!" Stopping here, he wiped his face with his sleeve and caught his breath. "Every day I wanted to say it but the words wouldn't come out. Finally, one afternoon in 10th period, I made my mind up to do it. Tak, I was so determined I ran all the way home from school. But when I got to my street and saw the ambulance, I knew it was too late!" With tears streaming down his face, Charlie shook his head in misery. "Tak, I never told my father I loved him! Don't make my mistake!"

Having vented his guilt, Charlie exploded into a mournful sob that lasted several minutes. Similar to another emotional event which occurred in the back of a Subaru just a couple months before, Charlie's feelings were so contagious, it was not long before I followed suit.

So there we were, two teenagers bawling uncontrollably on top of one another.

Knock, knock, knock!

"Who's that?" Charlie demanded in a stern tone unlike the one he had been narrating his story with.

"It's me, Craig," said the familiar voice. "Hurry up and unlock the door, it's raining out here!"

The darkness of night plus the windows being fogged were all that saved us from getting caught by our friend. Had Craig busted us crying that night we never would have lived that down!

Reflecting thus with a chuckle, my thought was again interrupted by Ruby when she exited the bathroom. As she ran toward the staircase, I heard Mrs. Willis tell her granddaughter to "Wake Tak up for dinner."

"Ruby, I'm already up," I announced before she had a chance to catch me glassy-eyed.

"Okay," Charlie's niece replied from the hallway without opening the door.

As Ruby descended the staircase, I relished my last moments in the darkness before sitting up and turning on a light. Wiping my face with a tissue, I took a deep breath to gather myself. "Everything's gonna be fine," I reaffirmed, balling-up the tissue. Using my left hand, I tossed it across the room into a wastepaper basket. *Swish!*

With a smile on my face, I stood up and walked to the bathroom.

On my final evening as a civilian, Mrs. Willis blessed us with an uncommonly tasty meal consisting of succulent baked chicken, macaroni with cheese, Uncle Ben's rice, and steamed broccoli. Three heaping servings later, with my appetite satisfied, Mrs. Willis asked me to help her with the dishes. After I agreed, she kicked Charlie and the others out of the kitchen. A second-mother to me, I was soothed by her words as I wiped the plates, cups, and utensils she handed me. Following our discussion, I walked to a convenience store with Charlie. On the way, Charlie fired-up a joint.

"I wonder if we'll still get high together when you come home on leave?" Charlie pondered aloud.

"Who knows?" I said before joking, "Yo pass that, it ain't a microphone, you know!"

As the time to meet Asia drew near, I found it more and more difficult to tear myself away from the niceties of

Charlie's home. Subtleties I never appreciated until this moment—I wondered what my mother and sister were doing. At midnight, Charlie and I hugged to end an adventurous chapter of our adolescent maturation. A process which had begun in middle school, not only did we play ball and party together, we also stretched the boundaries of our imaginations with novels and comic books.

In both his bedroom and mine, we spent hours laying on the floor reading. We would only interrupt each other to cite cool passages from scenes unfolding in our stories. Charlie was the first black person I met who liked books.

After refusing his offer to give me a ride, I embarked on the forty-five minute walk to Asia's. Strolling down the driveway, I passed Charlie's beat up Torino. Teary eyed to say the least, I noticed it was parked in the same spot it had been on the night we were tripping. This caused me to gaze toward the heavens and wonder how Mr. Willis was doing before I crossed the street and stepped into the night.

"I can't believe you're leaving tomorrow," Asia softly murmured through her screen.

"You mean today," I corrected, staring into her eyes.

Being my last night, we decided to risk detection by her mother. Once inside her warm bed, I was optimistic about getting her panties off. Nonetheless after an hour of on-and-off intimacy between reprimands of *"Shh!* I think my mother's coming—get under the bed!" I surrendered the remainder of our time to dialogue.

Soon it was time to go.

"Takuan, don't forget about me!" Asia whined with tears in her eyes. "And don't forget I love you!"

Hearing the only words that were important to me, I kissed Asia. "I love you too." After I climbed out the window, we kissed again. "And I won't forget you," I said grabbing my bag and putting the strap over my shoulder.

I arrived at Herb's house with just enough time to shower, pack my belongings, and smoke a joint before my mother and Mrs. Clark unexpectedly showed up. I was overjoyed to see them.

Herb said my mother and I were cold and without emotion in our exchange because he did not understand that Japanese rarely express emotion in public. When I hugged my mother, I felt the souls of a thousand Samurai warriors stirring within me. Staring into her dark eyes, I wondered how many women in her lineage had likewise sent their sons off to military training. I also thought about how beautiful my mother was.

"Good morning everyone." Arriving at six-thirty on the dot, Sgt. Thompson was coldly polite in his Class A uniform.

The last person I hugged was Herb. By this time, Sgt. Thompson had checked his wristwatch several times. With a final nod toward everyone, I got in the recruiter's car before my eyes got too watery.

Twenty minutes later, we picked up another recruit named Albert Tasman. Before I could match his face with a place, he pinched his index finger to his thumb and placed his hand to his lips like he was smoking a joint. Seeing this plus his blood-shot eyes, I imagined he had bought a dime from me in the past. Once I smiled my affirmation, he grinned to let me know my intuition was correct.

Introductions completed, we compared our orders and found we were in the same company. Not only that, Sgt. Thompson pointed out since I had scored high on the ASVAB, I had been promoted to E-2. So, despite *Taz* being the same age as Malik and Chris, I outranked him.

"So Amaru, you can tell Tasman what to do," the recruiter stated with a chuckle like he was trying to drive a wedge between us. Since Taz and I were both trainees, we ignored Sgt. Thompson's divisive tactic and related to each other as peers.

Tasman will always be remembered for making everyone laugh at lunchtime during the first week of boot camp. That day was extremely hot and humid so everyone was exhausted. In a low-morale moment of silence, out of nowhere, Taz expressed his grief by blurting out his colorful rendition of Rakim's lyrics in *'Eric B. is President.'*

"Drill Sergeants don't phase me 'cause they're crazy, they playin' me like a doughnut they're trying to glaze me!"

End of Book I

If you enjoyed Book I, please consider leaving a review here:
https://www.amazon.com/review/create-review/?ie=UTF8&channel=glance-detail&asin=4908556016

https://www.goodreads.com/book/show/28349177-gaikokujin---the-story

Thank you so much!

In Book II, subtitled "Making of a Soldier," we follow Takuan on his journey into basic training. Still black-and-blue from the fight with his father, his 'get over' mentality is instantly put to the test when he meets his new, government-issued father—a U.S. Army Drill Sergeant. In such a stressful environment, Tak's depression from being away from Asia begins to mount. Does he have what it takes to become a soldier?

For a peep into what you can expect from Book II, check out the Afterword.

Afterword

"Amaru, yo Amaru, what's up cuz? I've been looking for you since I got here," said an olive-complexioned man in his early-twenties. Like most of the people seated in the vicinity, he was dressed in a green, Army Class-A uniform.

"What's the deal?" I asked in response, stifling a yawn. I was too tired to even bother with seeing who was calling me. When I finally looked up, I realized my visitor was Private Colón.

Seeing his face, I flashed back to two nights ago when Colón and I found ourselves in a dicey predicament. We were smoking a joint in the restroom of a Petersburg night club when a cop walked through the door. Remembering that situation, I had an idea of what he would say next.

"How the fuck did you get away?" Colón inquired with an incredulous expression.

"Whoa, whoa," I said before standing up and leading him away from the other trainees in my company. "Come on, let's take a walk. You can leave your duffle bag here."

"Nah, I'll take it with me," Colón said, picking it up and re-strapping it on his back.

Together, we strolled across the spacious waiting area

241

toward the restrooms. Once we had covered about ten yards, I figured everyone was out of earshot. Before replying to his question, I asked one of my own. "He let you go, didn't he?"

"Yeah, but afterwards I saw that same cop chasing your crazy ass through the parking lot. Yo, Jefferson said you kicked him in the chest. Is that true?"

"I had to. Homeboy grabbed my leg when I was climbing a fence behind the club. He was trying to pull me down."

"I can't believe you got away!" Colón expressed his disbelief by staring me up-and-down like I was a ghost.

"What I can't believe is, that the rent-a-cop called the MPs just 'cause we were puffing on a joint!" I said wrinkling my brow in a quizzical fashion.

"You know damn-well that ain't why he called the MPs!" Colón exclaimed, looking at me like I was stupid. "Muthafucka, a bunch of brothers in my company told me you had the whole club laughing at him. And he was a real cop, you know that right?"

Playing dumb, I said nothing.

"After the cop kicked me out, they said you and him were walking around the club together like y'all were friends. What's up with that?"

Instead of responding directly, I decided to tell the story from the point where we parted ways. "Cuz, after we walked out the latrine, you turned left even though the cop told us to walk straight to the exit."

"Yeah, I saw the shorty I had been *kickin-it* to that night. She was standing in line to use the ladies' room when

242

we came out. I at least had to say goodbye."

"Word?" I responded with a grin. "You get her digits?"

"Hell no! I was supposed to meet back up with her after I took a piss. But when I saw homie in there selling dime-bags, that ganja started callin' me *bee!* And then your ass magically appears waving a five dollar bill, grinning like a mad scientist—"

"Oh, so now it's my fault you didn't get no pussy?"

"Nah, I ain't saying that," Colón's tone turned serious.

"I'm just playing," I said cracking another smile. "Yo, lemme get back to the story." Following a casual glance around to make sure no one was nearby, I resumed. "So I walked toward the door like he said, but when I saw him chasing you down, I put on my jacket, grabbed a fly honey, and headed for the dance floor."

"The dance floor? You're crazy, Amaru!"

"No I'm not!" I replied with equal emphasis. "That was the first time we had been around any quality putang since boot camp started. How many times you'n jerked-off since then? Cuz, my dick wouldn't let me leave without putting up a fight."

"So what happened?" Colón asked between chuckles.

"After that fool threw you out, he started making his rounds looking for me. I figured he'd search the darkest corners of the club, so I decided the dance floor was the safest place to be."

"And he didn't see you?" Looking stupefied, Colón

243

grabbed my shoulder before stopping and placing his bag on the ground.

"Not for a while," I said, pivoting toward Colón. "Every time he walked by, I slowly turned to keep my back facing him—while of course, rockin' to the rhythm!" To further illustrate, I balled-up my hands and raised both fists into the air.

Seeing me swaying my head, arms, and shoulders to an imaginary beat, Colón clapped his hands and busted out laughing. When I resumed speaking, I continued to demonstrate my dance prowess.

"After he made about five passes, I didn't see him no more. Oh, and may I add, the deejay wasn't that bad once he got warmed up."

"What?" Colón exclaimed, struggling to control his laughter. "That muthafucka played the same ol', country-ass bullshit we always hear. You were just high, that's all! Not only pussy, Amaru, it's been four months since you smoked, right? Me too. And you best believe, I was blitzed outta my mind!"

"Yeah I guess you're right," I replied with a chuckle before dropping both arms to my sides. "Anyway, grab your bag, let's go," I ended my dance performance and we continued walking. "When girlie suddenly looked uptight and said she was tired, I knew something was up. When I turned around to walk off the dance floor, you-know-who was standing there with his arms folded, just staring at me."

"The cop?"

"Yeah."

"And that's when you bolted for the door?" Colón's eyes grew bug-eyed with curiosity.

"Hell no!" I frowned. "There were three, huge muthafuckas guarding that door, remember?"

"So what'd you do?"

"Relax *Colo,'* I'm 'bout to tell you. Let's sit down for a sec." I scanned the area and noticed we were approaching a departure gate that was boarding the last of its passengers. "We can chill right here," I said gesturing with my head.

As we entered the vacated seating area to further discuss our adventure, I took a cursory look at the guards manning the gates and the distant trainees. Not seeing anything amiss, I sat down next to Colón and continued my story.

"So I looked straight at dude and complained like I never saw him before. 'Why you staring at me? Damn man, you just busted my groove.' Then I tried to walk away." Thinking back to that moment made me grin.

"Get the fuck outta here!" Colón expressed his astonishment. "And he fell for that?"

"Kind of. When he stepped in my path, I stopped and acted surprised. After he accused me of being the guy he caught smoking weed in the bathroom, I denied it, saying it must've been my twin brother, 'Michael'."

"Hell yeah, I can see that dummy falling for that!" Colón started cracking up. "Especially 'cause he was definitely drunk, if not high too."

"Nah I mean!" I exclaimed in agreement.

245

"What happened next?" Colón asked impatiently.

"That's when we started walking around the club together—to look for my 'twin brother.' Whenever I saw somebody I knew, I whispered in their ear: 'My name's Larry, I have a twin brother named Michael, and you don't know where he is.' And sure enough, the dumb-ass cop would ask them the exact same questions—damn-near in the same order."

"Yeah! Yeah! That's what Jefferson and them were laughing about in the barracks!" Colón said, struggling to speak and laugh at the same time.

"Then I saw Hawk, and guess what?" I asked.

"What?"

"That muthafucka saved me again."

"Again? Get the fuck outta here! How?"

"He pointed out the second dance floor was being opened up. Once they folded that wall back, the only thing I saw was a lit-up exit sign," I replied with a wry grin.

"The fire exit?"

"Hell yeah!" I responded. "By this time, there were at least four different groups of people pointing at us, laughing. Those giggling dickheads clued homie in that he was gettin' played. When he tried to grab me, I knew the gig was up, and the chase was on after that!"

The public address system crackled to life just as Colón asked for more details.

"Shh!" I snapped. "Might be my flight info."

Directing our attention to the metallic, female voice reverberating through the airport intercom, we heard the announcement that TWA flight 751, to JFK International Airport, was now boarding its first class passengers.

"That's me," Colón said. "Before I jet, there's something I gotta tell you, Amaru."

"What's up?"

"Remember back in boot camp I said you reminded me of a dude who lived on my block?"

"You talkin' about that drug-dealing brother who got your hood on-lock? What's his name again? Barry?"

"Yeah, but his name's Larry," he corrected. "Larry Davis. And he isn't really a drug dealer. Larry's more like a talented entrepreneur who got caught-up fuckin' with some crooked-cops. I'm talkin' about real criminals and killers, nothing like that off-duty *pogue* you drop-kicked on Saturday."

P.O.G. is the Army acronym that soldiers used to describe cowards. Pronounced 'pogue,' the letters stood for Personnel Other than Grunts.

"You ain't even got to tell me!" I interrupted with a knowing grin. "Fuck coming back to Fort Lee after Christmas Exodus, right? You gonna start working for your man Larry, huh?"

"Hell no!" Colón responded, looking at me like I was dumb. "I might smoke a li'l ganja but I don't deal with no crack. Sheeit, that's the only reason I joined the Army: to escape getting swallowed up by the streets! Nah cuz, I'm telling you this because Larry got arrested a few weeks ago."

"Word up? That's ill."

Although this reflected my true sentiments, I was wondering why he was breaking his neck to tell me about this guy. As I began losing interest, Colón, seeming to read my thoughts, added some thought-provoking details to enhance his story.

"Yesterday when I called my brother, Jose, to make sure I had a ride home from the airport, he told me Larry shot up the cops, the FBI, and the SWAT team back in November. Then, the insane muthafucka was on the run for like two and a half weeks. My brother said Larry's face was on the news every night. He said it was the biggest man-hunt in New York City's history!"

Nothing Colón was saying seemed to add up. I suspected that at best he was embellishing the facts, or at worse he was straight-up lying, so I challenged him. "FBI? SWAT? All that to snag one neighborhood, candy man?"

"L.D. wasn't just some brother peddlin' dovesacks," Colón replied. "Everybody around my way knows who he was working for. Last year, Larry showed us photos of his dirty dealings with po-po. Jose said Larry tried to double-cross them by dipping out with their dough. He threatened to go to the news and drop dime if they didn't leave him alone."

"Word?" I replied, clapping my hands to show my appreciation. "He tried to vick the feds? You know that's a no-no. What happened?"

Now I was the bright-eyed bunny rabbit waiting to hear a tale.

"That's when the cops raided his sister's apartment.

248

And according to the word on the street, Larry took *their guns* and blasted like twenty of 'em before *they* ran out!"

"Hold up, hold up," I interrupted to get clarification. "Did you just say five-o ran from him?"

"Yeah," Colón replied matter-of-factly. "And the best part was, no one in his family got hurt. That plus he got away."

"Oh shit!" I blurted-out amidst my laughter. "Now that's what I'm talking about! Some real gangsta shit!"

"Jose said Larry spanked NYCs Finest, all by himself. Supposedly, he was shooting cops through the walls."

"Good for those crooked bastards!" I replied with passion, waving a 'black power' fist in the air. "But you know what? I bet those cowards were shooting each other too, because in a fire fight you know all they do is close their eyes and start squeezing off shots."

"Indeed," Colón declared as he gave me a pound. "And check this out," he resumed, "when my brother said Larry escaped by leaping like thirty feet to a hill behind his sister's building, I thought about you right away."

Before he could finish his story, another announcement interrupted us. Colón's plane had begun seating economy-class passengers. Hearing this, he stood up to leave.

"Gotta go, but word-up Amaru, you're the only other person I know that could pull off a stunt like that. That's why y'all remind me of each other." Saying this, he reached out to shake my hand.

In a confused state, I held his palm firmly in my grip.

249

I was not about to let him leave until he explained further. "What's that supposed to mean?"

"Are you being serious?" Colón asked, wearing a surprised expression. "Back in boot camp, weren't you the crazy bastard who was sneaking out at night by jumping from a second-story window? Cuz, you did some insane shit in basic—and got away with *all* of it!"

"That may be so," I admitted, letting go of his hand, "but I've never done anything that led to being the target of a city-wide manhunt." Standing up, I was about to dismiss Colón and his eccentric conversation. It was then he said something that caught my attention.

"That muthafucka Larry is a *Beast!* Just like you! You and him both got that power!"

"Power? What power? What the hell are you babbling about, Colo'?"

"I'm talkin' about that dark, chaos energy that possesses you when you're in trouble," he scrutinized me closely as he spoke. In spite of my bewildered expression, Colón was nodding like we had agreed on something. "The first time I saw you in action, I knew I had seen that Beast before. When that Spirit's riding with you, you're unstoppable…unbeatable!"

"Oh-kay," I replied, creasing my features into a smirk. "I see it's time for you to get on your plane, Colo'. You're starting to sound delirious." I held out my fist to give him a farewell pound.

"Nah hold up, hear me out!" As Colón said this, the final boarding call for flight 751was announced over the intercom. "It's interesting you called yourself 'Larry' when you were lying to the cop in the club."

"I was just making up a name."

"I know. But aren't you the one who's always saying, there ain't no such thing as coincidence? What happened to that?"

"Yeah but—"

"Amaru!" An odd urgency laced Colón's tone when he interrupted me. "I don't have time to convince you, but I'm sure of this. So I'm gonna leave you with some names that might ring a bell: Nat Turner, Crazy Horse, Toussaint Louverture, Sitting Bull, and even ol' John Brown, himself!" Colón stated with confidence. "What did they have in common?"

Only knowing fragments of information about these ancestors, I shrugged my shoulders. "What the fuck I look like? A history teacher?"

"The Beast, that's what!" Colón shouted. "And all of them—*just like Larry*—were only captured because they surrendered. They never could've been taken alive otherwise. Cuz, you know the whiteboys that were searching for 'em were shittin' bricks. Like you said earlier, 'all they do is close their eyes and start squeezing off shots.' They would've killed any of those legends on sight…I mean straight-up riddled them with bullets!"

Realizing I still did not get the point, Colón drove it home in his closing remarks.

"Amaru, no matter what happens, never let them talk you out of your power. Remember, there've been others like

251

Harriet Tubman and Assata Shakur who were enslaved, jailed, raped, or beaten but their fighting spirit never gave up. Did you know that both of them ended up free? It's unbelievable that Harriet Tubman goes down in history as a hero, despite all the trouble she caused them crackas. And you know they'll never catch Assata again!" Then Colón pointed at me. "Just like them, nobody can fuck with you as long as the Beast got your back. And it'll have your back so long as you don't surrender. Word is bond, I saw it in Larry, and I see it in you. Whatever happens, never stop fighting!"

With that we hugged.

Then Private Colón grabbed his duffle bag and sprinted to gate thirteen. He was just in time to be the last passenger to disappear through the portal.

Acknowledgements

First and foremost, I must give praise and respect to
the entity called "God"—but also known by many other
names. I want to thank my family and everyone I was ever
cool with in my hood. To the old heads—especially the
coolest cat in the world—Arnold. A big shout-out to "big-
head" Chucky; also to the only guy who gunned more than
me, Dwayne; and the coolest geek, Jay. To some of my first
homies: Stevie-Ron, Danny D, Eric T, P-Mo, and Bryan A.
To the hardest-hitting brother who ever lived, Forrest. To
Winky & Troy, and the grimiest crew in the Boro—and much
respect for the times y'all stopped other posses from jumping
me! To the baddest street-dancers I ever witnessed, the
Serious Rockers: Special K, Ice E, Exotic Rocker, Crazy
Knees, Sir Spin-a-Lot, etc., sorry I can't remember all y'all
names, but I do recall when y'all took out that group that
eventually starred in a blockbuster, Hip Hop movie. Plus, the
Midnight Express could never deal with y'all! Also, big
respect to the Puppeteers and the South-side Poppers (even
though there was no 'south-side' in our suburb...lol!). Deejay
squads like the Scientists of Sound (SOS) and Emcees like
Hi-C, Stevie Gee, and them dark-skinned twins from
Brooklyn...what was their names again? All of y'all held it
down at the high school jams! To my youngboys, Hank "the
Tank" and Ty—back when y'all used to be the "Philly
Brothers." To the Memory of anyone I ever busted with my
"Money" jumper at the Courts...'fess up, you know who you
are! To all of my classmates, teachers, coaches, teammates,

and girlfriends growing up. Not enuf love to spread around to Karen L, Krista, Frenchie, Nina, Renate, Dee (RIP), Chauntay, and Robin & Nicky. I could never forget the bruthas from "the Pack" like Chris and Quincy, or black-ass Calvin, Nigel, Aaron (the baddest human beatbox), youngboy John M. (RIP), Kevin M, Joe H, Derrick & Nicole, Shirelle & Wink (not same as above), Tonia (the girl who threw all the parties!), my homies Terry, Keith & Scott. Pete F you was a funny mutha! Kevin & Carl, Myron, and my man Froggie…please forgive me homeboy, and I got you when I see you—madd love & respect!

None of this would have been possible without the support I received from my wife, Mai. Thank you very much! To my brother from another mother, Sterlyn: Like they say, when you're down and out, that's when you see who your friends are…peace & respect Sun! To my editor, Josh: I almost want to forget some of those grueling wee-hour editing sessions in Kanoya. Then again, they were highly inspired and we really went in—thanks!

Of course, I cannot forget the very idea to write this book started from a reading by Ms. Blue Rasberry Wind. I wanted to write a book but not when she told me to. Just like she said, once I started, all hell broke loose! And lastly, I'd like to acknowledge the guidance and advice I received from seasoned authors. Justin Thomas, DjaDja N Medjay, Beverly A. Terry, Tracy M. Riva, A.D. Koboah, and Denis Ledoux. Your help is greatly appreciated.

Sincerely,
Tak Amaru
August 2015

Glossary of Terms, Historical Figures, and Events

(3 Volumes)

A – B

ACAP is the abbreviation for: Army Career and Alumni Program

Affirmative Action is a policy that seeks to redress past discrimination practices through measures to ensure equal opportunity in education and employment

Air Jordan is a nickname for Michael Jeffery Jordan (1963 -), who is considered by many to be the greatest basketball player of all time

Air-ball is a shot attempt in basketball that misses both the backboard and rim *(see Brick)*

Akashic Records: According to *Robert Bruce* (2009), it is a frequency that permeates all dimensions. An interdimensional broadcast containing records of all past events and future probabilities (pg. 277)

Akitu (or *Akītum*) means: cutting of barley; it was the Sumerian spring festival in ancient Mesopotamia

Albert Hofmann (1906 – 2008) was the Swiss scientist credited for synthesizing the psychedelic effects of LSD

Alfred is the butler and father-figure to the famed Marvel Comics super-hero, *Batman*

All the Way Live! Refers to: an exceptionally cool vibe at a party; popularized by a 1978 single by Lakeside

Alvin Ailey (1931 – 1989) is the choreographer who is credited with popularizing modern dance

Amazing Grace is a Christian hymn written by poet and clergyman John Newton in 1779

Amazon Warriors were called *Oiorpata* in the Scythian lexicon. According to Greek mythology, they were a nation of all-female warriors

Amen (also *Amon, Amun*) is an ancient Egyptian god who, together with his spouse Amaunet, rose to the position of patron deity of Thebes during the 11th dynasty of the Old Kingdom (c. 21st century BC). The name itself signifies the 'hidden one,' and according to Dr. Muata Ashby (2000-2001), the concept of Amun is the central theme of every world religion – and of modern physics as well (p. 77)

American: Until the 19th century, *Negro, Indian, Colored, Black,* and *Moor* were used interchangeably with *American;* Caucasians were referred to as

'Europeans' or 'settlers' (in their history texts)

Amos 'n' Andy: In the 1920s - 1950s, two Caucasians in *black-face* portrayed 19th century, racist stereotypes on radio and television shows

Angkor Wat [អង្គរវត្ត] is a vast temple complex built by Suryavarman II, the Khmer King. It was dedicated to the god, Vishnu. It is still the symbol of Cambodia and appears on its present day national flag

Anomaly: Deviating from what is standard, normal, or expected; i.e. an inconsistency

Anubis is also known as *Anpu*. This ancient Egyptian god is the 'opener of the way' into the Underworld

Apollo Theater: Reference to: the *World Famous Apollo Theater;* located on historical 125th Street in Harlem, NYC

Apostle-hood: In classical Greek, *Apostle* means: one who is sent away; this is what the disciples were called after Jesus' death

ARCOM is an acronym for: Army Commendation Medal

Area J: A rugged training area located on Fort Bragg, NC

Aretha Louise Franklin (1942 -) is one of the best-selling female artists of all time; known as the 'Queen of Soul'

Arizona Brown is marijuana from Mexico that is rumored to be smuggled into the US through Arizona

Arms Room: a secure area for stocking military armaments

Army Slogan: "Be All You Can Be!" was the official Army slogan from 1980 – 2001. It was featured on a commercial with another popular phrase: *"We do more before 9 am than most people do all day!"*

As the sound of many waters is a quote in Revelation 1:14-15. It states: *His head and his hairs were white like wool as white as snow; and His eyes were as a flame of fire; His feet like unto fine brass as if they burned in a furnace; and His voice as the sound of many waters*

Asiatic: the Original Man; we have existed for aeons preceding anything documented in western history books. The Noble Prophet, Drew Ali, referred to black, brown, red, and yellow people as *Asiatics*

Assata Olugbala Shakur (also known as JoAnne Chesimard) (1947 -) is a former member of the Black Panther Party and Black Liberation Army. Between 1971 and 1973, Shakur was accused of several crimes and was the subject of a multi-state manhunt. In May 1973, Shakur was involved in a shootout on the New Jersey Turnpike. She was wounded while BLA member, Zayd Malik Shakur, and New Jersey State Trooper, Werner Foerster, were both killed in the incident. Assata was accused of murdering the officer and assaulting fellow Trooper, James Harper. Between 1973 and 1977, Shakur was indicted on many charges. Some of which included: murder, attempted murder, armed robbery, bank robbery, and kidnapping. (Note: it is documented fact that many of these crimes occurred while Shakur was in legal custody. Many claim this illustrates she was being framed by the state of NJ). The charges resulted in three acquittals and three dismissals. However, in 1977, she was convicted of the first-degree murder of Officer Foerster, and of seven other felonies related to the shootout. Shakur was incarcerated in several prisons in the '70s. This includes serving time in a men's prison where, as a "cop killer", she was subjected to regular vaginal-and-anal strip searches. *Is this equivalent to saying she was repeatedly raped?* In 1979, she escaped from prison, and is now in Cuba, where she has been living in political asylum since 1984. Since 2005, the FBI has classified her as a 'domestic terrorist' and offered a $1 million reward for assistance in her capture. In 2013, the New Jersey Attorney General doubled the reward for her capture to $2 million. Shakur is the first woman on the FBI's Most Wanted Terrorist List. According to Ms. Shakur herself, she is a "20th century escaped slave"

ASVAB is the initials for the Armed Services Vocational Aptitude Battery. This entry test is administered by the United States Military Entrance Processing Command. It is used to determine qualification for enlistment in the US Armed Forces

Ate up is military slang meaning: far below the accepted standard; i.e. bad, terrible, fucked up

Awesome God is a contemporary worship song by Rich Mullins on his 1988 album, *Winds of Heaven, Stuff of Earth*

AWOL is a military acronym for: Absent Without Official Leave; i.e. a deserter

Baba Dwame Ishangi (1934-2003) the artistic director of the world renowned Ishangi African Dancers is also an accomplished African folklorist, dancer, percussionist, choreographer, lecturer, storyteller, sculptor, yoga instructor, nutritionist, poet, family counselor, spiritual advisor, and teacher

Babbit is marijuana with very low levels of THC; i.e. bad weed

Back Slide is Christian term meaning: to return to a prior state of sinful living; i.e. to regress

Baller is slang for: basketball player; it later adopted attributes of street hustling and womanizing

Balls: This term makes reference to the testis. It means: courage, brashness, boldness. "Having balls' is military slang for: having the nerve to do something

Bama means a southerner (from Alabama) trying to blend in up north, but is so obviously 'country'

Bar-Mitzvah is a Jewish coming-of-age ritual. It is akin to the female version, *Bat Mitzvah*

Barrio is a Spanish term for the *Hood*. In the US it is the Latino equivalent of *Ghetto*

Battle Creek, MI is the home of *Kelloggs;* a multinational manufacturer specializing in breakfast cereal products

B-Boys is terminology for: a participant in the Hip Hop culture of the early

'80s; there were also *B-girls*

BDU is the initials for: Battle Dress Uniform. It is the olive-drab, camouflage uniform

Be Down: This phrase is questioning if a person is worthy to be included. It's a shortened form of 'down by law'

Bean Pie: A pie often sold by representatives of the Nation of Islam

Beating Meat is slang for: masturbating, i.e. jerking off, choking the chicken, etc.

Beef: 'Having a beef' is slang for: holding a grudge against someone and wanting to fight them

Beemer is a nickname for: Bavarian Motor Works; BMW

Beethoven: [ˈluːtvɪç fan ˈbeːt.hoːfən] (1770 – 1827) was the son of a Moorish woman. Most people have no idea that one of the most famous composers of all-time was, in fact, a 'black-a-moor'

Benjamin Banneker (1731 – 1806) was an astronomer, mathematician, inventor, author, farmer, engineer, and social critic. This African man was an internationally known polymath who lived as a 'free man' during the chattel-slave era of the Americas. A few of his many contributions include being the original publisher of the *Farmer's Almanac,* the architect who laid the plans for Washington DC, and inventing the modern clock. For this reason, according to Dr. Booker T. Coleman, the clock in London is called 'Big Ben'

Bensonhurst: This section of southwest Brooklyn is predominantly populated by the descendants of Italian immigrants

Bent: 'To get bent' is street terminology for: getting intoxicated / high

Bento [弁当[: refers to: a lunchbox

Big Gulp: A super-sized 20-64 ounce soft-drink introduced in 1980

Billy Bad-Ass was my shit-talking alter-ego. He is not to be confused with the Beast, who rarely spoke

Binghi: The *Nyahbinghi Order* is the oldest of all the Rastafari mansions and was named after Queen Nyahbinghi of Uganda, who fought against European invaders in the 19th century

Bite or Bitin' is the act of intentionally trying to pass another artist's lyrics off as one's own in a plagiaristic context

Bite out (someone's) Back is a phrase meaning: talking negatively about someone in secret; i.e. talking behind someone's back

Black: Beyond denoting a race or color, this term symbolizes many things (see Melanin, Moors, Negro)

Black Hawk is a nickname for the UH 60 series of military, utility helicopters

Black History Month is held annually in February to celebrate important people and events in the history of the African diaspora

Black Man's World is another reference to BMW

Black Ops is a loose reference to government, covert operations with negative overtones

Black Panther Party (for Self-Defense) was a revolutionary socialist organization promoting the Black Power movement in the US from 1966 to 1982

Black Sheep is an idiom for: an odd or disreputable member of a group; especially within a family unit

Black-and-White is slang for: police car

Blazing is street slang for: high-level; it can refer to anything from a beautiful woman to very potent cannabis

Blessed are the pure of heart, for they shall see God is a quote from Matthew 5:8 of the New Testament

Blow is one the various street-names for cocaine; i.e. *yayo, nose-candy, snow white, etc.*

Blue Devils is the nickname for: Duke University athletic teams

Blue Light Special: In a US department store named *Kmart*, a flashing blue light is turned on to indicate a short-term discount

Blues (or Dress Blues) are the Air Force dress uniform; i.e. their version of the Army's Class A uniform

BMO is the abbreviation for: Battalion Maintenance Officer

B-More is the nickname for: Baltimore, Maryland

Body-Boxing is a brutal form of boxing wherein punches to the legs, abdomen, and chest are thrown as hard as possible

Bogart: 1. The act of shoving someone out the way. 2. Cutting in front of someone. 3. Taking more than one's fair share

Bokuto [木刀] is a wooden sword commonly used in *Kendo*

Bon-odori[盆踊り] is a dance commemorating the Buddhist custom of honoring the spirits of one's ancestors

Bonaparte: A comical reference to Napoleon Bonaparte becoming a tyrant due to his 'short man' complex

Bones is slang for 'dollars'

Box is a street name for: a large portable radio/cassette player; whites labeled them "ghetto blasters"

Brainiac is a term for: studious individuals

Brick: In basketball, this is a bad shot that bounces hard off the backboard or the rim

Brickhouse is jargon for: an irresistibly sexy woman; made famous in a song by the Commodores

BRM are the initials for: Basic Rifle Marksmanship

Broomhilda is a comic strip by Russell Myers depicting a man-crazy, cigar-smoking, beer-guzzling, 1,500-year-old witch. In ancient times, the Celtic people had an entirely different image of the witch, or 'crone'. She was revered as the 'dark mother', the healer, the wise woman. The buffoonish images of women, or those of the 'wicked witch', are wholly concepts created by western society

Brother: Many ethnicities and groups use 'brother' to address its male members. However, 'a brother' or 'a sister' typically refers to melanin-rich people

Brown-Round is the Army's nickname for: a drill sergeant's hat

Brown-nose is Army slang for: ass kisser; supposedly, these individuals 'kiss ass' so often, they have brown, fecal residue on the tips of their noses

Brown People are generally Latinos, Indians, and dark-skinned Asians

Bruce Lee: [李小龍] *Lee Jun-fan* (1940 – 1973) this Hong Kong fighter and filmmaker, who founded *Jeet Kune Do,* is perhaps the most influential martial artist of modern times. Bruce Lee's widow, Linda Lee Cadwell, asserts that Bruce created the concept for *Kung-Fu* (with himself as the star) before Warner Brothers outright stole the idea. It is believed that David Carradine was inserted because of opposition to a Chinese man being cast in the role of a hero

Brut is a brand name by *Fabergé* for a line of men's cologne

Buck is slang for: firing a gun

Buddah is a nickname for marijuana because THC is known to cause a deep level of meditation

Buggin' out is slang for: having fun or acting crazy; popularized by a 1985 song by Whistle entitled *Just Buggin*

Bumming (something) is slang for: receiving something for free

Bumple-stiltskin is a comical reference to the imp-like creature in the German fairy tale, *Rumplestiltskin*

Burner is another reference to a handgun

Bushido [武士道]: is the samurai's moral code emphasizing frugality, loyalty, and honor unto death

Bust (someone's) Balls is Army slang for: to embarrass or humiliate

Bust a Nut means: male ejaculation; i.e. to cum

Busta is slang for: an uncool person; i.e. a nerd

Buster Brown is a comic strip character created in 1902 by the *Brown Shoe Company*

BX is an acronym for: Base Exchange; these are huge retail stores for Air Force personnel and their families (similar to PX)

C – D

Cadre means: the military personnel in charge

Cammied-up is the act of using camouflage paint and clothing in order to blend into the surrounding environment; i.e. a guerilla

Candy Shop: A metaphor for: a place where illegal drugs are sold

Carl Wade Stiner (1936 -) is a retired US Army, four-star general

Caught Out There is slang for: getting caught doing something wrong plus the consequences that go along with it

261

Chakra is a *Sanskrit* term. Often thought of as 'spinning wheels of energy', they represent the seven subtle energy centers aligned from the base of the spine to the top of the head. In Hindu metaphysical and tantric/yogic traditions, it is believed that when all seven chakras are in alignment, a person's life force *(kundalini)* can travel up the spine to the crown of the head

Challenge-Password is Guard Protocol. A question is posed to the oncoming party who must provide a valid answer to be authenticated

Chaptered (Out): Army Regulation manual 635-200 covers all types of less-than-honorable discharges

Charlie Chan: This Chinese-American detective, created by Earl Derr Biggers, is viewed as a racist stereotype by many Asians

Charlton Heston: John Charles Carter (1923 – 2008) was an actor known for his portrayal of *Moses* in *The Ten Commandments*

Cheeba is a street name for: cannabis or marijuana

Cherry Blast: is the nickname for the first parachute jump after Airborne school; i.e. the sixth jump

Chi; or *Qi* [氣] is an active principle forming part of any living thing; frequently translated as 'natural energy', 'life force', or 'energy flow', it is the central underlying principle in traditional Chinese medicine and martial arts

Chicken George: A reference to the subservient, fearful character in *Roots,* played by Ben Vereen

Chill-Guill was my nickname for Perez. It was also to honor one of *Doug E. Fresh's* deejays named *Chill Will*

Chink was originally a British slur for Chinese. Nowadays, this pejorative refers to Asians in general

CIA: On August 18, 1996, the *San Jose Mercury News* published the first installment of a three-part series of articles concerning crack cocaine, the Central Intelligence Agency, and the Nicaraguan Contra Army

CID are the initials for the Criminal Investigation Command. This unit investigates crimes within the US Army; akin to Internal Affairs

City of Brotherly Love is a nickname for Philadelphia; i.e. Philly

Civvies is military slang for: civilian clothes

Clap is a nickname for: Gonorrhea; a sexually transmitted infection (STD)

Clinton Eastwood, Jr. (1930 -) is another icon actor for white masculinity

Clockin' Dollars is a euphemism for: making money; i.e. working around the clock

Cloud 9 is an idiom meaning: a feeling of euphoria; i.e. floating on clouds

Clowning (someone) is slang for: making fun of; to ridicule someone

CO are the initials for: Commanding Officer

Coca-cola: Prior to the 20th century, cocaine was a legal ingredient used in this popular, carbonated soft drink

Cold Lamping is an alternate form of *chilling* or *cold-chilling*

Colored: An outdated Jim Crow reference meaning: black or African-American

Colt: A horse in its infancy stage is actually called a 'foal'

Columbian Gold is a a native strand of marijuana grown in Columbia. It is known for its golden hairs and powerful psychedelic effects

Commie is short for 'communist', but really meant anyone not agreeing with US policy during the Cold War. This code word for 'the enemy' was changed in the 21st century to *Terrorist*

COMMO is the Army abbreviation for: the communications platoon

Conan the Cimmerian is a sword and sorcery hero created in 1932 by Robert E. Howard

Concertina Wire is sharp, barbed wire that is formed in large coils. Also called 'Dannert Wire'

Confucius [孔子] (551 – 479? BC) was a teacher and philosopher who emphasized human morality; he is credited with being the first to write the *Golden Rule* and is the author of many famous texts including the *Five Classics*

Cool Jay is a shortened form of LL Cool Jay

Cop is slang for: a police officer. Or a verb meaning: to receive something by either purchasing or stealing it

Coqui 900 is a malt liquor brew by *Pabst Brewing Company.* It was popular in Philly for its potency

Cowardly Lion is a reference to the timidly fearful character in the 1939 musical-film, *The Wizard of Oz*

Cowboys and Indians: In this make-believe ritualistic role-play, children re-create the massacre of the original Americans

CPA: Certified Public Accountant

CQ is an abbreviation for: Charge of Quarters; the NCO in charge overnight

Cracka is a term used to identify the class of societal slave drivers; i.e. the foreman who *cracks* his whip

Cracka Theology is my way to express the system of white supremacy. Dr. Neely Fuller and **Crackhead** is slang for: a person addicted to crack-cocaine; it also suggests poor personal hygiene and kleptomaniac behavior

Crazy Horse: Tȟašúŋke Witkó (1840? - 1877) was an American hero who defended the territories and way of life of the Oglala-Lakota branch of the Sioux Nation; he earned a reputation for being 'untouchable – un-killable' amongst the invading 'pale-face' soldiers

Crib is slang for: a person's house. According to Dr. Francis Cress Welsing, we unconsciously equate the bed of an infant with our home due to being reduced to 'child status' (minority) by white supremacy

Cum is slang for: semen

Curious George: Comical reference to the monkey in a popular children's book by Hans Augusto Rey and Margret Rey

Dap: Slapping hands or exchanging pounds (bumping fists); it is a sign of respect or group solidarity

Darth Vader is the main villain in George Lucas' *Star Wars* saga. After turning to the 'dark side', he evolves into a menacing character known for punishing his subordinates' mistakes with death

Daruma: *Bodhidharma* was a dark-skinned man born in the Indian state of Tamil Nadu during the 5th/6th century CE. Credited as being the transmitter of *Ch'an* to China, he also began the physical training of the *Shaolin* monks that led to the creation of *Shaolinquan*

Debarge: A family, music group that was revered by females who adored the light-skinned, wavy hair type of guy

D-Day refers to the Normandy landings of the Allied invasion. It occurred on June 6, 1944

Delta Force: 1st Special Forces Operational Detachment-Delta (1st SFOD-D) is one of the four secretive, tier-one counter-terrorism and special mission units

Deuce and a Half: The M35 series of trucks are large utility vehicles in the 2 ½ ton weight class

Dick-down is slang for: having sex

Diesel is short for *cock-diesel,* which is slang for: an extremely muscular physique; i.e. like a body-builder

Dime-piece or Dime is a metaphor for: a rating of 10. It is used to describe a good-looking female. Or, it is $10 worth of marijuana

Dimples Dee is the emcee moniker for Crystal Smith

Dissed is Hip Hop terminology for: being disrespectful toward someone

Dixie is the brand name of a line of disposable paper cups

Dizzy Gillespie: John Birks Gillespie (1917-1993), is one of the jazz pioneers credited with ushering in the 'Be-Bop' era

DJ Cash Money: Jerome Hewlett is a Philadelphia-based *turntablist* who is well-known for winning deejay contests worldwide

DJ Chuck Chillout: Charles Turner (1962 -) was a featured deejay on NYC's 98.7 *Kiss FM*

DJ Debonair & Tricky D are two progenitors of Miami Bass music in the late '80s

DMZ are the initials for: Demilitarized Zone. In spite its name, this area, which runs across the Korean peninsula, is the most heavily militarized border in the world

Dog Star is the brightest star in the night sky. Many believe *Sirius* is the original home of melanin-rich people

Don is loosely derived from Italian and Spanish; we used it to mean a cool guy with the girls – i.e. a playboy

Dove Sack is drug-dealing terminology for: a bag of marijuana or cocaine

Down by Law is slang for: having respect in the streets. It was popularized by MC Shan's 1987 album entitled, *Down by Law.* In the '90s, this expression was eclipsed by *Keep it Real* as the preferred catchphrase in Hip

Hop

Dr. Dunkenstein is a moniker created by Darryl Dawkins to describe his thunderous, backboard-shattering dunks

DRF are the initials for: Division Ready Force. Combat brigades rotate in the planned deployment sequence of readiness

Dr. Ben: Dr. Yosef A.A. Ben-jochannan (1918 – 2015) taught us about many of Africa's ancient civilizations as a professor at numerous institutions including Cairo's University of Al-Azhar and Cornell University. A fellow historian and contemporary, Dr. Asa Hilliard III, described him as "fearless, audacious, and driven." He claimed that *Dr. Ben* did not "merely ask us to accept his testimony" but rather "put the primary evidence for his conclusions before us."

Dr. Frances Cress Welsing state that a system is practiced by the global white minority, on both conscious and unconscious levels, to ensure their genetic survival by any means necessary. Accordingly, this system attacks people of color (particularly people of African descent) in nine major areas: economics, education, entertainment, labor, law, politics, religion, sex, and war

Dr. J: Julius Winfield Erving II (1950 -) is the player credited with launching the modern style of playing 'above the rim'; the *Doctor* is considered one of the best dunkers of all-time

Dr. John Henrik Clarke (1915 – 1998) was a pioneer at Cornell University and Hunter College. Beyond revealing the truth about black people's history, he was famous for confronting and defeating western historians in public debates, most notably Wellesley College European classics professor Mary Lefkowitz. According to Dr. Clarke: "the first light of human consciousness and the world's first civilizations were in Africa." He taught us that the so called Dark Ages were dark only for Europe

Dravidian: Due to their dark skin, the original descendants of India have been relegated to a low-caste called *Untouchables*

Drop: the command to get down and do push-ups. Or, it means: a knockout (KO) in boxing

Drop Dime is street vernacular for: snitching or ratting

Dropping Knowledge is terminology for: teaching; usually by lecturing

Dumbed Down: This form of mental exploitation contains elements of *misinformation* and *disinformation*

Dun is a Moorish title; similar to El, Bey, Ali, AL, Dey, etc.

E – G

Earth, Wind, and Fire is one of the most successful bands of the twentieth century; *EWF* was one of the first black groups to claim a spiritual lineage in ancient Egypt

Eating out the palm of your hand is an idiom meaning: to have someone under a spell which leaves them helplessly gullible

Edward Leo Peter McMahon Jr. (1923 - 2009) was famous for being the set-up man for Johnny Carson

Egg McMuffin is the signature breakfast sandwich sold by McDonalds

EIB are the initials for: Expert Infantryman Badge

Elaine Brown (1943 -) the former Black Panther Party chairperson (and mistress of Huey Newton) is a prison activist, writer, and singer

Elvira: *Elvira, Mistress of the Dark* is a comedy horror character created by James Signorelli

Embed Miltarism: Since the 1980s, embed militarism in movies has been funded by a taxpayer subsidy through the military and its contractors. This process of Pentagon-Hollywood collusion includes military officials producing, collaborating on screenplays, line-editing scripts, and even changing plot and dialogue in order to guarantee the film is pro-military (Sirota, 2011)

Emotional Pain Body: As explained by Dr. Umar Johnson: an EPB is a "chip of self-hatred" that is suppressed in the subconscious of a person and can be activated suddenly and without warning if she/he is put in a stressful situation

End of Cycle Test (EOCT): is the final examination in basic training

Enquiring Minds is a reference to: the gossip tabloid newspaper, the *National Enquirer*

Enterprise is a reference to a spacecraft commandeered by *Captain Kirk* in *Star Trek*; i.e. the USS Enterprise

Ernest "Ernie" Eugene Barnes, Jr. (1938 – 2009) was an artist. His piece entitled *Sugar Shack* became famous on the sitcom, *Good Times*

Ernesto 'Che' Guevara (1928 - 1967) was an Argentine revolutionary, physician, guerrilla leader and author

ETS is the military abbreviation for: Expiration Term of Service

Everclear is a brand of rectified alcohol distilled from grains; it is bottled at 190-proof (95% ABV)

Extra Sensory Connection was a classic 'slow-jam' radio program broadcast on WDAS

Eye for an Eye: In Exodus 21:23-24, it is written: *And if any mischief follow, then thou shalt give life for life, eye for eye, tooth for tooth, hand for hand, foot for foot*

Failure to Adapt: AR 635-200, chapter 11, states the measures for dismissing personnel due to 'failure to adapt to the military environment'

Fart is slang for: flatulence; i.e. breaking wind

Fayette-nam was a nickname given to Fayetteville in the '60s by protesters of the Vietnam war

Field Negro: As explained by Malcolm X, in slavery, the 'house negroes' worked inside as butlers and maids while the others performed manual labor outside (see House Negro)

Fire Guard is a night guard-duty for trainees only; i.e. the soldier must stay awake and patrol the barracks while others sleep

Fireman's Carry is a technique for a person to carry another person without assistance by placing the body across their shoulders

First Call signals the start of the day; i.e. wake up

Fishers of Men and Women is written in Mark 1:17 in the New Testament

Five-O is slang for: police; it is derived from the TV drama, *Hawaii 5-0*, which aired from 1968-1980

Flat-line: To register as having no brain waves or heartbeat on an electronic monitor; i.e. dead

Flower Child was a nickname for idealistic young people during the 1967 Summer of Love

Fly Girl is Hip Hop slang for: a fashionably sexy female

Forties (40s) is terminology for: a 40-ounce bottle of malt liquor

Fortune 500 is a magazine which annually lists the top ranking corporations by their gross revenue

Foxy 99 FM: WZFX is a radio station in Fayetteville, NC

Fresh Fest: The first major Hip Hop tour; it featured the hottest names of '80s Rap

Frogmen was a nickname for the SEAL trainees

Front or Frontin' is Hip Hop jargon meaning: to assume a phony or disingenuous stance

Front-Leaning Rest is Army terminology for: the push-up position

FSU are the initials for: Fayetteville State University

Ft. Leavenworth is the US Army installation which serves as the military's corrections complex. The Department of Defense's only maximum security prison is located in Kansas

FTX: is the abbreviation for: Field Training Exercise

Furious Five: Joseph 'Grandmaster Flash' Saddler (1958 -) is the pioneering deejay who is credited with inventing the 'cross-fader.' His five emcees: *Melle-Mel, Mr. Ness, Raheim, Kid Creole* and *Cowboy* formed this pioneering Hip Hop group from the South Bronx

Gaijin [外人[is a bigoted word originally reserved for Portuguese, Dutch, and other Europeans sailors; i.e. non-human, barbarian, savage. In modern Japan, it has become a pejorative to signify any non-Japanese person

Ganja is slang for: marijuana; derives from *Ganjika* in Sanskrit

Gasface is 80s slang meaning: to make a stupid face to show disrespect toward someone you don't like. It was popularized in a song by *3rd Bass*

General Order: Orders to Sentry is the official code of conduct governing guard duty in the US armed forces

Gentrification: the Urban renewal (1949 Housing Act), or 'slum elimination,' is a mechanism of racial discrimination used to force a change of residence upon people who lack resources to cope in a biased housing or business market. Once the people are removed, upscale neighborhoods, resorts, freeways, or golf courses are erected. According to James Baldwin (1963): "Urban renewal means Negro removal" (Standley, 1989, pg. 42)

Get Ghost is slang for: disappearing from the scene, i.e. to leave

Get Jacked means being a victim of a car-jack or a strong-arm robbery

Gettin' New is the act of being two-faced or phony in a new environment or social situation

Gettin' Nice: Slang for the 'high' feeling one gets from marijuana or liquor; i.e. a mild euphoric state Gettin' Puffed is slang for: getting high on marijuana

GI is the abbreviation for: Government Issue; sometimes it is short for GI Party

GI Bill: A range of benefits including cash for college. GI's in the program donated $100 bucks a month and received payments after being honorably discharged and enrolled at an approved institution

GI Party: Soldiers collectively cleaning the barracks on the weekends or before an inspection

Globe Trotterish is a reference to the *World Famous Harlem Globetrotters* – most notably Marques Haynes

Go [围棋; 圍棋; 囲碁; 바둑[: literally means: encircling game. It is a board game involving two players that originated in ancient China more than 2,500 years ago. In antiquity, it was considered one of the four essential arts of a cultured scholar.

Golden Rule: The traditional maxim stated: 'One should treat others as they would like to be treated'; however, the contemporary version has become: 'The man with the gold makes the rules!'

Goliath: In 1ˢᵗ Samuel 17, *Goliath of Gath* was a giant Philistine warrior who was defeated by *David*

Good Times is a popular sitcom portraying the projects of Chicago, Illinois; it aired from 1974 - 1979

Good Hair: Part of the *Willie Lynch Doctrine* states that non-Caucasian hair textures are 'bad hair.' A documentary by Regina Belle, entitled: *My Nappy Roots: A Journey through Black Hair-itage* explores this subject in detail

GP Mediums have been the most used 'general purpose', canvas tent in the US armed forces since World War II

Grapevine: An unofficial source of rumors, news, or gossip spread by spoken communication

GrandMixer D.ST: Derek Showard is the deejay credited for establishing the turntable as a fully improvisational music instrument

Grasshopper refers to a *Kung Fu* flashback scene in which *Master Kan* says to Caine as a boy: "Grasshopper, quickly as you can, snatch the pebble from my hand". After Caine tries and is unable to do so, the master replies, "When you can take the pebble from my hand, it will be time for you to leave".

Great White Hope: John Arthur "Jack" Johnson (1878 – 1946), nicknamed the 'Galveston Giant,' became the first 'colored' champion in 1908. This was at the height of the Jim Crow era. Ever since then, every few years, a new 'great white hope' (i.e. a white man or group who can defeat the 'black threat') surfaces in the media

Grimace is a large, purple character in a fantasy world used by McDonald's to attract children, called *McDonaldland*

Grinch refers to the comically heartless character created by Dr. Seuss in 1957

Gringo: Similar to *Gaijin* and *Toubob (West Africa)*, this is the pejorative term used by Latinos to describe the melanin-deficient invaders of their country

Grittin' on (someone) is the act of staring at a person with the intention of provoking a fight

Grizzly Adams is the main character in a movie about a California mountain man / trainer of wild animals; i.e. an updated *Tarzan*

GURU: Keith Edward Elam (1961 – 2010) became known as *Gifted Unlimited Rhymes Universal* with his partner, DJ Premiere

Guy-Smiley: A game-show host character on *Sesame Street* who is known for his broad smile

H – K

Haile Selassie I (1892 – 1975) was the Emperor of Ethiopia from 1930 to 1974. He was the heir to a dynasty that traced its origins by tradition from *King Solomon* and *Queen Makeda (also known as the Queen of Sheba)*

Half-Klick is an Army slang for: half of a kilometer. One klick equals a kilometer

Hanafuda [花札] are Japanese playing cards used for a number of games; it literally translates as 'flower cards'

Happy Face: A popular picture-design used on blotter sheets of LSD

Hard Rocks: tough guy or hoodlum; this term evolved into *thug* in the '90s and was popularized by Tupac Shakur

Harriet Tubman (1820 - 1913) Nicknamed *Moses* due her role in orchestrating rescue missions to free people from slavery, ironically, she actually had to threaten many 'dumbed-down' negroes to get them to leave their bondage. *"Live North or die here!"* This was the phrase she used while pointing her double-barreled shotgun in their faces

Heat Miser's Lyrics: The actual lyrics are: *"He's Mr. Heat Miser, he's Mr. Sun..."*

Hee Haw is a reference to a 1970s television show featuring country music; *i.e. redneck, hillbilly, or honky*

269

Heisman Trophy: the annual award given to the most outstanding player in collegiate football; i.e. college football's MVP
Hi-C is a neighborhood emcee
High Speed is Army slang to describe extreme people or situations. It can be either positive or negative. It is also used for cool stuff in order to express the cutting-edge greatness of it
Hitting the Pipe is street terminology for: smoking crack
Hoagies are a popular torpedo-shaped sandwich in northeast US cities; also known as a *submarine*
Hombres is Spanish for: men
Homegirl: In '80s Hip Hop slang, it means: a female friend who is almost like a sister; there were also *homeboys*
Honkie is a nickname earned by Caucasians in the early 1900s. Especially during the 'depression', many melanin-rich women were forced into prostitution. This is what the families of these women called the European men outside their homes honking their horns at all hours of the night
Hood is short for: neighborhood. However, since black people don't live in actual communities, the result is a *hood*. And according to Dick Gregory, "a hood is something you put over your head to hide something you're ashamed of"
Hood Ethics: The dictated customs which are created in a volatile, aggressive environment in order to survive
Hoopty is slang for: a car in poor condition; i.e. beat up, busted, etc.
Hoosiers is the nickname for: Indiana University athletic teams
Houdini: Erik 'Harry Houdini' Weisz (1874 – 1926) was a Hungarian stunt performer billed as an Escape Artist
House Negro: this label refers to people who disown their own racial identity to please Caucasians
House Nigger: The slave who imagines himself as being closer to his master than the field hands because he lives inside the house
Housing: Military service members with a spouse receive extra money as part of their allowance for living quarters
Howitzer is a type of 105 mm, anti-aircraft cannon
Huey Percy Newton (1942 – 1989) Dr. Newton formed the BPP along with co-founder, Bobby Seale
Hustle: This popular disco dance became the name of its own song in 1975
Hustler is a pornographic magazine published by Larry Flint
ICU is an abbreviation for: Intensive Care Unit at a hospital
Ijime [苛め[is a form of bullying someone deemed different from the group; it is very popular in Japan
Iron Mike: 1. A statue of a paratrooper. 2. A forward lunge exercise. With legs shoulder-length apart and hands on hips, a person steps forward with one leg at a 90 degree angle, then pushes back to the start position and repeats the process with the other leg

Iron Mike Tyson: Michael Gerard Tyson (1966 -) was perhaps the most dynamic KO artist of all-time. He dominated the heavyweight division similar to how Jack Johnson, Joe Louis, and Muhammad Ali reigned during their time as champion

Jabber Jaw is an idiom for: a person who talks too much

Jack Frost was an actual baller from my hood. This guy's reputation for dunking on people rivaled Jo-Jo's KO fame

Jackie Robinson (1919 – 1972) Jack Roosevelt Robinson was NOT the first African / Black to play professional baseball alongside white players. He wasn't even close. Blacks played for decades following the Civil War. Incidentally, in 1944, 2nd Lieutenant Robinson was assigned to the *761st Tank Battalion (nicknamed the "Black Panthers")* at Camp Hood, Texas. He was court-martialed for refusing to move to the back of the bus after being ordered to do so by a Caucasian bus driver

Jack is short for 'jack shit', it's slang for: nothing; i.e. diddly

Jam is street terminology for: a party

James Arthur Boeheim (1944 -) is the head coach of the men's basketball team at Syracuse University

James Clavell: Charles Edmund DuMaresq Clavell (1924 – 1994) was a novelist best known for his Asian Saga series

Jammy: Slang for: gun

J'd: Street terminology for: smoking a joint

Jegna is an Amharic (Ethiopian) word meaning: a brave person, elder. Note: Jon instructed me to *never* refer to him or Curt as a 'mentor'. This was because the duties of a 'mentor' were derived from the mythical Greek character who educated *Odysseus'* son, *Telemachus.* Jon said that a significant part of *Mentor's* role was to introduce the boy to a pederasty lifestyle (i.e. men raping children)

Jehovah's Witness are a modern spin-off Christian denomination created by Charles Taze Russell

Jenny Craig is the name of a weight loss, weight management company founded in 1983 in Melbourne, Australia

Jesus Christ Superstar was a musical staged on Broadway in 1971

Jewish American Princess is a Jewish girl. The term sometimes incorporates a stereotype implying materialistic, selfish behavior

Jim Crow are laws that mandated de jure racial segregation in all public facilities; i.e. apartheid, open racism

Jimmy is short for 'Jimbrowski'. This is a comical euphemism for 'penis' made popular by the *Jungle Brothers, KRS-1,* and *De La Soul*

John Brown (1800 – 1859) electrified the nation after he and his gang of 21 killed several Caucasians – including Mayor Fontaine Beckham. Believing he was the instrument of God's wrath for the sin of owning slaves, he was a heroic martyr and a visionary. His response to being sentenced to death: "Had I so interfered in behalf of the rich, the powerful, it would have

271

been all right".

John Wayne: Marion Mitchell Morrison (1907 – 1979) was an actor who epitomized white masculinity in his movies

Johnnie Law is slang for: the police

Judas is a reference to *Judas Iscariot* (Hebrew: יהודה איש־קריות). One of the twelve disciples of Christ, he is infamously known for his kiss and betrayal of Jesus, for a payment of 30 silver coins

Juice: 'Having Juice' is equivalent to being respected; i.e. down by law

Jump Street is slang for: the beginning of any sequence; i.e. the starting point

Kata: is a fundamental martial arts stance with the feet placed shoulder-width apart. Also called a 'horse stance'

Kayumanggi: In *Tagalog,* this means: brown

Kelloggs Sugar Smacks is the name of a children's breakfast cereal by the Kellogg's Company

Kent State University: On May 4, 1970, the Army National Guard opened fire on this campus at an anti-war protest killing 4 students and wounding 9 others

Kick Game is slang for: to woo; i.e. to enchant or seduce

Kickin' it is a phrase meaning: to hang out with, or spend time with. Or, it is synonymous to 'Kick Game'

King David: According to the bible, he was the second king of Israel, and an ancestor of Jesus

Kissing the Sky: This phrase is taken from the lyrics of Jimi Hendrix's song, *Purple Haze*

Kiwi is a brand of shoe polish commonly used by US Army personnel

Knight's Creed: The Code of the Knights is: *'Protect the weak, defenseless, helpless, and fight for the general welfare of all'*

Knock It Down is street vernacular for: having non-romantic sex with a girl; i.e. hit it

Kodak Moment: A priceless moment that is captured by a photo, or should have been. This phrase is attributed to the Eastman Kodak Company

Kool Herc refers to: Clive Campbell (1955 -) This Jamaican-born deejay is the first in the recognized 'Trinity of Hip Hop Architects' along with *Afrika Bambaataa* and *Grandmaster Flash*. Note: it is debatable as to whether other deejays such as *Grandmaster Flowers, DJ Hollywood, Pete DJ Jones,* and others preceded them

Kool-Aid is the name of a soft drink known for its mascot: an anthropomorphic grinning pitcher

Ku Klux Klan: A highly advanced secret society. Although the KKK is infamous for 'rednecks' and public lynchings known as *pick-a-niggers* (which later became *picnic),* many people fail to realize this white supremacist group has its roots in Moorish science. Nowadays, it is believed by many the Klan has disrobed to become the *Tea Party* (Booker

T. Coleman, *Hidden Colors 2*, 2012)

Kumbaya is a reference to a children's spiritual hymn from the 1930s

Kundalini: Literally meaning 'coiled power,' it is believed that awakening this primeval energy results in evolving to higher levels of consciousness

Kurombo [くろんぼ[is a racial slur for: dark-skinned peoples; akin to the word *nigger* or *sambo*

Kwai Chang Caine is the main character in the television series, *Kung Fu*

L – M

Laid: 'Getting Laid' is slang for: having sex

Land Speeder: An anti-gravity craft featured in *Star Wars*

Land of Make-Believe refers to the *Neighborhood of Make-believe,* which is an imaginary town for puppets on the show, *Mr. Rogers' Neighborhood*

Larry Davis (1966 – 2008) later changed his name to Adam Abdul-Hakeem. He gained nation-wide notoriety after winning a shootout with NYC Police officers in November 1986. Davis's defense attorneys claimed that the police were trying to murder him because of his knowledge of the involvement of corrupt police in the drug business. After escaping unscathed, Davis was the target of a 17-day manhunt. *The Larry Davis Story,* a documentary directed by Troy Reed, alleges the NYPD was involved in narcotics trafficking, and claims that the shootout came after Davis backed-out of a drug deal. Incidentally, Adam Abdul-Hakeem was the first person in US judicial history to be found innocent by reason of self-defense in a police-shooting case

Larry, Moe, and Curly: are known as 'the Three Stooges'. This is a famous 20th century, American vaudeville, slapstick comedy team

Latin Rascals: In 1981, Tony Moran & Albert Cabrera began splicing together hit songs on a NYC dance radio station, WKTU

LEG: This condescending term is used by paratroopers to describe non-Airborne personnel. The letters stand for: Lacking Enough Guts (similar to POG)

Lemon is an idiom meaning: unsatisfactory or defective; i.e. a hoopty or a piece of junk

Len Bias: Leonard Kevin Bias (1963 – 1986) was a basketball player drafted in 1986. He died two days later from cardiac arrhythmia induced by a cocaine overdose

Lone Wolf McQuade: In this 1983 film, J.J. McQuade is a tough-guy who prefers to work alone; he lives in a dirty trailer with a wolf

Lotta-Mo: 'I got a lotta-mo' is a phrase popularized by Mr.T in the movie *Rocky III*

LSD: Lysergic Acid Diethylamide

Lunch is modified terminology for: missing a sure opportunity; i.e. out to lunch

Lyndon B. Johnson (1908 – 1973) was President of the US from 1963–1969

Mac and Tosh are an animated cartoon duo created by Warner Bros. They are known for their over-exaggerated, polite gestures

Make Money was Curt's way of saying: to make significant gains in a chosen endeavour

Make Way for the Bad Guy is a *Scarface* quote by the character *Tony Montana,* played by Al Pacino

Malcolm X (1925 – 1965) changed his name to **Al-Hajj Malik El-Shabazz** (الشباز مالك الحاج). He was a Muslim minister and spokesman for Black Nationalism; he is noted as one of the greatest Americans in history

Man's man: A rugged leader; according to some, what all men should aspire to be; akin to the concept of the *Alpha Male*

Manzai [漫才] is a traditional style of Japanese, stand-up comedy involving two performers

March Madness is the official nickname for: the Division I college basketball tournament held each spring

Mark: A person identified as an easy target; i.e. a sucker

Mason-Dixon Line: Surveyed by Charles Mason and Jeremiah Dixon in the 1760s, it became the border between the North and South

Master Jay is a deejay moniker. He spun rap on WKDU long before it was accepted on mainstream, Philly airwaves (not to be confused with *Jam Master Jay,* of *Run-DMC)*

Mayari: In *Tagalog* mythology, she is the lunar goddess. The daughter of *Bathala,* the king of the gods, she is revered as the most beautiful deity in Bathala's court

McGuire Air Force Base is located in South Jersey, near Wrightstown and New Hanover Township

Medal of Honor is the USA's highest military honor. It is awarded for personal acts of valor, above and beyond the call of duty

Melanin: Derived from the Greek *melanos,* which means 'black', this is the most important, the most complex, and the most perfect molecule in the human body. This biological living light-source, which connects organisms to the universe, is influenced by the electro-magnetic field, light waves, and sound vibrations. Because of its magnetic properties, according to Anthony Browder (1989), "People with higher concentrations of melanin in their bodies are more in tune with nature...more spiritual".

Melanin Challenged: Scientific research has shown that some 85% of people with high concentrations of melanin in their skin produce 'melatonin', while only 15 percent of people lacking melanin cannot produce this spiritually inducing substance (Browder, 1989, pg. 94)

Melanin-Deficient refers to the state of lacking a functioning pineal gland; in scientific terms: the absence of the polymerization of oxidation products of tyrosine and dihydroxyphenol compounds. Note: Melanin deficiency has been connected with various genetic abnormalities and disease states

Melanin-Rich: In this book, this term is synonymous with 'black' or 'brown' people. Popularized Dr. Frances Cress Welsing and Yaffa Bey, it represents the condition of a healthy, functioning pineal gland; i.e. uncalcified

Melle Mel: Melvin Glover (1961 -) is an original member of the Furious Five. He is credited with coining the term 'MC' for 'Master of Ceremony'. Simply put, he is one of the greatest of all-time.

Messy Marvin is a reference to a sloppy boy in a popular, *Hersey's Chocolate* syrup commercial

Miami Vice was a television crime-detective series that aired from 1984 - 1989

Michael Joseph Jackson (1958 – 2009) is recognized as the most successful entertainer of all time. A global figure in popular culture virtually his entire life, he is often referred to as the 'King of Pop'

Mickey: 'To slip someone a mickey' describes surreptitiously slipping drugs into a person's drink

Midas Touch: In Greek mythology, the God *Dionysus* granted *King Midas of Phrygia (modern day Turkey)* the power to transmute whatever he touched into gold

Midnight Oil is an idiom referring to: studying late into the night; i.e. pull an all-nighter

Mighty Mouse is an anthropomorphic, superhero character created by the Terrytoons Studio in 1942

Miles Dewey Davis III (1926 – 1991) was a jazz musician, trumpeter, bandleader, and composer; widely considered one of the most influential musicians of the 20th century

Military-Industrial Complex: The aggregate of a nation's armed forces and the industries that supply their weapons and materials

Mind-Control is a systematic method to manipulate others' thought patterns

Money Mike is where my street-ball moniker came from

Monie-Love: was my nickname for Monica. Coincidentally, the identical moniker was made famous by Simon Gooden a couple years later

Moolie: Derived from Italian for *eggplant,* it's a pejorative for a dark-skinned person; akin to *nigger*

Moor / Moors / Moorish: Until the 19th century, *Negro, Indian, Colored, Black,* and *Moor* were used interchangeably with *American;* Caucasians were referred to as 'Europeans' or 'settlers' (in their history texts). Many people know the Moors ruled Spain from 711 to 1492, and are credited with bringing Europe out of the Dark Ages. However, there's much more. According to Hakim Bey, the Moors are the aboriginal / indigenous inhabitants of North, Central, and South America, including all of the

275

adjoining islands. The Moorish empire extended from Africa & Europe to the Americas; which was known in ancient times as *Amexem*

MOS is an acronym for: Military Occupation Specialty

Moses: Arabic [مو سى] Hebrew [מֹשֶׁה] 1. According to the Qur'an, Baha'i scripture, and the Hebrew Bible, he was a religious leader, lawgiver, and prophet. 2. Nickname for: Harriet Tubman

Mozart: ['vɔlfgaŋ ama'deus 'moːtsaʁt] (1756 – 1791) *Is it possible the most prolific composer of the Classical era was taught by an Austrian Moor?* Angelo Soliman (1720-1796) was a native of Central Africa. Kidnapped as a child, he was presented to the imperial governor of Sicily in 1734. By adulthood, Soliman was known to be an expert in many fields. As a renowned musical-composer, it is said he had a large influence on the young prodigy while serving as Prince Georg Christian's confidant

MRE are the initials for: Meal Ready to Eat; they are self-contained field rations

Mr. Magic was the moniker for John Rivas (1956 – 2009). He hosted the *Disco Showcase* on WHBI, which later had its 'world premiere' as the *Rap Attack* on WBLS. Marley Marl was his deejay, and the first member of the legendary *Juice Crew*

Mr. Magoo is a near-sighted cartoon character created in 1949 that, by luck, avoids disaster after disaster

Ms. Piggy is an animated pig-like puppet played by Frank Oz on *The Muppet Show*

MTV is a popular US cable and satellite music video channel

Muhammad Ali (1942 -) was known as Cassius Marcellus Clay before he embraced Islam and changed his name. Recognized as 'The Greatest', he'll always be remembered for his famous quote when he refused to fight in the Vietnam War: "Ain't no VietCong never called me 'nigger'. They ain't my enemy – *you* my enemy!"

Mushroom: Psilocybin or "magic" mushrooms are fungi that contain psychoactive indole alkaloids

Musk: The aroma obtained from a gland of a musk deer. Believed to have originated in ancient Egypt, Queen Cleopatra was known to wear this oil

Mustangs are one of the first-generation Ford Mustangs; known as a 'pony car'

N – P

NCAA Championship: The 1987 NCAA Finals was held on March 30, 1987, at the Louisiana Superdome in New Orleans. The Finals are the culmination of March Madness

Noriega: Manuel Antonio Noriega Moreno (1934 -) This Panamanian leader is one of the many publicized enemies who was either inserted into the leadership position by the US, or was known to be a collaborator of the CIA. Noriega has been serving sentences in various prisons since surrendering to US troops in 1990. Other notable 'public enemy' types fitting this criteria are: *Mohammed Reza Pahlavi (the Shah of Iran), Saddam Hussein,* and *Osama bin Laden*

Nappy is a description of: natural African-textured hair

Nathaniel Turner (1800 - 1831) was a prophet who saw visions that prompted him to lead one of the most effective rebellions in US history. Stating he was "Intended for some great purpose", although there were many such revolts, his ignited a culture of fear amongst Caucasians which still exists today

Nature: It is reported that many indigenous people called the planet 'mother'. However, the ancient Egyptians referred to the land as a male deity, *Geb*. His wife, *Nut,* was the goddess of the sky

NCO is the initials for: Non-Commissioned Officer

NCOIC are the initials designating the Non-Commissioned Officer in Charge

Negro denotes 'black' in Spanish. In contemporary usage, it means: a dark-skinned person manufactured in the likeness of a European (see Black)

Neo-Colonialism is a policy whereby a major, world power uses economic and political means to continue ruling its former colony from behind the scenes; i.e. the puppet master

New Yorkers are very thick, stylish laces made popular in NYC Hip Hop culture in the early '80s

Newbie means an inexperienced newcomer; i.e. noob

Nigger: Since colonial times this has been the main ethnic slur directed at peoples of African descent. Most believe it is synonymous with 'ignorant person'. However, the origin of this word is debatable. Some claim it derives from the Sanskrit and Pāli word: *Nāga.* This is a god taking the form of a great snake; specifically the king cobra. It is found in Hinduism, Buddhism and Jainism. Still, others believe it comes from *Negus;* meaning King, or Ruler in Amharic. The scholar, Taj Tarik Bey, teaches that Caucasians were the original niggers, in the form of the *Troglodyte Niger.* This is a type of pale-face chimpanzee

Nippon [大日本帝國] was a world power before the inhabitants of the *Land of the Rising Sun* became *Japanese* in 1947

Non-Commissioned Officers (NCO) are military personnel in positions of authority (E-5 – E-9), but not in positions of 'command' per-se. All commanders must be commissioned officers (O-1 – O-10)

Nori [海苔]: refers to: seaweed

North Cackalackee is a nickname for North Carolina

Northern Lights is a pure *indica* strain of weed with bud crystals that glimmer, i.e. the resemblance to the northern lights sky

Nose Wide Open is a term usually for a male who is crazy in love or lust over a girl, and as a result will focus his total attention on her, ignoring his friends; maybe a hint she is exploiting him

Nubia: The Kingdom of Kush (the Land of Gold) was located on the Nile River, to the south of *Kemet* (ancient Egypt)

NVG is the initials for: Night Vision Goggles

NWA: This group from Compton, California is considered one of the seminal acts of 'Gangsta Rap'. The original group also featured *Arabian Prince*

Nyquil is a brand of cold medication containing alcohol

Occipital Lobe: Located at the rear of the brain, it is the main visual processing center

OCS are the initials for: Officer Candidate School

OG are the initials for: Original Gangster; this street terminology shows respect for an older hustler

Ol' E is an abbreviation for: a 40 ounce bottle of *Old English 800* malt liquor

OPFOR is an acronym for: Opposing Force; this unit represents the enemy during war-game scenarios

Orangemen is the nickname for: Syracuse University athletic teams

Orgone Energy is a hypothetical universal life force closely associated with sexuality. It was proposed in the 1930s by Wilhelm Reich

Original People is a reference to: the indigenous people of the planet; i.e. Asiatics

Othello is a tragedy about the *Moor of Venice,* by William Shakespeare. It is based on *Un Capitano Moro,* by Cinthio

Oxy 10 is a skin cream for acne

PAC is an acronym for: Personnel Actions Command

PAL is an acronym for: Police Athletic League

Parris Island is a military installation used for the Marines' basic training. It is located in Port Royal, South Carolina

Pathfinders are covert soldiers who set up helicopter landing sites in hostile territory

PATS is an acronym for: Program for Academically Talented Students

PCS is the abbreviation for: Permanent Change of Station

Peeping Tom is a person who gets pleasure (usually sexually related) from secretly watching others; i.e. a voyeur

Perpetrating means: the act of faking something or being phony; it was a popular idiom in '80s Hip Hop

Peter Brian Gabriel (1950 -) is a musician most known as the lead vocalist of the rock band, Genesis

Peter Edward Rose (1941 -) Nicknamed 'Charlie Hustle', Rose is the MLB all-time leader in hits. Ironically, he is not in their hall of fame due to being accused of illegally betting on games

Peter Tosh (1944 – 1987) was a Jamaican reggae musician; he was a core

member of *The Wailers*
PHAT is an acronym for: Pretty, Hot, And Tantalizing
Phenom is short for: phenomenon. It is slang for: a person or thing of outstanding abilities or qualities
Pig: Derogatory slang for: police; it was commonly used in the '60s and '70s
Pinocchio is a fictional protagonist in the children's novel *The Adventures of Pinocchio* (1883), by Carlo Collodi. This animated wooden-puppet's nose grew longer whenever he told a lie
Pirates is the nickname for: Seton Hall University athletic teams
PLF is the abbreviation for: Parachute Landing Fall. This is the landing technique taught at Airborne School. Properly executed, it allows a paratrooper to land without sustaining injury
PLL are the initials for: Prescribed Load List
POG, or Pogue, is an acronym for: Personnel Other than Grunts. This condescending term is used to describe weak soldiers
Po-Po is an acronym for: Police Officer
Point-Man: means to assume the first and most exposed position in an advancing combat formation
Police Call is a brief reconaissance / clean-up mission
Popeye: *Popeye the Sailor* was a comic strip character created by Elzie Crisler Segar in the 1920s
Post Traumatic Stress Disorder (PTSD) is a severe anxiety disorder that develops after being exposed to extreme psychological trauma
Postwar Japan refers to: the period immediately following the end of World War II in 1945 to the present day
Pothead is slang for: a habitual cannabis smoker
Pound: Also called *dap* or a *fist pound;* Caucasians later adopted it and called it a *fist bump,* and by many other names. This hand-gesture, which is a symbol of respect, is commonly used by athletes to celebrate with teammates
POV is a military acronym for: Privately Owned Vehicle
Predator: Also called 'Yautja,' these extraterrestrial hunters use advanced technological weaponry to hunt any being they consider a worthy opponent
Presidential Unit Citation is awarded to units of the US Armed Forces for extraordinary heroism. It's on par with the Medal of Honor
Prima donna means: the leading woman soloist in an opera. However, sports writers adopted it to label vain, star athletes
Prodigal Son: In Luke 15:11–32, a wayward son squanders his inheritance but returns home to find his father has forgiven him
PT is a military acronym for: Physical Training
Pu-tang is slang for: vagina; i.e. pussy
Public Enemy: Consisting of *Chuck D, Professor Griff, Flavor Flav, Terminator X,* and the *S1Ws, PE* is famous for their Black Power charged

lyrics and criticism of the establishment

Puerto Rico: The ancient name the *Tainos* used was *Borinquen,* which means 'Land of the Valiant Lord'

Pups was a nickname for the SEAL trainees

PX is an acronym for: Post Exchange; these are huge retail stores for Army personnel and their families (similar to BX)

PYT are the initials for: Pretty, Young, Thing. This is a song by Michael Jackson on the album, *Thriller*

Q – S

Quiet Storm is a nationwide, late-night radio program featuring love songs

Quincy's: A buffet restaurant in Fayetteville, NC

Rainbow Coalition: This is not to be confused with Jesse Jackson's diluted organization. The original coalition was led by Chairman Fred Hampton, and comprised of several extremely radical melanin-rich groups. When Hampton was assassinated by Chicago Police, this multi-cultural assembly was on the verge of creating a rival to counter the racist ruling class in the Windy City

Rangers are the elite infantry unit of the US Army

Rastaman is terminology meaning: an adherent of *Rastafari*

Ray Charles Leonard (1956 -) this 1976 gold-medalist was named *Boxer of the 1980s*

Ready Rock is street terminology for: crack rock; i.e. cocaine that is ready to smoke

Red Alert: Fred Crute (1956 -) was a deejay for the *Almighty Zulu Nation* before gaining popularity on KISS FM; he is credited with popularizing dance hall music on the radio

Redneck is a nickname for: Caucasian slaves who spent an extended amount of time working in the sun

Red Wolf: This North American canid was once the alpha-predator in the woods throughout the Southeastern states

REM 4: Rapid Eye Movement is the deepest stage of delta sleep

Replacement Centers are temporary living quarters for personnel until they process into their new unit; i.e. a reception station

Rev. Albert Greene (1946 -) is famous for singing both gospel and (secular) soul music

Rev. Dr. James Cleveland (1931 - 1991) Crowned as the 'King of Gospel', this singer/composer popularized the modern gospel sound

Richard Franklin Lennox Thomas Pryor (1940 – 2005) Perhaps the funniest stand-up comedian of all-time, he was known for his social examinations of racism while consciously probing history; most notably, ancient Egypt

Richie Cunningham is a character from the sitcom *Happy Days*. He was a pip-squeak, redhead with freckles

Richie-Rich is slang for: a person who grows up in a wealthy family. It originates from the 1950s cartoon

Rick James: James Ambrose Johnson (1948 - 2004) popularized funk music in the late 1970s and '80s

Riddler: is a comic book super-villain appearing in *Batman* comic books, published by DC Comics

Roach: the remains of a joint, blunt, or rolled-up cigarette after most of it has been smoked

Robert Ludlum (1927 – 2001) was an author of suspense novels about governmental conspiracy theories

Robert Montgomery Knight (1940 -) is a retired Indiana University basketball coach

Roberto Clemente (1934 - 1972) was a pro baseball player from Puerto Rico. Arguably the best right-fielder of all-time, he died in a plane crash on New Year's eve while delivering aid to earthquake victims in Nicaragua

Rock is street slang for: a basketball. Or, a cluster of cocaine

Rockin' the Cradle is a crass reference for: having sexual relations with a person deemed too young; i.e. statutory rape

ROK is the abbreviation for: Republic of Korea; i.e. South Korea

Roody-poo is a combination of the word 'rude' and 'poo'; i.e. a lame, easy, soft, cowardly, etc.

Roots is a best-selling novel by author Alex Haley; it was later aired as a historical TV drama in 1976

Roscoe is a nickname for: handgun; i.e. gat, heater, etc.

ROTC: The Reserve Officer Training Corps prepares students to be a commissioned officer

Rubber to hit the Road is an idiom meaning: the most important point; i.e. the moment of truth

Rumble in the Jungle is a reference to: the *Rumble in the Jungle* boxing match on October 30, 1974, in the Democratic Republic of Congo, between George Foreman and Muhammad Ali

Run-DMC: Joseph 'Run' Simmons, Darryl 'DMC' McDaniels, and Jason 'Jam Master Jay' Mizell comprised this influential rap group

Running a Train is a ritualistic re-enactment of slave owners raping one slave; i.e. post-traumatic slave behavior

R&R is an abbreviation for: Rest and Relaxation

Sakura [桜] means: cherry blossoms

Salem Witch Trials: In Massachusetts, between February 1692 – May 1693, 14 women and 5 men were executed after being accused of doing witchcraft; i.e. the "devil's magic". Hundreds more were imprisoned resulting in many more deaths

SAT: The Standardized Admissions Test was the most widely accepted college admissions test in the US

Sayonara [さようなら] means: Good-bye

Scared Straight: The act of abandoning a life of crime due to stark fear; this phrase was popularized by a 1978 documentary

Scarface was originally a 1932 film portraying the life of gangster Al Capone. The 1983 remake about a Cuban immigrant turned drug dealer is more well-known

Scarlet Letter: In this 1850 sadistic work by Nathaniel Hawthorne, a European community humiliates a woman by forcing her to wear a scarlet 'A' on her dress as a punishment for allegedly committing adultery

School Boy: This belittling term meaning *nerd* is also the name of a style of frames

S-Curl: Reference to the *Luster* hair-care product that slightly straightens 'nappy' hair into curls and waves

SEAL is an acronym for Sea, Air, and Land Teams; they are the special operations force of the US Navy

Sell-out is slang for: A person who betrays his people to promote his own personal advancement

Seminoles is the nickname for: Florida State University athletic teams

Senioritis is an informal term referring to a reduction of academic focus characteristic of some high-school seniors, especially after they've been accepted into a university

Sensei [先生] is defined as: teacher; literally, it means a 'a life before another'

Sent-up is street terminology for: getting sent to prison

Separate Rats is short for separate rations. Service members with a spouse receive extra money as part of their allowance for meals

Serpentine Fire is an indirect reference to a song by Earth Wind and Fire.

In Sanskrit, *Prana* [प्राण] means *Kundalini Energy*

Sess: Meaning high-quality, female cannabis; this is a shortened form of the Spanish word, *Sensimilia*

Setting-Up Camp is slang for: the act of preparing for rulership or leadership in any significant venture

Sev is an abbreviated form of *7- Eleven*. It was also Takuan's street-hustling moniker. Tak's friends called him this due to his proclivity for shoplifting

Seventh Heaven means: a state of intense happiness or bliss. The number 7 is prevalent all throughout Creation. From the number of notes, the days of the week, to the number of orifices on the human body, there are numerous examples. Accordingly, many spiritual systems profess there are 7 heavens, with the 7th being the highest

Shakespeare, William (1564-1616): It is rumored the famed poet either assisted in the compilation of the King James version. Or, he and the king are the same person

Shammer is military slang for: a person who shirks his duty; i.e. lazy or shiftless

Shibumi: This novel, by *Trevanian,* incorporates the philosophy of the Japanese game *Go* to create the 'perfect assassin'

Shirley Ann Caesar (1938 -) is the gospel singer nicknamed the 'First Lady of Gospel Music'

Shit on Lock is slang for: having a situation under control

Shittin' Bricks is slang for: being extremely petrified, nervous, or upset

Shock and Awe is a US military doctrine utilizing the use of overwhelming power to paralyze an adversary's will to fight

Shogun: [征夷大将軍] *Sei-i Tai-Shogun* means: 'Barbarian-subduing Genralissimo'. This was the most sought after military rank in *Nippon* for over a thousand years. A Samurai named *Sakanoue no Tamuramaro [坂上田村麻呂] (758? – 811?)* was the first to assume this exalted position. Depicted as a "paragon of military virtues," according to historian, Dr. Alexander Francis Chamberlain, he was a "Negro." This warrior is venerated at *Kiyomizudera* [清水寺], which is the temple Sakanoue established in Kyoto City

Shook and Shook-Daddy are slang for being scared; i.e. petrified

Shorty is slang for: either a child or a young lady

Shuckin' and Jivin' is slang referring to: deceit, mischief, or involving lies

Sitting Bull: Tȟatȟáŋka Íyotake (1834? – 1890) was a Hunkpapa-Lakota Sioux holy man who, in June of 1876, led a united coalition of American tribes in the *Black Hills* to massacre Gen. **George A. Custer** and his 7th Calvary

Skeezer is '80s slang for: a girl who is known to be sexually promiscuous; i.e. a whore

Skunk: Perhaps the most fragrant strain of cannabis in the world, it is also known for its sweet flavor and pleasant high

Slap-boxing was a contest using open hands to penetrate an opponent's defense and smack him in the face

Slow Jams: In modern America, with the exception of the Latin dances (salsa, merengue, etc.), melanin-rich men and women rarely dance in each other's arms. However, back in the day, it was an essential segment of every party

Sneak is slang for: punching someone in the face when they aren't expecting it; i.e. a sucker-punch

Sole Survivor Policy: see DD 1315.15

Soror is Latin for: sister

SOCOM: US Special Operations Command (USSOCOM); i.e. the Special Forces

SOS is the abbreviation for: *Scientists of Sound.* They were deejay crew in my town.

Soul Train was created and hosted by Don Cornelius. The "hippest trip in

283

America" aired in syndication from 1971 until 1993

Soul to Soul is a British music group comprised of: Jazzie B, Caron Wheeler, Simon Law, Daddae, and Nellee Hooper

Spades is a card game played in pairs. It is very popular in black and brown communities

Special Forces: US Special Operations Command (USSOCOM)

Spicoli: *Jeff Spicoli* is a character from the comedy film, *Fast Times at Ridgemont High,* played by Sean Penn. He is depicted as a 'surfer-dude' who enjoys smoking marijuana

Spike Lee: Shelton Jackson Lee (1957 -) is a film director well known for examining race relations

Spit-shine: A meticulous method for polishing boots which leaves the surface of the leather as reflective as a mirror

Spliff is slang for: a cone-shaped marijuana cigarette

Sports Center is a daily sports, news program on ESPN

Steady B: Warren Sabir McGlone (1969 -) is infamous for being an emcee who actually lived the life of a 'hustla' – not just rapped about it. *Steady B* is currently serving a life sentence for his part in the murder of a police officer during a botched bank robbery in 1996

Steatopygia means an extreme amount of fat on the buttocks region

Stevie Gee is a neighborhood emcee

Stick is a designated group of paratroopers jumping together from an aircraft during an Airborne mission

Stick Ball is a street version of baseball. This game was popular in US cities because it only required a stick, a ball, and some space

Stogie is slang for: a cheap cigar

Straw Man: According to the Redemption Theory, the US government creates a fictitious person corresponding to each newborn citizen and pledges them as collateral to borrow money; i.e. foundation of slavery

Street Entrepreneurship is the ability to hustle or make money; sometimes by selling illegal merchandise

Super Six: This was the name of an actual posse in my hood. Comprised of six members, they were known for their various shades of sheepskin coats and stomping kids in the ground

Sun Tzu [孫武[(544?–496 BC) was a high-ranking Chinese general during the Zhou dynasty's Spring and Autumn Period

Survival of the Fittest: According to Wayne Chandler, Darwin's theory of evolution contradicts every ancient codex on how humans and animals evolved. Claiming it "lacks convincing evidence", Chandler also talks about a "pervasive genius" which encompassed the ancient world. He goes on to describe a time "when humans were truly advanced beings" and "walked in harmony with God and Nature" (pg. 215)

SWAT is an acronym for: Special Weapons and Tactics; it is an elite paramilitary unit that was created to combat 'radical' organizations like the

Black Panthers

Sweating is slang for: obsessing over a person

Synagogue of Satan: Revelation 3:9 states: "Behold, I will make them of the synagogue of Satan, which say they are Jews, and are not, but do lie; behold, I will make them to come and worship before thy feet, and to know that I have loved thee"

S-2 is Military Intelligence; they collect data on enemy movement, strengths, and battlefield deployments

T – Z

T-10: The most common static line-deployed parachute used for combat, mass-assault, Airborne operations

TA-50: Table of Allowances is the standard issued gear; i.e. kevlar helmet, ruck sack, canteens, etc.

Taino-Arawak are the indigenous peoples of the Caribbean Isles

Takuan is the family name of Takuan Soho [沢庵宗彭] (1573-1645) He was a Zen monk, calligrapher, painter, poet, gardener, tea master, and author. His collected writings total six volumes and over 100 published poems, including his best known treatise, *The Unfettered Mind*. A central figure in the Rinzai School of Zen Buddhism, his list of accomplishments include being the inventor of the pickled, *daikon* radish that was named after him. At the moment before his death, it is said he painted the Chinese character [夢] 'dream', laid down his brush, and died

Tall, Young, Legend in Leather is a title used by LL Cool J in his lyrics to describe himself

Tamahu: The ancient Egyptians spoke of a group of uncouth nomads that were described as having pale skin, red to blond hair, and blue eyes.

Tarzan is a *very* fictional character who rules the "African jungles" all by himself. This icon has been a tool for white supremacist imagery since the early-1900s

Tet Offensive: At 3 am on Jan. 31, 1968, North Vietnamese and Vietcong forces launched simultaneous attacks on South Vietnamese and American forces all throughout South Vietnam. The fighting, the heaviest of the Vietnam War, coincided with the Lunar New Year, or *Tet*. It was the military turning point in the war and a political and media disaster for the US

The Christ is a title for Jesus in the New Testament. It is Hebrew for 'Messiah' [מָשִׁיחַ], meaning: the Anointed One

The Clark Sisters are comprised of Jacky, Elbernita, Dorinda, Denise and Karen. They are credited as being pioneers in bringing gospel music to the mainstream

The Doors: Led by Jim Morrison, this rock group took its name from Aldous Huxley's book *The Doors of Perception*

The System is a government structure imposing biased inequality. The discrimination is viewed as 'normal', or even 'ethical', by the law / media simply because they are part and parcel of the very same infrastructure

The Winans are a family, gospel quartet from Detroit, Michigan. The members consist of four brothers: Marvin, Carvin, Michael, and Ronald

Thrasher is someone who listens to heavy-metal music; i.e. a metal-head or a headbanger.

Timbuktu: This city, in the West African nation of Mali, is just north of the River Niger. In its Golden Age, the city's extensive trade network along with the *University of Sankore Madrasah* were internationally famous

Timothy Francis Leary (1920 – 1996) was a psychologist known for his advocacy of psychedelic drugs

Titties is slang for: breasts; i.e. jugs, boobs, knockers, etc.

Toby: In a scene in *Roots, Kunta Kinte,* played by LeVar Burton, was whipped into accepting his slave name, Toby

Top is the officially recognized nickname for a US Army 1st Sergeant

Toussaint Louverture: Francois-Dominique Toussaint Louverture (1743 - 1803) led the rebellion at Saint Domingue, in 1791, which led to the Haitian Revolution. A military genius, not only did he outwit Napoleon on the battlefield, he helped found the independent state of Haiti – that to this day, is still being punished for defeating France

Townies: is a condescending term describing the local people; akin to hillbilly

Tramaine Davis (1951 -) is a well-known gospel singer

Triathlons are competitions consisting of a 2.4 mile swim, a 112-mile bicycle ride, and a 26.2-mile marathon

Trim is slang for: vagina

Trippin': Negative terminology meaning: to behave in an irritating way. Or, it means: using LSD

Trips is slang for: tabs of LSD

Tsunami [津波[refers to: tidal wave

Turned-out: is slang related to the sexual act. Usually negative, it can mean raping someone; or satisfying a person to the point they're sexual orientation is altered; i.e. from heterosexual to homosexual

UCMJ is the abbreviation for: Universal Code of Military Justice. It is the military's list of laws and statutes

Ultra Man [ウルトラマン] first aired in 1966, and is still a popular Japanese television series amongst children

Uncle Sam is a popular nickname for the 'US' government

Uncle Tom is the title character in Harriet Beecher Stowe's 1852 novel, *Uncle Tom's Cabin;* it is also an epithet for a person who is slavish and excessively subservient to the ruling class

Underage is a reference to persons who are below the legal age limit to procure or consume alcohol

Undercover Brother is a reference to a movie starring comedian, Eddie Griffin (see bibliography)

Underground Railroad: A secret network of routes and safe houses used by people in the 19th century to escape slavery in the Americas

Unit Colors is the flag identifying the brigade, battalion, company, etc. This practice of marking the location of the commander originated in ancient Egypt

Up North is street terminology for: prison; i.e. up state

Uprock is a soulful type of street-dance consisting of foot shuffles, spins, and freestyle movements

UPS: United Parcel Service is a US-based, global package, shipping company

Up-State is street terminology for: prison; i.e. up north

US Military Installations: The NATO watch committee reveals that the US operates between 700-800 bases in at least 63 countries. There are over 90 in Japan alone

Vapors means: being high in a chemically-poisoned way; this phrase was made famous by Biz Markie in a 1988 song

Vatos is *Calo* slang for 'dude'

Vaya con Dios: In Spanish, this phrase means: to go with God

Venus was the goddess of love and beauty in ancient Rome. She is also known as *Aphrodite*

Vick is street terminology for: robbing or stealing

Video Music Box: Created in 1983 by Ralph McDaniels, it was the first TV show to give mainstream exposure to Hip Hop

Visine is a brand of eye drops that constricts the eye's superficial blood vessels; i.e. "it gets the red out"

Vogue: was a dance imitating super-model poses. Developed in NYC gay clubs, it was later popularized by *Madonna*

WKDU is a Philadelphia college-radio station at Drexel University *(see Master Jay)*

Wack is slang for: something uncool; i.e. corny

Wench is a derogatory word for: an unvirtuous woman; i.e. a bitch or slut

West Point: The preeminent four-year military academy located in West Point, New York

When the Saints go Marching in is a famous gospel hymn often played by Jazz musicians

Whiteboy is a derogatory term meaning: fearful, having no rhythm, or any trait associated with melanin-deficiency

White Devil: Wallace Fard Muhammad was one of the co-founders of the Nation of Islam (NOI). He taught the original humans were melanated and that Caucasians were 'artificial, white devils' created on the Greek island of *Patmos,* by a mad scientist named *Yakub*

White Lie is a diplomatic or well-intentioned untruth; a fib

287

Who's Zoomin' Who? This phrase means: turning the tables on someone. It was popularized by a 1985 song by Aretha Franklin

Wild Styles is a reference to: the 1983 motion picture produced by Charlie Ahearn

Wile E: Referring to the Warner Brothers character, *Wile E. Coyote*

William Franklin Graham, Jr. (1918 -) is a Christian evangelist, ordained as a southern Baptist minister

Willie Lynch: Allegedly, in 1712, a British slave owner named Willie Lynch delivered a speech in Virginia detailing tactics to pit the indigenous tribes against one another; i.e. the secret to controlling the majority population

"Willie" Wilver Dornell Stargell (1940 – 2001), nicknamed 'Pops', was a left fielder on the Pittsburgh Pirates for 21 years

Wop: the name of a popular dance in the 1980s

Ye are Gods: Psalm 82:6: *I said, 'You are gods, sons of the Most High, all of you';* John 10:34: *Jesus answered them, 'Is it not written in your law, I said, ye are gods?'*

Yeshua [יְהוֹשֻׁעַ]: This was a common spelling in many translations amongst Jews of the Second Temple period

Yin-Yang: In Chinese cosmology, *Yin* represents female energy while *Yang* expresses the masculine principle

Yoni [योनि] is a Sanskrit word meaning: vagina or womb; symbolic of the goddess, *Shakti*

Young Boy means: younger kid. However, this label can also be a term of endearment, or an insult toward an actual peer

Your Arms Too Short to Box with God is a Broadway musical based on the biblical book of *Matthew*

Youse: a phrase meaning 'you guys' which is commonly used by people of Italian descent in the New Jersey / New York area

Zacchaeus: According to the Gospel of Luke, he was a tax collector in Jericho; his name means 'pure and righteous one'

Zested is slang for being intoxicated or getting high

Zooted: the state of being overly intoxicated; i.e. fucked-up

Numbers

007 is the codename of author Ian Fleming's legendary MI6 agent, *James Bond*

144,000: In Christianity, this number represents the sum of God's people going to heaven

7-Eleven is the world's largest chain of convenience stores

808: A 3-way speaker system utilizing 5 drivers mounted in a bass-reflex enclosure

Bibliography

Articles

Bishop, J. (1988, Aug. 26). To fend off the sun, researchers are using body's own chemistry. *The Wall Street Journal*. Retrieved from ProQuest databases.

Chamberlain, A. (1911, Apr) The contribution of the negro to human civilization. *Journal of Race Development 1*(1). Retrieved from https://archive.org/details/jstor-29737886.

King, R. (1986). Black dot, the black seed of humanity. *Ureaus, The Journal of Unconscious Life, 2*(1). Los Angeles, California: Aquarian Spiritual Center.

Sirota, D. (2011, March 16). How your taxpayer dollars subsidize pro-war movies and block anti-war movies. *The Huffington Post*. Retrieved from http://www.huffingtonpost.com/david-sirota/how-your-taxpayer-dollars_b_836574.html.

Blog

The Remix with MsBlue. (2010, October 15). "The psycho-sexual war against black girls!" Bro Umar Johnson [Audio file] Retrieved from http://www.blogtalkradio.com/theremix/2010/10/16/the-psycho-sexual-war-against-black-girls-bro-umar-johnson

Books

Ashby, M. (2005). *The Egyptian Book of the Dead: The Book of Coming Forth by Day*. Atlanta: Sema Institute.

Barnes, C. (1988). *Melanin: The Chemical Key to Black Greatness*. Houston, Texas: Lushena Publishing.

Browder, A. (1989). *From the Browder File, 22 Essays on the African-American Experience*. Washington DC: Institute of Karmic Guidance Publishing.

Bruce, R. (2009). *Astral Dynamics: The Complete Book of Out-of-Body Experiences*. Newburyport, Massachusetts: Hampton Roads Publishing.

Chandler, W. (1999). *Ancient Future: The Teachings and Prophetic Wisdom of the Seven Hermetic Laws of Ancient Egypt*. Baltimore, Maryland: Black Classic Press

Howard, R., Sprague De Camp, L., & Carter, L. (1968). *Conan*. New York: Ace Books.

Kingseed, C. (2006). *Old Glory Stories: American Combat Leadership in World War II*. Maryland: Naval Institute Press.

Muhammad, E. (1965). *Message to the Blackman in America*. Arizona: Secretarius MEMPS Publications.

Rashidi, R. (1985). *African Presence in Early Asia*. Rutgers – The State University of   NJ, Piscataway, NJ: Transaction Publishers.

Standley, F. (1989). *Conversations with James Baldwin*. Mississippi: University Press of Mississippi.

Whitaker, R. (1979). *Shibumi*. New York: Crown Publishers.

Music

Baker, A. (1985-1986). Been so long [Recorded by Anita Baker] *Rapture* [Vinyl]. California: Elektra Records. (1986)

Baker, A. (1985). Sweet love [Recorded by Anita Baker] *Rapture* [Vinyl]. California: Elektra Records. (1986)

Barrier, E., Griffen, W. (1986). Eric B. is president [Recorded by Eric B. & Rakim] *Paid in Full* [Vinyl]. New York: 4th & B'way/Island. (1986)

Blackmon, L., Jenkins, T. (1986). Word up! [Recorded by Cameo] *Word up!* [Vinyl]. New York: Atlanta Artist. (1986)

Cameo (1983-1984). She's strange [Recorded by Cameo] *She's Strange* [Vinyl]. Casablanca. (January 16, 1984)

Chandler, J. Bell, F., & McDonald, C. (1981). Silly [Recorded by Denise Williams] *Silly* (single) [Vinyl]. Pennsylvania: Columbia/ARC. (1981)

Dewese, M. (1986). Go see the doctor [Recorded by Kool Moe Dee]. *Go See the Doctor* [Vinyl]. New York: Jive. (1986)

Dixon, M., Murphy, D., Dechalus, L., Withrow, K., Brickell, E., Houser, J., Bush, J., & Aly, A. (1989 -1990). Slow down [Recorded by Brand Nubians] *One for All* [Vinyl]. United States: Elektra Records. (1990)

Edwards, B., Rodgers, N. (1978). Le freak [Recorded by Chic] *Le Freak/Savior Faire* [Vinyl]. Atlantic. (January 1978)

Edwards, B., Rodgers, N. (1978). We are family [Recorded by Sister Sledge] *Easier to Love* [Vinyl]. Cotillion. (1979)

Elam, K., Martin, C. (1990). Just to get a rep [Recorded by Gang Starr] *Step in the Arena* [Vinyl]. New York: Chrysalis/ EMI Records. (1991)

Fekaris, D., Perren, F. (1978). Shake your groove thing [Recorded by Peaches & Herb] *2 Hot* [Vinyl]. Polydor. (1978)

Fequiere, S., Campbell, J., Reeves, F., & Bailey, M. (1985). Roxanne roxanne [Recorded by UTFO]. *UTFO* [Vinyl]. New Jersey: Select Records. (1985)

Gamble K., Huff, L. (1978). Use ta be my girl [Recorded by The O'Jays]. *So Full of Love* [Vinyl]. Philadelphia: Philadelphia International (1977-1988)

Gamble, K, Huff, L., Jackson, A. (1972). Foe the love of money [Recorded by The O'Jays] *Ship Ahoy* [Vinyl]. Philadelphia: Philadelphia International Records. (1973)

Ginyard, R., Bryce, R., Riley, T., & Brown, J. (1988). It takes two [Recorded by Rob Base and DJ E-Z Rock]. *It takes two* [Vinyl]. New York: Profile. (1988)

Green, R., Aleem, T., Aleem. T. (1984). Cosmic blast [Recorded by Captain Rock]. *Captain Rock* [Vinyl]. New York: NIA. (1984)

Greene, S. (1984).Let the music play [Recorded by Shannon]. *Let the Music Play* [Vinyl]. New York: Mirage. (February 1, 1984)

Griffey, D., Sylvers, L. (1978). It's all the way live [Recorded by Lakeside]. *Shot of Love* [Vinyl]. California: Solar Records. (1978)

Hancock, H., Laswell, B., & Beinhorn, M. (1983). Rockit [Recorded by Herbie Hancock]. *Future Shock* [vinyl]. (August 1983)

Hanson, A., Davis, E., Mantronik, K. (1986). Hungry for your love [Recorded by Hanson & Davis] *I'll Take You On/Hungry For Your Love/Hold On To Yesterday EP* [Vinyl]. Fresh Records. (1986)

Hardy, A (1986-1988) Vapors [Recorded by Biz Markie]. *Goin' Off* [Vinyl]. New York: Cold Chillin' Records. (1988)

Hardy, N.S., McDaniels, Jr., Simmons, J., & Smith. (1983). Sucker M.C.'s (Krush Groove 1)[Recorded by Run-D.M.C.] *Run-D.M.C.* [Vinyl]. Profile, Arista. (1984)

Hendrix, J. (1967). Purple haze [Recorded by The Jimi Hendrix Experience] *Are you experienced* [Vinyl]. United Kingdom: Track Records. (1967)

Hutchins, J., Fletcher, J., Carter, D. (1984). Friends [Recorded by Whodini] *Escape* [Vinyl]. Jive/Arista Records (October 17, 1984)

Jabara, P., Shaffer, P. (1979). It's raining men [Recorded by The Weather Girls] *Success* [Vinyl]. New York: Columbia. (1982)

Jackson, M. (1982). Beat it [Recorded by Michael Jackson] *Thriller* [Vinyl]. Epic. (November 30, 1982)

Jackson, M. (1982). Thriller [Recorded by Michael Jackson] *Thriller* [Vinyl]. Epic. (1982)

293

Johnson, H., Gill, P., O'Toole, M., Nash, B. (1983-1984). The World is my oyster [Recorded by Frankie Goes to Hollywood] *Welcome to the Pleasuredome* [Vinyl]. London: ZTT. (1984)

McCoy, V. (1975). The hustle [Recorded by Van McCoy & the Sould City Symphony]. *Disco Baby* [Vinyl]. New York: Avco Records. (1975)

Moltke, S. (1986). The bridge [Recorded by MC Shan] *Down by Law* [Vinyl]. New York: Cold Chillen/Warner Bros. Records. (1985)

Myers, D., Parrish, G., Dixon, T., & Ferrell, F. (1986-1987). The overweight lover's in the house [Recorded by Heavy D & the Boyz] *Living Large* [Vinyl]. New York: Uptown Records. (1987)

Pryor, R. (1975). That nigger's crazy [Recorded by Richard Pryor]. *That nigger's crazy* [Vinyl]. San Francisco: Warner Bros. Records. (1974)

Richie, L., McClary, T., Williams, M., King, W., La Pread, R., Orange, W., & Dean, C. (1980). Jesus is love [Recorded by The Commodores] *Heroes* [Vinyl]. United States: Motown Records. (1980)

Ridenhour, C., Sadler, E., Boxley, H., & Boxley, K. (1990). *Fear of a black planet* [CD]. United States: Def Jam / Columbia Records.

Ridenhour, C., Sadler, E., Boxley, H., & Boxley, K. (1989). Fight the power [Recorded by Public Enemy] *Fight the power* [Vinyl]. United States: Motown Records. (1989)

Robinson, J., Glover, M., & Robinson, S. (1982). Message II (Survival) [Recorded by Melle Mel & Duke Bootee of Grandmaster Flash & The Furious Five] *Message II (Survival)* [Vinyl]. England: Sugar Hill Records. (1982)

Simmons, J., McDaniels, D. (1983). Jam-master jay [Recorded by Run-D.M.C.] *Run-d.m.c.* [Vinyl]. United States: Profile / Arista Records. (1984)

Simmons, J., McDaniels, D. (1985). My adidas [Recorded by Run-D.M.C.] *Raising hell* [Vinyl]. United States: Profile / Arista Records. (1986)

Smith, C., Williams, Kaye, & Montnegro. (n.d.). Sucker DJ's (I Will Survive) [Recorded by Marley Marl] *Sucker DJ's (I Will Survive)* [Vinyl]. Party Time. (1983)

Smith, J. (1986-1987). I'm Bad [Recorded by LL Cool J] *Bigger and Deffer* [Vinyl]. New York: Def Jam, Columbia, CBS Records. (1987)

Smith, J., Jay, J., & Rubin, R. (1984). I Need a Beat [Recorded by LL Cool J] *Radio* [Vinyl]. New York: Def Jam/Columbia/ CBS Records. (1985)

Tosh, P. (1975). Legalize it [Recorded by Peter Tosh] *Legalize It* [Vinyl]. Jamaica: Columbia Records. (1976)

Williams, J. Mantronik, K. (1986). Cold Gettin' Dumb [Recorded by Just-Ice] *Back to the Old School* [Vinyl]. Fresh/Sleeping Bag Records. (1986)

Withers, B., Salter, W., & MacDonald, R. (1981). Just the Two of Us [Recorded by Grover Washington & Bill Withers] *Just the Two of us (B-side: Make Me a Memory)* [Vinyl]. Elektra. (1981)

Movies

Beckerman, S., Feitshans, B. (Producer), & Milius, J. (Director). (1984). *Red dawn* [Motion picture]. United States: MGM/UA Entertainment Co.

Ben-Ami, Y., Carver, S. (Producer), & Carver, S. (Director). (1983). *Lone wolf Mcquade* [Motion picture]. United States: Orion Pictures.

Bregman, M. (Producer), & De Palma, B. (Director). (1983). *Scarface* [Motion picture]. United States: Universal Pictures.

Canton, N., Gale, B. (Producers), Zemeckis, R. (Director). (1985). *Back to the future* [Motion picture]. United States: Universal Pictures.

Chartoff, R., Winkler, I. (Producer). Avildsen, J. (Director). (1976). *Rocky* [Motion picture]. United States: United Artists.

Curtis, K., Harris, T., Ross, D. (Producer), & Murray, D. (Director). (1970). *The cross and the switchblade* [Motion picture]. United States: 20th Century Fox.

Donner, R., Silver, J. (Producers), Donner, R. (Director). (1987). *Lethal weapon* [Motion picture]. United States: Warner Bros. Pictures.

Feitshans, B., Kassar, M., Vajna, A. (Producer), & Kotcheff, T. (Director). (1982). *First blood* [Motion picture]. United States: Orion Pictures.

Fox, T., Henderson, G. (Producers), O'Bannon, D. (Director). (1985). *The Return of the living dead* [Motion picture]. United States: Orion Pictures.

Gordon, L., Silver, J., Davis, J. (Producer), & McTiernan, J. (Director). (1987). *Predator* [Motion picture]. United States: 20th Century Fox.

Grazer, B. (Producer). (2002). *Undercover brother* [Motion picture]. United States: Universal Pictures.

Kennedy, K., Jones, Q., Marshall, F., Spielberg, S. (Producer), Spielberg, S. (Director). (1985). *The color purple* [Motion picture]. United States: Warner Bros. Pictures.

Kopelson, A. (Producer), & Stone, O. (Writer/Director). (1986). *Platoon* [Motion picture]. United States: Orion Pictures.

Lee, S. (Producer/Writer/Director). (1989). *Do the right thing* [Motion picture]. United States: 40 Acres and a Mule Filmworks.

Lester, D., Miller, D., Rappaport, M. (Producer), & Shelton, R. (Director). (1992). *white men can't jump* [Motion Picture]. United States: 20th Century Fox.

Linson, A., Azoff, I., (Producer), & Heckerling, A. (Director). (1982). *fast times at ridgemont high* [Motion picture]. United States: Universal Studios.

Nasheed, T. (Director). (2011). *Hidden colors 1* [Motion picture]. United States: King Flex Entertainment.

Nasheed, T. (Director). (2012). *Hidden colors 2* [Motion picture]. United States: King Flex Entertainment.

Nicolaides, S. (Producer). Singleton, J. (Writer/Director). (1991). *Boyz n the hood* [Motion picture]. United States: Columbia Pictures.

Puttnam, D. (Producer), Hudson, H. (Director). (1981). *Chariots of fire* [Motion picture]. United Kingdom: The Ladd Company.

Raymond, C. (Producer), & Wei, L. (Writer/Director). (1972). *Fist of fury* [Motion picture]. Hong Kong: Golden Harvest Miramax.

Roddenberry, G. (Producer), Wise, R. (Director). (1979). *Star trek: The Motion Picture* [Motion picture]. United States: Paramount Pictures.

Shapiro, A. (Producer), Shapiro, A. (Writer/Director). (1978). *Scared straight!* [Motion picture]. United States: Golden West Television.

Silver, J. (Producer), & Lester, M. (Director). (1985). *Commando* [Motion picture]. United States: 20th Century Fox.

Simpson, D., Bruckheimer, J. (Producer), & Scott, T. (Director). (1986). *Top gun* [Motion picture]. United States: Paramount Pictures.

Solo, R. (Producer), Hopper, D. (Director). (1988). *Colors* [Motion picture]. United States: Orion Pictures.

Spielberg, S., Marshall, F. (Producers), Hooper, T. (Director). (1982). *Poltergeist* [Motion picture]. United States: Metro-Goldwyn-Mayer.

Wachs, R., Wayans, K. (Producers), & Townsend, R. (Director). (1987). *Eddie Murphy raw* [Motion picture]. United States: Paramount Picutres.

Television

Barbera, J., Hanna, W. (Producer). (1977). *Captain caveman and the teen angels* [Television series]. United States: Hanna-Barbera Productions.

Barbera, J., Hanna, W. (Producer). (1980). *Richie Rich* [Television series]. United States: ABC.

Bass, J., Rankin, A. (1974). *The year without a santa claus* [Television animation]. ABC.

Carsey, M., Werner, T., Kukoff, B., Leahy, J. (Producers). (1984). *The Cosby show* [Television series]. United States: Viacom Enterprises; Paramount Domestic Television; Carsey-Werner Distribution.

Cornelius, D. (Producer). (1971). *Soul train* [Television series]. United States: Tribune Entertainment.

Correll, C., Gosden, F. (Creators). (1951). *The Amos 'n' Andy show* [Television series]. United States: WMAQ AM.

Davis, A. (Director). (1947). *The goofy gophers* [Television series]. United States: Warner Bros. Pictures.

Dozier, W., Horwitz, H. (Producer). (1966). *Batman* [Television series]. United States: Greenway Productions/20th Century Fox Television

Freston, T., Pittman, R. (Founders). (1980). *MTV: Music television* [Television series]. United States: Viacom Media Networks.

Healy, T. (Creator). (1925). *The three stooges* [Television series]. United States: Columbia Pictures Corporation.

Levitt, G. (Creator). (1977). *Fantasy island* [Television series]. United States: ABC.

Margulies, S. (Producer). (Jan. 23, 1977 – Jan. 30, 1977). *Roots* [Television miniseries]. United States: ABC.

McDaniels, R. (Creator). (1983). *Video music box* [Television series]. United States: WNYE-TV.

Michaels, L. (Producer). (1975). *Saturday night live* [Television series]. United States: Broadway Video.

Monte, E., Evans, M. (Creators). (1974). *Good times* [Telvision series]. United States: CBS.

Peppiatt, F., Aylesworth, J., Brillstein, B. (Creators). (1969). *Hee haw* [Television series]. United States: CBS-TV.

Ruby, J., Spears, K. (Creators). (1976). *Jabberjaw* [Television series]. United States: Hanna-Barbera Productions.

Takamoto, I., Lovy, A. (Producer). (1973). *Inch high private eye* [Television series]. United States: NBC.

Terry, P. (Creator). (1942). *Mighty mouse* [Television series]. United States: 20th Century Fox.

Tsuburaya, E. (Creator). (1966). *Ultraman* [Television series]. Japan: TBS.

Walsh, J. (Creator). (1979-). *SportsCenter* [Sports news program]. United States: ESPN.